PRESENTS

THE FUNKY BASS BOOK

BASS PLAYER PRESENTS

THE FUNKY BASS BOOK

EDITED BY BILL LEIGH

Backbeat Books

AN IMPRINT OF HAL LEONARD CORPORATION

Portions of this book are adapted from articles that originally appeared in *Bass Player* magazine.

Published in cooperation with Music Player Network, New Bay Media, LLC, and *Bass Player* magazine. *Bass Player* magazine is a registered trademark of New Bay Media, LLC.

Published in 2010 by Backbeat Books
An Imprint of Hal Leonard Corporation
7777 West Bluemound Road
Milwaukee, WI 53213

Trade Book Division Editorial Offices
33 Plymouth St., Montclair, NJ 07042

Printed in the United States of America

Book design by Damien Castaneda

Library of Congress Cataloging-in-Publication Data is available upon request.

ISBN 978-0-87930-994-7

www.backbeatbooks.com

To generations of musicians everywhere, who, through their hard work, tireless dedication, and unbounded creativity, continue to give up the funk

And to Chandrika and Olivia, who always give me more of what I'm funkin' for

CONTENTS

FOREWORD

Back in the day, when I was coming up as a bass player, bass was still a behind-the-scene backup part that nobody really thought of as an out-front lead instrument. I really stood out because I had a certain Sick-O-Pation, an energy that was saying, "Out of the way, boy; you bother me." James Brown is the One who taught me about playing on the One, and once I enrolled in P-University I could stretch out and develop my own style. I was considered by the best to be one of the best.

But before all that, before I got with James Brown, Marshall Jones of the Ohio Players was a big up-close-and-personal influence on me. Guys like James Jamerson were really setting the stage for what was to come. Jimi Hendrix caught my ear with a signature sound and style that other guitarists wanted, which is what guys like Larry Graham did for bass, and what I was trying to do with a signature sound of my own. I took my interpretation of what Marshall and Jamerson were doing to what I believed was the next level, partly because I started off playing guitar, thanks to my baby big brother, Catfish.

In other words, in order to stay on a solid foundation, we must be reminded at certain intervals of how we all got there from here in the first place. That's where *The Funky Bass Book* comes in. Please don't get a big fart head and start to believe that your thing on bass is all what you as an individual have done on your own. You are part of a continuum. It begins with upright players like Jamerson, Ron Carter, and my friend John B. Williams to name just a few, who infused low-end frequencies into all kinds of music. It continues down through young-generation bass cats who have developed their own style and signature riffs.

There's no reason for you and the next generation to not be the greatest ever. After all, you have control of the vertical and horizontal. You have YouTube and a whole new world right there in the palms of your bass-playing hands. In my era, we didn't have things like *Bass Player* magazine and *The Funky Bass Book* to provide us with full knowledge, but you do. Knowledge and practice may not always make you perfect, but they will always keep you in pursuit of the funk perfection.

Bootsy Collins
Founder and Professor, Funk University
www.thefunkuniversity.com

INTRODUCTION

What makes funky music funky? Is it the way the rhythms swing with and against each other? Is it the tension of a groove unbroken, until just the perfect moment of release? Or is it something more abstract—the pressures and blues of hard living, being worked out in taut expression of stanky yet sanctified attitude?

It could be all of those things, or something else entirely, but whatever it is, there's almost always some funky bass involved. From Detroit to the Deep South, from Buffalo to the Bay and around the world, bass has consistently been the backbone—or maybe the *buttbone*—of funky grooves, from the dawn of electrified R&B and soul, through straight-up funk, disco, and hip-hop.

So if that's part of the *what* of funk and funky bass, *The Funky Bass Book* is about exploring precisely *who* and exactly *how*. For more than 20 years, *Bass Player* magazine has been piecing together those parts of the story through in-depth interviews, lessons, and analyses. *The Funky Bass Book* gathers many of these efforts into a comprehensive history that tells a coherent story, one that illuminates the evolution of funky bass playing through insights of the pioneering players who developed and nurtured it.

Part I starts with the Funky Founding Fathers, including James Jamerson at Motown, the homegrown Southern soul stylings of the Memphis and Muscle Shoals studio players, the early brilliance of Chuck Rainey, and the moment Larry Graham changed everything with his monstrously musical thumb. Part II examines the pantheon of players who developed the funk bass idiom on stages and in studios in the '70s and early '80s, whether in self-contained bands or as professional studio or side players. Part III explores what we've come to think of as modern funk bass and how it came to be, from the innovations of Anthony Jackson, Marcus Miller, and Victor Wooten, to new applications of bass in hip-hop and gospel music.

Along the way there are suggested recordings—Deep Cuts—for you to seek out and explore, as well as in-depth analyses—Deeper Cuts—that consider how a notably funky bass part came together, and just what makes it *so . . . dang . . . funky*. I encourage you to consider adding many of these tracks to your personal collections, but there are many online resources, from streaming audio services to popular video sites, where you can easily follow along with the groove.

A recurring theme throughout this book is how much players learned from each other—both from those who came before them and from their peers. I hope this volume presents you with the same opportunities: first, to discover or rediscover some of the great musicians who got us where we are today, and then, to pass on their groove wisdom generously.

★ OMISSIONS ★

While we tried to be as comprehensive as possible, there are a few bassists *Bass Player* has not covered (sometimes because they were difficult to find or contact). As such, there are some worthy players who aren't included in this book. Here are a few who come to mind, with some classic cuts for you to add to your listening list: Ron LaPread (the Commodores' "Brick House"), Al McGrier (Teena Marie's "Square Biz"), Robin Duhe (Frankie Beverly & Maze's "Joy and Pain"), Lequeint "Duke" Jobe (Rose Royce's "Car Wash"), bassist/producer Leon Sylvers III (the Whispers' "And the Beat Goes On"), and studio ace David Shields (think Cheryl Lynn's "Got to Be Real"). In addition, props must go to bass innovator Jaco Pastorius, who's funkier side was directly influenced by Rocco Prestia and Jerry Jemmott, as well as to early "Fender bass" pioneers Carol Kaye and Joe Osborn, the great Los Angeles session legends who, during their expansive careers, chiefly recorded rock, pop, and TV and film sessions, but also contributed capably to the funky bass idiom.

PART I:
THE FUNKY
FOUNDERS

It was almost a decade after the 1951 introduction of Fender Precision bass that electric bass guitar slowly began to gain acceptance among a small, mostly unconnected group of studio musicians. While players like Paul McCartney, Jack Bruce, and John Entwistle were experimenting with new rock sounds in the U.K., and pioneering session players like Carol Kaye and Joe Osborn were trying out the "Fender bass" on a range of pop sessions in Los Angeles, those cutting R&B and soul sides—James Jamerson in Detroit, Chuck Rainey and Jerry Jemmott in New York, and a handful of players in Memphis and Muscle Shoals, Alabama—were developing the vocabulary of funky bass that would become the language for generations of musicians.

Meanwhile, as the '60s went on, James Brown's band developed into an intensely funky unit that drove audiences crazy. In New Orleans, a young group of friends and family members were cooking up a syncopated sound steeped in the rhythms of the Crescent City. And in San Francisco, a young guitarist named Larry Graham had no idea the revolution he was starting when, making up for the lack of a drummer, he began thumping and plucking the strings of a rented bass.

1.
JAMES JAMERSON AND MOTOWN

★ THE HEARTBEAT OF MOTOWN BY CHRIS JISI ★

There's a scene in the 2002 film *Standing in the Shadows of Motown* where Nathan Watts and Ralphe Armstrong take turns lying on their backs in Hitsville's Studio A while playing the bass line from Marvin Gaye's "What's Going On," trying to recreate how James Jamerson reportedly recorded his part. It's a fitting image, because Jamerson has been flooring bassists for years. Unfortunately, mass recognition for the pioneering electric-bass genius didn't come until after his 1983 death at age 47. Six years later, Allan "Dr. Licks" Slutsky's essential Hal Leonard book/CD package, *Standing in the Shadows of Motown: The Life and Music of Legendary Bassist James Jamerson*, brought on the first wave of props, culminating in Jamerson's election to the Rock and Roll Hall of Fame in 2000. Slutsky and the surviving Motown backing musicians, the "Funk Brothers," partnered soon afterward, intent on making a documentary of what Slutsky calls "the last great untold story in rock & roll."

Bassists today, though, are well aware of his legacy. Born on January 29, 1936, James Lee Jamerson was raised on the sounds of gospel, jazz, and blues radio stations. Following his parents' divorce, Jamerson's mother relocated from Charleston to Detroit to find work in 1953, sending for James a year later. While attending Northwestern High School, he picked up an acoustic bass in the school's music room and discovered his "voice." He quickly sharpened his skills at jam sessions with Detroit's top jazz musicians and came under the influence of bass heroes like Paul Chambers and Ray Brown. James got club work in jazz, blues, and R&B nightspots, and before long he was recording for Detroit's labels, including Motown—where, in 1959, he met his future soulmates, the Funk Brothers.

In '61, at the urging of friend and fellow bassist Horace "Chili" Ruth, Jamerson strapped on a Fender Precision. The planets must have been aligned over Detroit that day, as Jamerson quickly took to an instrument he didn't particularly care for at first. Gradually he began applying melodic fills, string-raked walking lines, chromatic passing tones, dizzying syncopations, and other innovations that forged the template for modern electric bass playing. In the process, his inspiration touched pioneering session peers Chuck Rainey and Carol Kaye and reached across the ocean to concurrent rockers like Paul McCartney and Jack Bruce. His pervasive influence continues to this day. Notes Nathan Watts, "His genius even extends to keyboard bass. The master of that idiom, Stevie Wonder, is a Jamerson disciple when it comes to his left hand."

Unfortunately, James Jamerson's tale has a sad ending. When Motown moved to Los Angeles in 1972, Jamerson followed, but he never quite fit in without his Funk Brothers surrounding him. Beset with personal problems and plagued by alcoholism, his performance suffered and work slowed. He was said to be broke and bitter about his lack of recognition at the time of his death from a combination of cirrhosis of the liver, heart failure, and pneumonia. Had he survived just a few more years, he would have heard the accolades he was due.

★ JAMERSON'S RHYTHM-SECTION LOCKUP
BY ALLAN "DR. LICKS" SLUTSKY ★

From 1958 through 1972, Motown cranked out one hit after another, and the rhythm-section musicians of that era—known collectively as the Funk Brothers— were the R&B equivalent of the 1927 Yankees. Tormented genius James Jamerson was their Babe Ruth; Benny Benjamin, the most explosive drummer of his time, was the band's Lou Gehrig. When they locked up on a recording date, the dance floors of the world began to shake. The final tally of No. 1 hits Jamerson & Co. played on during this period exceeds the total No. 1 output of the Beatles, Stones, Elvis, and Beach Boys . . . combined!

> "Sometimes I'd just look at a flower, and the way it would sway would make me feel like playing a certain way."
>
> —JAMES JAMERSON

Jamerson erupted on the scene like a super nova. A converted upright player, he set the music world on its ass with his unprecedented use of syncopation and chromaticism in a pop/R&B format. "You couldn't write for him," muses former Motown arranger Gil Askey. "You'd give him a chart and he'd look at you with that grin and say, 'You really want me to play this?', and you'd say, 'No, I want you to do your thing.' So he'd tear up the chart and throw it on the floor and play something way better than anything the arrangers could dream up."

Armed with his old German upright and a '62 Fender Precision he dubbed "The Funk Machine," James got inspiration from a variety of sources. "Sometimes I'd just look at a flower, and the way it would sway would make me feel like playing a certain way," he once mused. In the same breath he admitted to conceiving a Temptations bass line by watching the way a fat woman's behind moved when she walked.

You need to hear only the intro to Martha & the Vandellas' "Dancing in the Street" to know where Benny Benjamin was coming from: energy and attitude.

He also excelled in subtle kick-drum shadings, deft brush work, and the originality of his beats. (Dig the war-dance toms on the Miracles' "Going to a Go-Go.") But above all, he was known for his constant quarter-note snare drum groove, which pounded the beat to oblivion on songs like Stevie Wonder's "Uptight" and "I Was Made to Love Her."

Benny wasn't the greatest shuffle player, which necessitated an additional Funk Brother: Richard "Pistol" Allen, master of the Motown shuffle. Benny's other flaw was his alcohol and drug dependence. You never knew what his condition would be when he showed up for a session—if he showed up at all. Enter Uriel Jones, the best Benny Benjamin clone this side of Stevie Wonder. Jones comments, "Papa Zita [Benny's nickname] invented that Motown beat, and he taught it to us. Because of all his problems, we probably played drums on more Motown hits than he did. But he was Funk Brother No. 1." Benny's abusive lifestyle finally stilled his sticks in 1968, when he died as a result of heroin addiction. The ensuing deterioration of Jamerson's physical and mental health caused Motown to bring in Bob Babbitt to fill the void. Eventually Jamerson's alcoholism caught up with him in 1983 when he, too, succumbed.

To this day, the surviving Funk Brothers still marvel at James and Benny's aggressive, unrelenting lock. "You really had to stay on top of the beat to keep up with them," recalls percussionist Jack Ashford. "If you laid back, they'd leave you in the dust. They were so bad, you could make a chicken squawk on *two* and *four* and if those two guys were playing behind it, it'd be a hit."

★ DEEP CUTS: ESSENTIAL JAMES JAMERSON ★

For an in-depth immersion into Jamerson's pioneering funk style, cue up these twelve Motown tracks …

"Bernadette" (the Four Tops)
"I Was Made to Love Her" (Stevie Wonder)
"I Heard It Through the Grapevine" (Gladys Knight)
"What's Going On" (Marvin Gaye)
"Ain't No Mountain High Enough" (Marvin Gaye and Tammi Terrell)
"(I'm a) Roadrunner" (Junior Walker)
"Home Cookin'" (Junior Walker)
"For Once in My Life" (Stevie Wonder)
"My Guy" (Mary Wells)
"You Keep Me Hanging On" (the Supremes)
"Shoo-Be-Doo-Be-Doo-Da-Day" (Stevie Wonder)

"Mutiny" (Junior Walker)
... *and these ten non-Motown hits.*

"(Your Love Keeps Lifting Me) Higher and Higher" (Jackie Wilson)
"Boogie Fever" (the Sylvers)
"Show and Tell" (Al Wilson)
"Rock the Boat" (the Hues Corporation)
"You Don't Have to Be a Star" (Marilyn McCoo and Billy Davis Jr.)
"Heaven Must Have Sent You" (Bonnie Pointer)
"Theme from S.W.A.T." (Rhythm Heritage)
"Boom, Boom, Boom" (John Lee Hooker)
"(Just Like) Romeo and Juliet" (the Reflections)

★ DEEPER CUTS: JAMES JAMERSON ON THE TEMPTATIONS' "I CAN'T GET NEXT TO YOU" BY CHRIS JISI WITH RON BROWN ★

When it comes to James Jamerson aficionados and experts, few rival Ron Brown. A top Los Angeles session bassist from the mid '60s to the late '70s, Brown befriended the Motown genius and became an authority on his style, often transcribing James's parts. Not that Brown didn't have it going on himself. Ron's credits range from Motown artists like Gladys Knight, the Temptations, and the Four Tops to the Monkees, B. B. King, and Freddie Hubbard. His '58 Fender Precision can be heard on such hit singles as the Jackson 5's "Never Can Say Goodbye," Marvin Gaye's "I Want You," Barry White's "I'm Gonna Love You Just a Little More Baby," and the Beach Boys' "Here Comes the Night."

Ron first met Jamerson in 1969, during a visit to the Hitsville studio while on a tour with the Fifth Dimension in Detroit. Ron recalls, "I was beside myself, but James was just as nice as he could be, letting me try his bass and read the chart for the session." When Jamerson moved to L.A. in 1973, the two hooked up and became good friends, frequently getting together to hang out and cook fish—a favorite activity of Jamerson's. Among Brown's prized possessions are a multi-song demo Jamerson cut at Ron's house for a female artist and a live tape of the Funk Brothers from Detroit's Chit Chat Club that "Jamie"—as Ron called him—played upright on and gave to Brown.

Like all Jamerson fans, he was elated by the release of the film soundtrack *Standing in the Shadows of Motown*, particularly The Deluxe Edition's "naked instrumental remixes of the original hits." One reveals Jamerson's brilliant, propulsive part on the Temptations' 1969 No. 1 hit "I Can't Get Next to You."

The groove kicks off after Earl Van Dyke's bluesy rubato piano intro, with Jamerson grabbing a unison line with the guitars and keyboard for the first verse. (If you don't have "naked" track handy, you'll have no problem following Jamerson's energetic part in the regular version.) According to Brown, the subtle swing feel present in everything Jamerson and the Funk Brothers played is an important element of his style, especially in straight feels like this one. Early in the song you can really hear the swing in the pickups to beats *one* and *four*, which feel more like triplets than 16ths. Jamerson stays with this figure until he introduces one of his trademark fills leading into the first chorus—a key shape that he will embellish and develop as the song goes along. Explains Brown, "The drop-down from *C* to the open *E* in beats *two* and *four* is a classic Jamerson move, probably rooted in his jazz upright background."

The chorus finds Jamerson slyly "spelling out" the *F* and *Fm* chords before adding a chromatic-laden fill. Offers Brown, "James's chromatic approach was also jazz-rooted. When I was over his house one day, he showed me the chromatic exercise I contributed to the original *Standing in the Shadows of Motown* book." ("Igor's Chromatic Exercise" appears on page 91 of the Jamerson tribute/instructional book.) Brown notes that Jamerson is able to get away with the occasional note that might seem odd. "They work in the context of the overall phrase and with James's deep, staccato sound—thanks to his touch, old flatwound strings, and the foam rubber under his P-Bass's bridge cover. Plus, it works perfectly in generating a feeling for the track."

In the second verse, Jamerson really digs in with syncopated figures and fills, injecting subtle rhythmic and pitch differences each time. "James had an uncanny sense of time that allowed him to trick the ear; he'd make you think he was going to do something out of time, but he always knew where *one* was, and he'd make it back."

In the breakdown, Jamerson answers the jangly, major-sounding guitar riff with cool, bluesy notes and alternate bar fills with tasty chromaticisms and open-string bounces. In the third chorus, Jamerson moves upward in motion and pitch for the first time, setting the stage for one of his trademark arpeggio drops on the measure's last four notes: *G, E, C,* and *E*. "He took great advantage of the range of the 4-string, and his use of open strings as passing tones to get around is well documented," says Brown.

"Dynamics were such a key part to his sound—accenting and emphasizing different notes and varying his touch within a measure," adds Brown. "His so-called ghost notes could vary from a dead thump to a dampened pitch: He would lightly fret a note with his left hand and also stop it with his right hand."

Ron concludes, "'I Can't Get Next to You' is a prime example of how Jamerson drove a track from the bottom while the vocalists drove it from the top. The presence of those two melodies is what made Motown unique and special. James was in a class entirely by himself. He set the tone and foundation for the electric bass guitar and brought it to the forefront of contemporary music."

★ THE JAMERSON STYLE BY CHRIS JISI ★

Chris Jisi asked a tribe of Jamerson disciples to analyze just what was so unique, so revolutionary, and so funky about James Jamerson's playing.

Chuck Rainey: Two ingredients are key to James Jamerson's style. One, he built many of his lines from the root-5th-octave shape, and then he'd add other scale tones, as well as non-scale chromatic passing tones, to create motion and melodic lines. That was his major influence on my style. A classic example is the kind of stuff he played on "Bernadette" by the Four Tops.

Second, the Motown drummers' Latin-influenced rhythms—a hidden *baiao* type of feel—also left open space for Jamerson. The dual result was that he had more room to stretch creatively, and he was more audible. On Motown tracks the bass is the most audible element other than the singer. Like all great musicians, James heard other things in his head while he played—such as polyrhythms from the drum patterns—and when he added those ideas they came through loud and clear, but they always locked with the groove and supported the song. Coming from his upright background, James plucked mainly with one finger, using all upstrokes. His heavy touch, high P-Bass action, and "real man" attitude resulted in strong, singing notes. I remember showing him my back-and-forth index-finger plucking technique, and he laughed and said, "that's sissy stuff right there."

Michael Henderson: James Jamerson's whole concept was melodic syncopated soul. He was all-melodic, like a saxophonist or pianist, but with a bass player's attitude. Rhythmically he could keep a syncopation going and developing through entire sections, and he knew it's what you *don't* play that makes the record go. And he never played the same thing twice. You couldn't get bored with what he was playing because you didn't *know* what he was going to do. He also had a way of getting notes that weren't on the bass. Like on the *E* string, he'd go between the *G* and *F*, but he wouldn't get an *F♯*—it was something else! He'd fret it just enough to get a ghosted note with some pitch to it. I think Jamerson had perfect pitch; at a club one night I saw him play a bass that had serious intonation problems, and he bent and pulled the strings so every note was in tune. His strings were dead flatwounds; [Philly session bassist] Ronnie Baker used to rub butter on his strings to try to get a sound like James had. And his action was so high, you had to get your friend to help you play *B♭*! But it made every note he played a nuclear weapon. He had a take-no-prisoners approach to playing; every song was a knockout.

FRED THOMAS WITH JAMES BROWN
(COURTESY OF ALLAN SLUTSKY)

2.
THE BASSISTS OF JAMES BROWN

★ THE RHYTHM SECTIONS OF SOUL BROTHER NO. 1
BY ALLAN "DR. LICKS" SLUTSKY ★

No one drove woofers and tweeters into fits of impassioned ecstasy like the bassists and drummers on James Brown records. Unlike the musicians at Motown and Stax, no single rhythm section was immediately identifiable with Brown's sound. The key element was the musical concept itself—a constantly evolving and, at times, combative vision between Brown and a band that reinvented itself more times than Madonna.

"When James hired me in 1956, he didn't have a bass player," says Bernard Odum, the closest thing to a permanent bassist the Godfather of Soul ever had

in the early decades. "His band at the time was just piano, sax, guitar, and drums. I was the fifth man." Brown's late '50s recordings consisted of derivative jump blues and 12/8 ballads that entertained many but broke little new ground.

Brown's rhythm and funk revolution finally began during a period from mid 1964 through mid '65. The arrival of a new drummer—North Carolina college student Melvin Parker—was the catalyst. Parker's cross-stick-driven, eighth-note hi-hat grooves fueled "Out of Sight," "Papa's Got a Brand New Bag," and "I Got You (I Feel Good)," a trio of blues-based hits that shook R&B to its foundation. Sam Thomas, the bassist on the first two, as well as David (Hooks) Williams, who played on "I Got You," were essentially rent-a-bassists. Nonetheless their rhythmic explorations were significant, as they may have produced R&B's first serious lockup between kick drum and electric bass.

Two years later, from the moment "Cold Sweat" hit the airwaves, the face of popular music changed forever. Drummer Clyde Stubblefield and his jaw-dropping backbeat fused with Odum and guitarists Jimmy Nolen and "Country" Kellum in a minimalist expression of jagged, angular lines that would have made no sense unless played together. Every instrument had essentially been turned into a drum working over a simple modal background. Harmony and pitch were irrelevant. Resistance was futile. Rhythm ruled.

The experiment continued through the next three years with the addition of two new bassists, Charles "Sweets" Sherrell and Tim Drummond, as well as two significant drummers: John "Jab'o" Starks and Nate Jones. Master tapes for such hits as "Funky Drummer," "Mother Popcorn," and "Licking Stick" were produced faster than the vinyl could be pressed. Things looked rosy for the Godfather, but a new revolution was brewing—this time from inside his band.

Frustrated by low wages and poor working conditions, Brown's group mutinied in 1970. His response was to can them and replace them with a Cincinnati club band called the Pacemakers. The new bassist was an unknown teenager named William "Bootsy" Collins; Brown immediately paired him with Jab'o Starks, the lone musician he had kept. The impact was as immediate and intense as it was short-lived. Bootsy's over-the-top style formed a perfect match for Stark's mature, Latin-tinged R&B groove, resulting in a staggering series of performances like "Get Up (I Feel Like Being a) Sex Machine" and "Talkin' Loud and Sayin' Nothing." Unable to deal with Brown's restrictive disciplinary code, Bootsy was gone within a year.

Tired of virtuosi and their attitudes, Brown went back to the streets to simplify his life and sound. With the addition of New York club musician Fred Thomas, Bootsy's syncopated 16th-note bombast was replaced by a simpler, more direct eighth-note style that once again paid off in gold and platinum for the Godfather.

What was the creative process like in the studio with Brown, and who came up with those ideas? "James sang most of my lines," explains Fred Thomas, "but he'd give it to you so blunt you'd say, 'What kind of line is this?' You had to lock into it and move it around to give it a good feelin'." Starks, Fred's funk partner, concurs: "James wanted everyone to think all the ideas came from him, but it wasn't like that. The trick was to work with his ideas, turn them into your own thing, and then make him believe it was his idea in the first place. That's how the James Brown grooves always came together."

★ SUPER BAD: PLAYING BASS WITH JAMES BROWN BY JIMMY LESLIE ★

The music made by James Brown and his ever-changing band is among the most influential of the 20th century. Not much remains to be said about James Brown that hasn't been covered by the media—or wasn't said by Mr. Dynamite himself. But not enough has been said about the amazing bassists who backed him up for five decades.

Scores of low-enders bounced in and out of Brown's band, but Fred Thomas held the bass chair in the world's premier funk & soul outfit for the better part of 33 years. He anchored the fort on such hits as "Hot Pants, Pt. 1," "Make It Funky, Pt. 1," and "Papa Don't Take No Mess." The sheer number of hip-hop tracks that use those lines prompted Brown to refer to Thomas as the "most sampled bass player in the world." If anyone is warranted to take issue with that statement, it's another Brown alumnus, William "Bootsy" Collins. Bootsy was involved with Brown's band only for a short time, but during his tenure he recorded several anthems, including "Get Up (I Feel Like Being a) Sex Machine," "Super Bad," and "Soul Power, Pts. 1 & 2," which ushered in an era of deeper funk that Collins later incorporated into his work with Parliament-Funkadelic and his own Rubber Band.

Almost as legendary as the man and the music is the iron-fisted manner in which James Brown ran his bands. Tales of fines for missed cues and unshined shoes have loomed large in the lore of working musicians. Two years before Brown's death, when he was still touring actively, we corralled Collins, Thomas, and the most recent co-holder of the bass chair, Ray Brundidge, to learn what it was really like to be a soul man in Soul Band No. 1.

When did you first encounter James Brown?

Ray Brundidge: I was 12 years old when "Mother Popcorn" came out in '69, and my friend and I took a bus to Buffalo to catch James's show. He had a bigger band than the one we have now—three drummers, multiple horns, dancers—and I think Bernard Odum was on bass. That was actually my first concert, and it made me focus on playing music.

Fred Thomas: I got a chance to see him live as James Brown & the Famous Flames when I was in high school in Georgia.

Bootsy Collins: I met him when I was 15. My brother [Phelps "Catfish" Collins] and I were in the house band at Cincinnati's King Studios, but when James and his band came to town, it was always a closed session. We couldn't get near him, but we would hang out with his group on their cigarette breaks. They were like our older brothers, our heroes. Then one day the band went to lunch while James was in the studio recording "Licking Stick." We were around the door, just buzzin', when his road manager, Bud, came to the door. He said Mr. Brown wanted us to come in and maybe lay down this bass line. That was my first encounter with him. We worked on it for a while, but we didn't get the chance to put it to tape before the band came back.

How did you come to be in James Brown's band?

Bootsy Collins: At first I thought they were kidding when we got the call to play with James that very night, and that his Learjet was on its way to pick us up. His management said they wanted us to "play with James Brown," but we didn't think they meant it literally. We thought, Even if this is true, we'll probably just be playing our regular set. They didn't tell us the band had walked out, so we kind of crossed the picket line—unbeknownst to us—until we actually got to the gig. Then we started seeing all these long faces on our friends and our heroes—Charles Sherrell and Bernard Odum were there—and it was like, "Wow, what have we done?" James said, "I want y'all to play the set with me. How much do you want?" We had no alternative but to go on! [*Laughs.*]

Fred Thomas: When I got to New York in 1965 I hooked up with [guitarist] Hearlon "Cheese" Martin and formed my first band, which I played with until I met James in 1971. One night we were working at this club in Harlem called Small's Paradise, which was owned by Wilt Chamberlain. James entered with his entourage, and everybody was hollering for him to come up and sing a song. "Sex Machine" was the hot record at the time, and he said, "Can I count it off?" We wore him out, and after that he said, "I want this band." We were rehearsing within a week or so, because Bootsy and those guys were having a conflict with James at the time. He needed a new band, and we were it.

Ray Brundidge: The funny thing is, I almost wound up in Billy Joel's band instead. They asked me to join, but I was busy with my band and Billy wasn't such a big deal then. A short time later I moved to California, and an old guitarist friend of mine who was in James's band brought me to Mr. Brown's attention. Years later, in 1998, they called me in to play with James so that Fred wouldn't get worn out.

How did you go about assimilating the tunes and making them work for your own style?

Bootsy Collins: We didn't go back and study anything. We just played it the way we felt it should be, which brought a freshness, and James liked it.

Fred Thomas: I already knew James's music, because my band did all the hot tunes from '66 until I joined. I did my own thing, which is to keep a nice bottom in the pocket. I never bothered with any fancy stuff because I always did the singing in my bands, and you can't be fancy and sing. I had to discipline myself to stick to the pattern. I pluck with my thumb and index finger in combination. It's kind of like a picking thing: down with the thumb and up with the index finger, which makes it more smooth and even than just playing the fast lick with my thumb. I go with the thumb until it goes fast enough that I need more notes, and then I grab them with my pinch [index] finger. For basic tunes like "Good Foot" and "Doing It to Death," I just scrape the strings with my thumb.

Ray Brundidge: Basically, you learn from the guy who came before you, and I learned by watching Fred. Everything sounded good, but there wasn't a lot of slapping and popping going on, so I figured that could be my niche. The first time I tried it, I turned up the treble on my amp so I could get a little pop. But James wasn't used to it and said, "Son, that doesn't sound like a bass. You don't know how to adjust an amp—let me do it for you!" Then he readjusted my amp so it was really deep and I couldn't get a pop out of it [*laughs*]. I held off on trying to pop again until I got to play "Living in America," which has a little bit of slap and pop. That was still a slow process because James likes Ampeg SVT amps, and for pluckin' and poppin' you need more of an SWR kind of thing. Finally, we did a show where no SVTs were available. They had an SWR with a horn in it, so I did some slapping on "Living in America," and James loved it. Now he'll point me in specifically to slap and pop.

What was it like to step onstage with Soul Brother No. 1 for the first time?

Bootsy Collins: I had been playing with everybody who wanted to be James Brown, but it took me a while to realize, I'm actually up here onstage with *the* James Brown. He told us, "All I'm going to do is call out the songs, drop my hand, and y'all are going to hit it," and that's actually what happened. After that first show he reassured us that everything would be fine once we rehearsed the songs and learned how he used his body movements and hand signals for the show. That was actually the first and only time he reassured us that everything was going to be on the *one* [*laughs*]. Once we learned the show and got it tight for real, he reversed the psychology on us—like we weren't happening—but years later I realized that it only made us tighter.

> "We just played it the way we felt it should be, which brought a freshness, and James liked it."
>
> —BOOTSY COLLINS

Fred Thomas: We rehearsed for about a week in New York and then we went to Toledo, Ohio, and played the first show. You had to have a memory like an elephant to remember two-and-a-half hours worth of hits, dips, and dancing cues. The gig went fantastic the first time out, and after that, all the butterflies were gone. To go from playing clubs to audiences in the 10,000 range, it was like, "Wow—this is show time!"

Fred, you've been with Brown's band for most of the last three decades. How has the show changed over the years?

Fred Thomas: The show runs basically the same with James. He's the man—nothing goes without his approval, and you don't add anything. But he isn't as strict now. He used to fine cats for unshined shoes, wrinkles in their suits, missed notes, and all kinds of other stuff. He did that diligently, man—I mean, all the time. You really had to mind your P's and Q's. At this stage, all he really wants is just for you to sound good so he can go out and do his thing.

Another difference is that there are less of us these days. Right now, we've got 11 people in the band: three horns, two bassists, two drummers, a percussionist, and three guitar players. We had four background singers, but now we've only got three. Back in the day we always had five or six horns; we used to have a keyboard player, too, and there would be players lurking around in the wings. He'd hold that over you, like, "Go ahead and mess up—I've got a cat right here, just waiting for your spot."

How is the stage set, how does the set work, and what exactly are some of these cues?

Ray Brundidge: The band sets up in a horseshoe configuration. Right now, Fred is in the center and I'm up on a riser on one side. James wants it that way because he wants to be able to make eye contact with everybody at all times, and he'll check to see if you're looking. You've got to see his hand signals; otherwise you're lost. Some of the signals are for individuals—in my case, to slap and pop, for instance. Others are for the whole group, like to move right or move left. He has his own language of signals and movements onstage, and you've got to be able to understand it, because you have only a split second to decide what he means before it's too late. He changes the songs, too; the basic idea might stay somewhat consistent, but he can add a lot of other parts until it winds up totally different.

Fred Thomas: He's got signals for things like "cutoff," or he might call a little name, like a "deaf bar"—where you play *D–E♭–F–B*—or he might throw a cue where everybody plays [*vocalizes a break part*] right in the middle of the song. And he doesn't have a particular order for the songs. He has a basic set to draw from, but you never know what song he might call. You've got to be prepared for anything.

Were there always two bass players in the show?

Bootsy Collins: I was the only bassist at the time. They always said they got two after I left to replace what I was doing [*laughs*].

Fred Thomas: I was the only one when I first joined, but then he used to bring in all kinds of guys; "Sweet" Charles [Sherrell] and Jimmy Mack were in and out. I think Bernard Odum even came back a couple of times.

How does it work onstage with two bassists?

Fred Thomas: Depending on the song, James will call who he wants to play. Some nights he might hear something different and switch up from the guy who normally plays a certain song. So you've got to know everything.

You and Ray play together at certain points. How do you work that out?

Fred Thomas: It's an experience playing the show with two bassists. Ray plays a 4-string and I play a 5, so we'll hook up on different songs and do complementary stuff, but we don't really play the same pattern at the same time. Like on "Try Me," I'll use that 5th string just to drop the low *C* on it, and then I'm out. Little stuff like that adds color. Or I'll play "Make It Funky" and Ray will just play a subtle little lick, but you can feel it. You can do a lot to help kick the funk, but we listen and make sure it's not interfering with anybody—that it's really helping and not just there. Of course, James looks at everything.

James seems to pay attention to every little detail of what you guys are doing.

Fred Thomas: Yeah, he does [*laughs*]. He's got big ol' beaver ears, believe me! That cat don't miss nothin'. One time when the band was rehearsing, Ray and I hooked up different lines for playing this song. When James heard it, he was like, [*in raspy James Brown voice*] "Nobody play—just the bass players." We played what we came up with, and he said, "Okay." He didn't take it out, because it was complementary to the melodic line, and it really worked.

Ray Brundidge: James is always searching for something different. One day on the road he wanted to change the "Sex Machine" bass line to more of a rolling, walking line. Fred did the walk-down line, and James gave me a part that I could put some snaps on. It sounded pretty good, and now it's in the show like that.

In the early years, how were bass parts conceived when a new James Brown song was being fleshed out?

Bootsy Collins: James would give you some grunts, and then you'd have to play it back and say, "Is this what you're talking about?" As long as what you played made him feel good, that was it—whether it was what he meant in the first place or not. The rhythm section didn't write anything down, because we played by ear and feel. Everybody seemed to like us for doing it that way, so that's what we built on. The first new James Brown song I played on was "Sex Machine." We were on the bus after a gig when he and [backup singer] Bobby Byrd hopped on. They didn't have any paper, so they tore up a paper bag and started writing the lyrics. My brother and I were sitting behind them with our guitar and bass, fooling around with the groove. We went straight from the gig to the studio, and that's where it all started happening.

Fred Thomas: The line on "Doing It to Death (Funky Good Time)" is the line I felt, but mostly, you played what he told you to play. If the line wasn't happening, you found your own way to make it funkier by adding a little space or attacking it differently. For instance, he gave me the "Good Foot" line, but it sucked. It wasn't saying jack, so I put a little James Jamerson-type ghost note in there. It was up to me to make it happen, and I think that was the case with all of his musicians.

Fred, inside Brown's *Star Time* box set, it says the bassist on "Papa Don't Take No Mess" was either you or Charles Sherrell. Can you clear that up?

Fred Thomas: It was definitely me—Sweets doesn't play like that. He has more of a thump and a light picking thing, whereas my notes are more laid down, more played. [Contrary to the liner notes] Sweet Charles did play on "The Payback," though. James gave him that line, but Sweets put a little pickup note in there that changed the feel and made it flow better.

Was the touring band and the studio band always the same entity?

Fred Thomas: Mostly it was, especially with the rhythm section, but the last of James's recording heydays were '71 through '76; after that, he did no more recordings that really made noise, except [1985's] "Living in America." I played on nothing after 1976.

Can you give us a story about being disciplined by James?

Ray Brundidge: I was studying Fred a lot, and I was amazed at the tone he was getting. Fred plays "down" with his thumb. That was something I had to learn. James said, "You play good, but I want you to play down." Most fingerstyle players like myself sort of play "up"—that's the direction the fingers are going when they pluck a note. But James thinks like a drummer—that when you are playing on a downbeat, your thumb should literally strike down on the string. That cleans it up so you aren't playing all those extra notes. James mentioned that he was going to charge me $25 every time he caught me not playing "down" [*laughs*]. After a couple of fines, I learned it's better to give him what he wants!

Fred Thomas: The last time I got fired was in 1995. I like to play with my eyes closed. I can just feel and hear better that way—but James is not with that. I usually manage to keep one eye cracked, but that last time he fired me, I had stayed under too long. When I did look up, he was right in my face throwing his hand down with his fingers pointing out, and every one of those means you're fined five bucks. He fined me 50 bucks and fired me, even though I didn't mess up anything. I was only out for about a month.

Bootsy Collins: James was like a father to me, and he treated me like a son. He lectured me every night after the show, and he would always tell me, [*in a low, scratchy James Brown voice*] "Son, I'm sorry. You just ain't on the *one.*" He kept doing that to me—so one night I took acid, and I cannot remember what happened during the set. All I remember is thinking that the bass turned into a snake. I broke all the strings, threw it down, and left the stage. I don't know how they finished the show, but afterwards, James called me back to the dressing room. He started lecturing me again, and I was trippin'—I just fell on the floor and could not stop laughing. James told his bodyguard, "Get that fool out of here!" They kicked me out of the dressing room, and from that night on, he never called me in there again for another lecture! [*Laughs.*]

Fred, you've been with James's band the longest. Can you offer some perspective on playing in his bands, and his music's place in history?

Fred Thomas: I have a lot to be proud of. I don't have a lot of money, but I'm fine—and I did something. I've been involved in one of the biggest, most legendary acts in the world. It's gone on for a long time—33 years, on and off—and I feel good about the musicians I've played with, like Bootsy and Ray. The Soul Music

Hall of Fame videotaped that show we all did together there, which is great because my grandkids and my great-grandkids can go there and see me long after I'm gone out of this place. I feel real good about the fact that I'll go down in history.

★ DEEPER CUTS: TWO TAKES ON JAMES BROWN'S "GIVE IT UP OR TURNIT A LOOSE" BY CHRIS JISI ★

The various JB outfits embody the concept that a rhythm section should be greater than the sum of its parts. A great deal of music flowed from the Brown machine, often on different versions of the same song. A good example is "Give It Up or Turnit a Loose."

The first version of the song was cut in October 1968, at Miami's famed Criteria Studios, with Charles "Sweets" Sherrell on bass and new drummer Nate Jones sitting in for JB drum institution Clyde Stubblefield. Sherrell himself had replaced Bernard Odum, ushering in a more aggressive, busy, and syncopated style. Sherrell's main verse groove is repeated twice to match up with the accompanying two-bar guitar phrase. While the drum part may be a bit too "peekaboo" to firmly hang your hat on, Jimmy Nolen's syncopated single-note guitar line is a virtual counterpoint to the bass line, and perfect to lock up with as it keeps time in the open spaces. The bridge bass line is pretty much the same part up a fourth, but with Alfonzo "Country" Kellum's chordal guitar part serving as hitching post. To cop the funky feel, be precise with your attack and keep all the back-end 16th notes short, but remember to relax and breathe to help make it funky and hypnotic.

Brown recut the song in July 1970 to capture what had become a showstopping live staple. Although six other tracks on the *Sex Machine* album were recorded in concert, this one was cut in the studio, with overdubbed applause. Still, the energy upgrade is immediate, from the brighter tempo to Phelps "Catfish" Collins's slightly more syncopated single-note guitar line and drummer Clyde Stubblefield's intense issuing of his classic "Funky Drummer"-style groove. Catfish's brother, a young William "Bootsy" Collins, gives the biggest push of all: He took the James Brown bass chair to its busiest, most in-your-face level. Bootsy extends the verse part to a true two-bar phrase (instead of Sherrell's one-bar phrase repeated twice) by ascending to the octave via chord tones and chromatics. He also adds more notes and bounces off an open *A*. Takin' it to the bridge, Bootsy's bass continues in a similar, slightly busier vein, cutting loose via climbs to an ear-grabbing octave.

3.
GEORGE PORTER AND THE METERS

★ GEORGE PORTER: NEW ORLEANS FUNKMASTER
BY BILL MILKOWSKI, FROM A 1996 INTERVIEW ★

Any discussion of funk must include the Meters, one of the all-time great instru-mental bands in popular music. In the late '60s the Meters came along and put a decidedly New Orleans spin on the genre with such infectious funk anthems as "Cissy Strut," "Chicken Strut," "Look-Ka Py Py," and "Funky Miracle." Their laid-back, loose-but-tight approach paved the way for '70s funksters like War, Cameo, Con Funk Shun, the Commodores, Kool & the Gang, Rufus, Slave, the Fatback Band, Mandrill, the Gap Band, and the Average White Band. And the Meters' influence can still be felt in the current hip-hop scene, as evidenced by

the many sampled grooves taken from their funky archives.

Formed in 1965 by keyboardist Art Neville, guitarist Leo Nocentelli, drummer Joseph "Zigaboo" Modeliste, and bassist George Porter Jr., the Meters captured national and later international attention with their ear-catching rhythms and soulful, syncopated interplay. Under the direction of producer Allen Toussaint and manager Marshall Sehorn, the Meters recorded three albums for Josie Records—*The Meters*, *Look-Ka Py Py*, and *Struttin'*—before they were picked up by Warner Bros. in 1972 and made five more albums: *Cabbage Alley*, *Rejuvenation*, *Fire on the Bayou*, *Trick Bag*, and *New Directions*. (Percussionist Cyril Neville, Art's brother, became the fifth member of the band during the Warner Bros. era.) *Funkify Your Life*, the two-CD Rhino anthology of their work from 1968 through 1977, is the perfect primer for would-be funk fans to delve more deeply into the Meters' unique brand of soul music.

Though the Meters officially disbanded in 1978, they have had various reunions and reincarnations over the years, usually with David Russell Batiste replacing original drummer Modeliste, and—with the band known as the Funky Meters—guitarist Brian Stolz replacing Nocentelli. The band still lays down super-funky versions of "Cissy Strut" and "Hey Pocky-Way," and Porter—whose muscular, inventive bass lines helped to define the Meters' slippery brand of funk from the very beginning—remains the backbone of the group.

Born on the day after Christmas in 1947, George Porter Jr. has long been highly regarded as one of the progenitors of funk bass. His work with the Meters alone merits him a place in Bass Valhalla, but Porter has also recorded solo albums and contributed his signature lines to recordings by such diverse artists as Paul McCartney, Robbie Robertson, Earl King, Robert Palmer, Patti LaBelle, Dr. John, Eddie Bo, Taj Mahal, Maceo Parker, Solomon Burke, Johnny Adams, Jimmy

Buffett, David Byrne, Tori Amos, Harry Connick Jr., and Snooks Eaglin. Aside from the Funky Meters he's stayed busy with his own seven-piece horn band, Runnin' Pardners, and with Porter Batitste Stoltz, and ongoing sideman work.

Was bass your first instrument?

No, I started on piano at age eight and went from there to acoustic guitar. I studied on Saturdays with Hamilton Brown; he would teach us cowboy songs because they were simpler, just to get us into the technique, so I was playing stuff like "Home on the Range." But on the way to my class, I would pass my friend Papee's house, and he'd be sitting on the porch playing "St. Louis Woman" and all this raunchy bluesy stuff with his grandfather. I'd say, "Man, that's what I wanna play." So on my second guitar recital I was supposed to play "Red River Valley," but I walked out onstage and played "St. Louis Woman" instead. The teacher threw me out; he said, "You're unruly, you got no discipline, you're never gonna be anything." That made my mom pretty upset, because the deal I made with my parents was that if I was going to play music, I had to learn the procedure—had to read, had to go through all the steps of playing, and had to have a teacher. But I had already learned how to read from my piano lessons; I just had to apply it to guitar. So I got Papee as my teacher, and he began teaching me the blues, which I wanted to play anyway. Through Papee I learned about Earl King and Snooks Eaglin, but it wasn't until years later that I actually got to play with those guys.

> "To me, syncopation is like jazz—it wasn't meant for the masses, it was meant for just a hip few."

Did your study of classical guitar, which is played with the fingers, help you when you got to bass?

Yeah, although I'm still very much a thumb player. If I'm doing anything that's swinging or really fast I'll use my fingers, but I actually believe my thumb is faster than my fingers. I've developed an up-and-down stroke that works well, and I use my thumb almost as a pick—sort of like Wes Montgomery.

Do you slap?

I do very little slapping. You might hear me do it for something like a turn-around. I'm trying to make a rule not to go in that direction, though; it's painful, and I'm too old to learn new tricks.

What were some of your first gigs around New Orleans?

I started playing with guys like Earl King and Benny Spellman when I was 14 years old, at little things like Friday night fish fries. I used to sit on the steps and work my way into the house, but most of the time youngsters didn't get a shot at getting into the room where these guys were jamming. So I'd just listen. I heard Earl King music and Snooks Eaglin music being played—I didn't meet Snooks 'til the '70s, but I'd been playing his songs for ten years by then. I started playing with Earl King in the mid '60s at fraternity parties. I wasn't even in the band; I was just helping them move equipment to and from the gig. When a guy in the band would get an eye for one of the girls in the audience, he'd leave the stage and I'd play his axe while he'd run off with the little chick for a while. I got to play bass, guitar, and drums that way.

Did you own a bass at the time?

No, I was playing bass lines on a guitar. In fact, the first bass I played was a 6-string guitar with the top two strings taken off. That's what I learned on; I'd sit on the steps with Papee playing acoustic guitars, and I would play the bass lines. My first gig was with Papee, playing in a sanctified church. He liked playing bass on that kind of uptempo sanctified music, though, so I wound up playing guitar that time. I think we got paid $2 each. I got my first electric bass around '63. A guy named Richard Dixon had a Fender Jazz Bass; he had painted it red and the *G* tuning peg was gone. He pawned it to me for $50, but he never intended on coming back for it—he took that $50 I gave him and bought himself a hollow-body Epiphone bass guitar. I was thrilled to have my own bass, even though it had only three strings. I played that 3-string bass for almost a year and a half with Art Neville & the Neville Sounds.

Where did you play with that band?

We played this place called the Nite Cap three nights a week; two of the nights we played for a flat fee, and Sunday night we would take the door. We built up the Sunday nights to where we were making lots of money, and then the manager of the club wanted to take our Sunday night away from us and pay us a flat fee. So we quit that gig and got a better one on Bourbon Street at a place called the Ivanhoe—and that's when all hell broke loose.

Who was in that band?

That band was Zig Modeliste on drums, Art Neville on keyboards, Leo Nocentelli on guitar, a saxophone player named Gary Brown, and myself. [Vocalist/percussionist] Cyril Neville was too young at the time to come into the joint, but he would sneak in every now and then and sing with the band. Aaron Neville would come by and sit in too; he'd sing "Tell It Like It Is," and the house would go crazy.

That 3-string bass made it through the whole year at the Nite Cap, but when Art called me up about the gig on Bourbon Street, he told me I had to get another string or I wasn't going to be able to keep the gig. So I told my mom I needed another bass, and she got me a Melody Plus, which was a Japanese copy of a Hofner bass. I played that at the Ivanhoe for a little more than a year, 1966 going into 1967. Near the end of '67, we recorded our first song as the Meters, "Sophisticated Cissy." That was actually a break song we used to play at the Nite Cap. There were several songs that came up later in the Meters repertoire that were created at the Nite Cap.

What do you recall about the Meters' first recording session?

When we went into the studio for the first time, we had only that one song, "Sophisticated Cissy." Just about everything we wrote back then got written in the studio, and that's the reason why we had such a large studio bill through our first three albums. We'd go in there dry and stay for 12, 13, 14 hours and just record until we got something. There's a lot of stuff that's come out recently that was material we never really finished.

In the very beginning, we started out as Allen Toussaint's rhythm section, backing up sessions with Lee Dorsey, Benny Harris, Lou Johnson, and a lot of artists we didn't even know. We were constantly cutting material; Allen used to just go in and cut, and we didn't know who the artist was. After Allen got tired, Marshall [Sehorn] might come in and say, "Well, why don't y'all lay down a couple tracks." Then we would stay for a few more hours and do more tracks.

"Sophisticated Cissy" came out and did really well, and that was the beginning of the Meters. Three weeks after that single was released, Marshall grabbed us and said, "Let's go in and cut an album." We had been doing pieces of stuff for Allen, so we already had plenty of material in the can. We went in there and laid down maybe four or five more tracks, and Marshall had an album. The first album had Art singing "Ride Your Pony" and "Darling Darling," but the rest was instrumental.

I recorded the first album on a Gibson hollowbody. On "Sophisticated Cissy," the *E* string was a little out of tune, but because of the way we recorded back then—straight to two-track—there was no separation, so we couldn't do the bass track over. It was a good take, so we all agreed, "Let's keep it." When we went to Atlanta for the second album [*Look-Ka Py Py*], I was having trouble keeping that Gibson bass in tune in the studio. At one point I was looking around, and I saw this old Fender Telecaster Bass sitting in the corner. It had cobwebs all over it, but man, it had such a ballsy tone. I used that bass to record a great deal of music.

What did you play after that?

I bought a fretless Precision Bass in 1970, but Art and Zig were saying I was playing out of tune, so when I got home from that tour, I acquired another bass from a friend of mine. His wife had retired him from the music business because he was always playing music for the women, you know? I mean, she took his Precision Bass and cut straight across the body with a chainsaw. But she didn't cut the neck, and that's the neck that's on the Precision that I'm using now. The body is a '70 and the neck is a '60-something.

What amp did you use on the early recordings?

I used a lot of Fender stuff until the year they came out with those Kustom 200s—that had to be '67 or '68. There was only one store in town that had those amps, and I bought two of them—black ones with 2x15 cabinets. So from that point on, I got away from the tube sound totally. Some people argue about the sound of tubes versus transistors, but I can make a tube amp or a transistor amp sound like what I want it to sound like.

Did any of the bassists on the early R&B records you listened to influence you?

No, I was influenced more by what I thought was the lack of bass. On a lot of those old R&B records, you can't hear the bass or the kick drum at all—it's all piano and voices and guitars. A lot of it was done with acoustic bass that wasn't recorded too well; that made me want to make the bass more punchy when I went to record with the Meters. I started off thinking there had to be lots of bottom, but I didn't realize that on the little bitty speakers you're listening to most of the time it's not the bottom you want but the punch. You want to hit a note and hear it come out clearly. So you get the sound to where you can hear the note, and then you add maybe 2dB of bass, just to round out the notes.

Do you use new strings for more clarity?

No, I like strings that are old and dull. My strings leave the bass when they break. Some people say I'm cheap, but I hate the sound of new strings. I would never, ever play a bass that has all brand-new strings on it; if I have to change all four of my strings, the bass is gonna sit around a while before I play on it. From the very beginning, there's never been more than two new strings on my bass at any one time.

How did the period with Warner Bros. differ from the early Josie years?

We started losing our identity because we were chasing after those elusive hit records, you know? We had been labeled too white to be black and too black to be white, so we were having trouble getting our records played on either black stations or white stations. Around that time, Leo and Zig wanted to write music that was styled like something that was already getting airplay. So when we did *Rejuvenation* in 1974, it became more of a vocal album; there was still some funky stuff, but we were trying to get a vocal hit. We thought "Africa" was going to be a hit off that album. So we went through that phase.

Did the band's chemistry change during this period?

Yes. I started removing myself further and further from the creative aspect of the band, because I wasn't willing to get in there and fight for positioning in the song pool. The last song I had written for the Meters at that point was "Same Old Thing," which was on the *Look-Ka Py Py* album maybe three years before. After *Rejuvenation*, we had lost the cohesiveness of being writers together. Everybody was staking out territory, and when certain people on the outside saw the lack of cohesiveness, they thought they could drive wedges between us. And that's what happened.

Both Art and Cyril Neville quit the band right before an appearance on Saturday Night Live that gave you incredible visibility.

Yeah, we did that gig without them. Art quit in December '77, so it might've been January '78 when we did that show. We used a keyboard player named David Batiste, whose son [David Russell Batiste] is now the drummer for the Funky Meters. At that point, Art began pursuing his real dream, which was to have a band with all of his brothers.

Was that SNL gig the beginning of the end for the Meters?

Yeah, because after that Warner Bros. got pissed off. They had what they believed to be a hit record on their hands [*New Directions*], and the two people who sang on it, Cyril and Art, weren't in the band anymore. So they just pulled the record. A few thousand copies went out, but after that—nothing. Maybe six months later I left, and Zig and Leo kept the band together for another year or so before they stopped speaking to each other.

Do you still get along with Zig? I had heard there was some kind of weirdness between you.

I don't think there's ever been any real weirdness between us, other than the competition thing. We're cousins, and our first music teacher was his older step-brother, Clinton Joshua, who taught us both how to play piano. There's always been a competition thing between us—and we're both Capricorns.

At the same time, you have this amazing chemistry.

Yeah, when we play. One thing that the Meters did great together was play music. We were all individuals, and we all lived different lives off the bandstand—but on the bandstand, the closeness we had was undeniable. We had some of our best gigs after having a big fight in the dressing room. We never got to fisticuffs, but there was howling and screaming and cussing and all of that shit. That was the craziness of it—we'd walk out of the dressing room not even speaking to each other, and then we'd play one of the ass-kickingest sets you'd ever want to hear.

Can you describe your hookup with Zig and what you developed together as a rhythm section?

I would say that bass players and drummers from New Orleans play it more together than bass players and drummers from anywhere else. In music from other places, there's more of a tendency for the bass player to play a note right after the kick drum. New Orleans bass players and drummers are more closely linked, so they're playing a note and the kick drum at the same time. Almost all the time, they are in sync rhythmically. The bass might venture away from the kick drum to play more notes, but at some point—maybe *two* and *four*—we always meet.

Zig and I created the bottom that everything grew on, and I think what Zig did on drums is undeniably the funkiest shit on the planet. But what he did, for some reason or another, has not made it to this time period. The drummers today do not have those tools in their toolbox.

The grooves you created together had a kind of natural flow.

Zig would start playing and I would find something that fit. On a lot of stuff that we wrote, Zig would just start a groove and Leo would be the second guy in. It usually took me a few minutes to figure out what the hell Zig was doing. I'd be sitting there listening and watching to make sure I had the same *one* that he had, because a lot of stuff Zig played could be interpreted differently. He used to throw off Art with some of those grooves. Art would say, "Where's *one?*" Where you come in can change the whole concept of where one is. It was all intuitive—we definitely did not write out any charts or anything like that.

Has the concept of funk changed over the years?

Definitely. I don't know what is considered funk today—I really don't. Funk music today is hip-hop, I guess. Syncopation is out. Syncopation is history. In my dealings with people at record companies, I keep being told that my music ain't funky. They say it's too syncopated.

People have to think about how to dance to music when it's syncopated, because it's not just straight 4/4 time. In the Meters, we never played anything straight 4/4. To me, syncopation is like jazz—it wasn't meant for the masses, it was meant for just a hip few.

★ DEEP CUTS: GEORGE PORTER ★

The Meters' "Cissy Strut." Porter bridges Modeliste's stuttering kick and Leo Nocentelli's slinky guitar line in "Cissy Strut."

The Meters' "Funky Miracle." Over Zig's wicked snare groove, Porter lays a bedrock vamp to open the song. Feel the forward motion created by the potent blend of George's driving, ascending eighths and Modeliste's splashy, behind-the-beat hi-hat.

LaBelle's "Lady Marmalade." With the Meters serving as producer Allen Toussaint's studio band, Porter manages to lay down a funky foundation with a lick that only fills half of the two-bar phrase.

4.
MEMPHIS AND MUSCLE SHOALS:
SOUTHERN STUDIO SOUL

★ TOMMY COGBILL: AN APPRECIATION BY CHRIS JISI ★

"Tommy Cogbill wove a major part of the fabric of American music, and he was a pioneering voice in the history and development of the electric bass." So says Nashville studio ace Michael Rhodes, and fellow Tennessee session stalwart Mike Leech agrees.

"From a historical perspective," says Leech, "he should be listed among the top five most important popular-music bassists of the last century."

"Unfortunately," says Rhodes, "he has remained anonymous to much of the musical community." Consider the credits Cogbill amassed as a Memphis and

Nashville session bassist from the late '50s until his death on December 7, 1982, due to a stroke. His résumé includes work with Aretha Franklin, Elvis Presley, Wilson Pickett, Neil Diamond, Dusty Springfield, Ray Stevens, Jimmy Buffett, and Dolly Parton, on hits ranging from Presley's "Kentucky Rain" and Diamond's "Sweet Caroline" to Springfield's "Son of a Preacher Man" and Franklin's "Natural Woman."

Rhodes, whom Cogbill took under his wing after the two met in Nashville in 1980, spoke to Cogbill's family to learn more about his musical hero. "Tommy was born in Johnson Grove, Tennessee, on April 8, 1932, and grew up in Brownsville. He started on guitar at age 6, later taking hourlong bus rides to Memphis for a year of lessons. At age 12 he began playing professionally with a fellow named Marcus Van Story. Tommy had a knack for doing whatever was needed, playing guitar, pedal steel, and—by his late teens—electric bass with Ron Jaffe and Ace Cannon. His sister even remembers him tooling around with the upright in the late '50s. Although he played all the regional styles from hillbilly to R&B, he loved jazz and was very steeped in bebop as a guitarist, with an encyclopedic knowledge of the standards—much like fellow electric-bass pioneer Carol Kaye.

"By the '60s, Tommy and his frequent partners Reggie Young and Chips Moman on guitars, Bobby Emmons on keyboards, and Gene Chrisman on drums became in demand as a traveling section doing dates in Memphis, Nashville, New York, and at Fame Studio in Muscle Shoals, Alabama, where they broke new artists for Atlantic's Jerry Wexler. When Moman bought American Sound Studios in Memphis, the five became the house section, and artists came from all over to work with them. That began a peak period from 1967–72 where Tommy's trademark 'busy' bass lines could be heard on such classic albums as *Dusty in Memphis* and Elvis's *Memphis Record*.

"Tommy played a '65 P-Bass, usually recorded through an Ampeg B-15, and he plucked with two fingers. His busy bass lines were likely the result of his guitar background plus his broad harmonic knowledge and understanding of jazz. That's what used to baffle other bassists: No matter how many notes he played, they all fit seamlessly into the chord and the groove.

"There are plenty of correlations between James Jamerson and Tommy Cogbill, including their jazz backgrounds and their parallel careers. Like James, Tommy was a take-charge guy in the studio; he would stand up and count off the songs, and basically run the session. He had such a strong presence in the music he played that there was a sort of natural deference by the rest of the band."

Examples of Cogbill's serious groove credentials include the notorious two-bar ostinato that runs the length of Wilson Pickett's '67 "Funky Broadway." "It's an example of Tommy's genius," Rhodes says. "He creates the definitive movement for the song, using a push-pull rhythmic phrase and down-up melodic motion. When I was a teenager, parts like this made me want to play bass." Then there's Aretha Franklin's '67 hit "Chain of Fools": "Tommy subtly varies his part rhythmically and melodically throughout this track, as opposed to a strict ostinato, because he's playing around—or answering—Aretha's vocal."

Of Cogbill's playing, Mike Leech says, "He's the only player I know who was able to use his knowledge on guitar, transpose it to bass, and make it believable. His dynamic interpretation on bass was uncanny; his sense of time was amazing. After a cut when he had played something outstanding, such as the bass line on King Curtis's 'Memphis Soul Stew,' and compliments were paid, he never claimed all the credit. He always passed credit around, usually by saying something like, 'Pretty funky groove, huh?'"

Another Cogbill classic is his driving bass line on "Respect," Aretha's 1967 No. 1 single. The song begins with a four-bar intro that outlines the chorus groove. "The drum part is pretty basic, so Tommy is creating all the motion and propelling the song," Rhodes points out. "The two-bar phrase he works for most of the track has a push-pull, tension-and-release feel, with aggressive 16ths in the first bar leading to laid-back eighths in the second bar."

The rest of the song remains faithful to the established groove, with occasional subtle variations. "Tommy obviously had the ability to change things up and fill more, but it wouldn't fit this genre of classic R&B, which consisted of short, ostinato-based songs. Once the band hit a groove they rode it, with everyone's parts working together like a machine. What's cool is how Tommy settles into a less busy, steady eighth-note pattern in the bridge to make room for the soloist.

"Tommy was very much a song player," Rhodes explains, "with an intuitive ability to hear dynamically and range-wise what was going to be most supportive for the song and the timbre of the singer's voice."

"Thomas Clark Cogbill was a father figure to me," says Leech. "During the many hours we sat and talked, bass technique seldom came up; musicianship between us was secondary. When I was down, he had advice to get me back up; if he saw me heading in a bad direction, he would point a finger in my face and order me to either stop or change my direction. Being a musician is not just a career move but a lifestyle, and that is what dictates your abilities. That's what Tommy taught me—not how to play, but how to *live*."

⋆ JERRY JEMMOTT: SOUTHERN SOUL STEW, BY WAY OF NEW YORK BY CHRIS JISI ⋆

"I make musical sense out of anything I hear," proclaims Jerry Jemmott. "If you knock over this table, I'll continue the phrase it creates in my head. That's basically what I do on bass." As a seminal '60s and early '70s session bassist, Jemmott had the music of Aretha Franklin, King Curtis, B. B. King, Wilson Pickett, Roberta Flack, and the Rascals to inspire him.

Bronx native Jemmott was one of the architects of the Atlantic Records soul sound, joining such peers as Tommy Cogbill and David Hood. He was also a key member of the versatile New York studio scene along with Chuck Rainey, Bernard Purdie, Paul Griffin, and Cornell Dupree. In 1984 one of Jerry's main bass disciples told *Guitar Player*, "When I was 15 I used to sneak into Criteria [Atlantic's Miami studio] and hide in the bathroom just to listen to Jerry. He was my idol, making the sounds I wanted to make. That stuttering kind of bass line, bouncing all around the beat but keeping it right in the groove." The disciple's name? Jaco Pastorius.

Raised in a musical household, Jemmott caught the bass bug after hearing Paul Chambers on his sister's recording of Miles Davis's "If I Were a Bell." Classical string-bass lessons followed at 11, and by the time he was 16 Jerry was playing jazz gigs, including a stint with Mercer Ellington's big band. Frustrated by the self-indulgent free jazz movement and inspired by an audience's reaction to an R&B band at a ballroom gig, Jemmott bought an electric bass and amp in 1962. "I discovered James Jamerson through Junior Walker's 'Shotgun,'" he remembers. "I took that line and developed it. In fact I was playing 'Shotgun' for many years!" Still, Jerry felt most electric bass playing lacked soul and emotion. "I thought to myself, I'm going to show them what to play using a combination of syncopation and nuance with a dose of the unexpected."

Jemmott's prowess on the uptown club circuit led Rainey to recommend him to R&B sax legend King Curtis in 1967. In addition to giving him a road-band bass slot, Curtis began calling Jerry for studio dates, leading to his breakout session for Aretha Franklin's *Aretha Now* in '68. Asked by King to bring his bass and "check out" the proceedings, Jemmott arrived to find a Muscle Shoals rhythm section—Tommy Cogbill, drummer Roger Hawkins, and guitarist Jimmy Johnson—struggling with the feel of the first song, "Think." "As soon as I heard it I knew it was a country song in a two feel," Jerry recounts. "After those guys took a break, producer Jerry Wexler told me to go in and take a shot at it. Two takes later we had it. An interesting side note: Tommy Cogbill, who was a great bassist, moved over to guitar and played an amazing, bubbling part." Jemmott finished the album and found himself in immediate demand. Within a year his name graced hits as diverse as Jerry Jeff Walker's "Mr. Bojangles," B. B. King's "The Thrill Is Gone," and the Rascals' "People Got to Be Free."

In 1972, in the prime of his career, Jemmott, Roberta Flack, and guitarist Cornell Dupree were involved in a serious auto accident on New York's Triboro Bridge. During the ten long years it took him to fully recover, Jerry fell victim to substance abuse and depression, which he eventually overcame through his conversion to Buddhism. In the meantime he turned his focus to music education, heeding the advice of his friend Richard Davis and Jaco Pastorius, whom Jerry finally met in 1982. (Their meeting led to Jaco's insistence that Jerry participate in the 1986 instructional video *Modern Electric Bass*.) "Jaco showed me a harmonized C major scale, and it was a revelation," Jerry says. "It was very rewarding watching the same reaction when I passed it on to my students." Getting back into playing shape, Jemmott learned new techniques while fronting his own band and gigging with a cross-section of artists that included Bette Midler, R&B singer/songwriter Don Covay, jazz trumpeter Jimmy Owens, and Duane Eddy.

In recent years Jerry has mostly been serving his Buddhist temple and his students, but he's focused on various music education projects as well. "Having been blessed with a rich playing and teaching career, my goal is to ensure the creation of good music throughout the world."

★ DEEP CUTS: JERRY JEMMOTT ★

Jerry Jemmott's jazz background made him a potent force when playing walking lines and shuffle feels—usually on his '69 Fender Jazz—with everyone from the Queen of Soul to the Kings of the Blues (B. B. and Freddie). And while he most enjoys his tasteful ballad work, his unique take on straight-16th syncopations has made an indelible impact.

King Curtis's "Memphis Soul Stew" from *Live at Fillmore West*. Dig Jerry's Latin-inspired bass breakdown figure, which he embellishes en route to his most famous recorded solo. (Tommy Cogbill played bass on Curtis's studio version.)

King Curtis's "You're the One" from *Everybody's Talkin'*. Though inspired by Larry Graham's part on the original Sly & the Family Stone version, Jerry came up with his own one-bar finger-funk ostinato, which has a James Brown-like interlock with Bernard Purdie's drums. Note the use of space and hammer-ons.

Aretha Franklin's "Think" on *Aretha Now*. Check Jerry's session-saving verse line. "Everything I needed to know was in Aretha's vocal-and-piano intro," says Jerry. "I just took the country two feel and added a little spice with 16th-note lead-ins, pickups, and turnarounds."

Aretha Franklin's "Love the One You're With" from *Live at Fillmore West*. Note how Jerry avoids the downbeat during his two-bar verse phrase. This epitomizes his contrapuntal, "sub-melody" approach. "I've always considered myself an accompanist to the melody—be it the singer or the soloist."

B. B. King's "The Thrill Is Gone" from *Completely Well*. Jerry injects a bossanova/samba feel on the blues master's minor-blues classic, "One of the nuances I used was hammering from the chromatic approach note up to the root or the 5th for a smooth, legato motion." Herb Lovelle's kick drum matches the two eighth-notes Jerry plays on *one*.

B. B. King's "You're Losin' Me" from *Completely Well*. Jerry's wicked 12-bar blues line is built in two-bar phrases and accented perfectly by Lovelle's upbeat open hihats. Typical of the *Completely Well* sessions: Jerry and Herb alter the groove slightly every chorus, as well as break it down subtly when B. B. sings and kick it up a notch when he solos.

B. B. King's "Get off My Back, Woman" from *Live & Well*. Check Jerry's killer opening. The part is a direct link to such future Jaco grooves as "Come On, Come Over" and "The Chicken." In contrast to his usual style, Jerry actually plays *less* as the tune unfolds. "Sometimes you can say it all in the first four bars," he laughs. "That's the overture, right there."

★ DONALD "DUCK" DUNN: STAX'S SOUL MAN BY CHUCK CRISAFULLI ★

It all happened in one homely little room in Tennessee. That's where Wilson Pickett waited for the Midnight Hour, where Otis Redding demanded Respect, where Sam & Dave pledged their devotion as Soul Men, and where Rufus Thomas Walked his Dog. Within the humble confines of the Stax studio, these performers and many others helped to create one of pop music's finest and most enduring legacies: the sound of Memphis soul.

The vibrant singers on the Stax roster all displayed distinctive personalities and unique talents, but there was a common groove in their music. A sly commingling of country & western shuffle and lazy blues—with a dramatic dash of gospel tossed in to keep up the heat—the Memphis sound came from bass, drums, guitar, and organ making music that was brilliantly simple and remarkably understated, yet tantalizingly rich. The lines were clean and cool, the groove warm and soothing; the singers could shout or whisper—the band was always right behind them. The Memphis groove was golden. And no one made that groove sound finer than the Stax house band: Booker T. & the MG's.

"I thought we sounded terrible in that room," laughs the esteemed MG's bassist, Donald "Duck" Dunn. "I hated it. They were always asking me to play with a lot of highs, and it just sounded too trebly to me. And the drums never sounded right. But we'd walk out and listen to the playback, and the bass would be just as round as it could be. I couldn't hear it when we were playing, but somehow our sound always made it to tape."

Stax was run by partners Jim Stewart and Estelle Axton, and their first hits were instrumentals from a loosely knit unit called the Mar-Keys. The lineup shifted frequently, but the core rhythm section featured guitarist Steve Cropper, bassist Lewis Steinberg, and drummer Al Jackson Jr., whose unfaltering beats had already made him something of a Memphis legend. Booker T. Jones had been picking up session work as a sax man, but his genius was in his masterful touch on the Hammond B-3 organ. In the summer of '62, Jones teamed up his organ sounds with the soulful groove the other three had perfected, and the MG's—which stood for "Memphis Group"—were born.

The MG's began at the top, scoring a national hit with the classic finger-snapper "Green Onions." And they got even better. When Steinberg left, Cropper brought in another ex-Mar-Key, his Memphis high school buddy Duck Dunn. With Jones and Cropper playing their lean, teasing melodies on top of Dunn's bass work and Jackson's drumming, the Memphis groove was raised to an art form.

"When I started playing with the MG's, it was just a treat to be in the same room with Al Jackson Jr.," recalls Duck. "He was the most respected drummer in Memphis, and I had enjoyed seeing him play plenty of times. He had the secret to that groove—that big pocket with the delayed feel. If there's any secret to my playing, I think it comes from what Al used to tell me: 'Just wait on *two*.' With him, it could be an awfully long wait."

Dunn grew up listening to R&B dance records like Bill Doggett's "Honky Tonk" and "Slow Walk." When he wanted to make his own music, he began strumming a guitar along with his pal Cropper. He made the switch to bass in order to follow Cropper into the Mar-Keys lineup, which already had a second guitarist. "I saw a picture of an electric bass somewhere and thought, Hey, four strings—I could play that! I bought a '58 Precision and started working. The electric bass was starting to show up on a lot of R&B records, but when I signed with the union in Memphis, I think I was one of only three players listed."

With his '58 P-Bass in hand, Duck joined the MG's at Stax, plugged into the studio's Ampeg B-15, and quickly became a part of the most sublimely powerful rhythm section ever recorded. "Al just had this amazing sense of time, and he knew how to shape a song," says Dunn. "A lot of what he did sounds so simple, but nobody else could play that way. You know, every band has its disagreements and arguments about how a song should go, but it became clear pretty quickly that when Al came up with something, it was going to end up being perfect for the song. I just stuck with him; we locked down, but we never hitched, and that's what gave us a lot of room in the groove. And like I always say, if the drums and bass ain't happening, *nothing's* happening."

By the mid '60s, the MG's were all over the charts. They continued to have hits of their own, such as "Boot-Leg" and "Hip Hug-Her," and also contributed to such smashes as Wilson Pickett's "In the Midnight Hour," Sam & Dave's "You Don't Know Like I Know," and Otis Redding's "I've Been Loving You Too Long." The amount and range of music the MG's took on might have fazed lesser players, but Dunn says the talent of the voices they backed made the work a pleasure. And competition kept the band from slacking off.

"When we started charting records, it just felt great. We all knew, even before the charts did, that we were working with great talent. I mean, Otis Redding—now *there* was a sense of time and feeling; you didn't have to understand any of the words he was singing to understand what he was saying. We did have an MG's sound, but we'd shift it around a little depending on whether we were playing with Otis or Wilson or Sam & Dave. And as we got more successful, there was definitely a little competition with Motown and Muscle Shoals. At first I used to think, James Jamerson—man, I'm not even in the same league with him. And Tommy Cogbill was a hell of a player, too. But that kind of competition keeps you focused on your playing. It keeps you working hard—real hard."

"In the Midnight Hour" was not only a successful single—it also pointed the way to an even fatter MG's groove. "That one really opened up the pocket for us," says Dunn. "We were working with [famed Atlantic Records producer] Jerry Wexler, and he started telling us about this 'jerk' dance that was popular in New York. He started throwing his arms around and said, 'That's where the beat should be—where the arms get thrown.' So that's where we played it. Al got that real delayed feel on *two* and *four*, and that gave me a little room for syncopation and for some of the little jumps I like to play."

It often takes a close listen to hear just how artful Dunn's lines are on the old records. What at first sounds like a simple stroll through a chord progression often turns out to be a mystifying stream of notes that moves through and around the beat, always pushing the song along but never drawing attention away from the melody. It's hard to believe that this master of understatement ever had to be reined in, but Duck says otherwise. "Oh, once in a while I stepped on some toes," he chuckles. "But I got pretty good at hearing myself. You listen to one playback and think, That's not it—I'll play half of what I'm doing, and it'll be right. Cut it in half, and I'm there. On 'Respect' I got to step out, and I cut loose a little bit on 'Walkin' the Dog,' but I think those worked pretty well."

Dunn has always been most comfortable playing with his fingers, but he developed an interesting technique for situations where he needed to get a little extra edge. "I thought that using a pick might make me sound too white, but I did start using my fingernail to pluck the strings. It was just for effect on a couple of tracks, but Jim Stewart liked the sound so much it seemed he was always calling for the fingernail. I could do it live sometimes, but I tend to play a lot harder live—so I'd get about three-fourths of the way through a song, and the nail would break right off. Then I'd have to go to my third finger and make the best of it."

As a live band, the MG's reached a lofty pinnacle of success during 1967's Stax/Volt Revue, which toured Europe with Redding and Carla Thomas. "That's when I realized we were really on to something. Flying into London we felt like stars, and the shows were great. Jim Stewart had told us to stick to the sound of the records, but Otis said, 'We're not going to let those songs just lie there onstage.' So we picked things up, and that was just fine with me."

Despite the acclaim the European concerts were receiving, Dunn often found that he was getting a little less credit than the rest of the band. "A lot of people thought I was a pickup bass player—they thought Duck Dunn was a black guy who couldn't make the tour for some reason." This comment points to the most important non-musical contribution the MG's made to the pop scene: the idea

---

★ DEEP CUTS: DONALD "DUCK" DUNN ★

Wilson's Pickett's "In the Midnight Hour." The verse pattern: Nothing to it, right? But listen to the way Duck's eighth-note placement meshes with Al Jackson Jr.'s delayed feel on *two* and *four* to give the tune its slinky swing—the perfect backdrop for Pickett's urgent vocal.

Booker T. & the MG's "Time Is Tight." On this 1969 instrumental, Duck doubles Steve Cropper's guitar line with deadly accuracy while Jackson uses crisp eighth-notes on the closed hi-hat to create a strong but subtle push.

that it was no big deal for black and white players to make music together. That may have been a radical notion back in the segregated '60s, but Dunn and his colleagues didn't think about it too much. "People always wanted to make a race thing out of our sound, but there wasn't any race thing there. In Europe they'd ask me, 'What's it like to play with a black man?' I never knew what to say; we didn't think that way—we just played. We got the soul sound by blending our country and blues influences. I grew up with some Grand Ole Opry, and when that feel got mixed with the blues, we got something new."

The sweet sound of the MG's seemed to be the perfect soundtrack for the hopeful mood of the mid-'60s, but that was shattered in 1968 by the assassination of Martin Luther King Jr. "It became really hard to go on," says Dunn. "We were so sad and confused. I didn't know what to say to anybody, because it always seemed

★ DEEPER CUTS: LEWIS STEINBERG ON BOOKER T. & THE MG'S' "GREEN ONIONS" BY CHRIS JISI ★

On the surface, Booker T. & the MG's' "Green Onions" stands as one of the grooviest and most famous instrumentals of all time. Peel away the layers, however, and there's more to this 12-bar minor blues than meets the watery eye. For one, it wasn't the great Donald "Duck" Dunn who played the simple, driving bass line but the band's original bassist, Lewis Steinberg, who Dunn would replace a year later.

One day while waiting for vocalist Billy Lee Riley to show up for a session, the four started noodling with a bluesy riff, out of which grew "Green Onions." Steinberg, who played his P-Bass on the three-take recording, named the song after the funkiest (meaning dirtiest or stinkiest) thing he could think of. Cropper brought the track to a local radio station, and it soon shot to No. 1 on the Black Singles charts and No. 3 on the pop charts.

The bass line is the backbone of the three-minute dialogue between Booker T. Jones's bouncing organ and Steve Cropper's guitar stabs. Listen to how both Booker T. and Cropper double Steinberg's bare-bones reading of the part, adding feel-defining ghost notes. Even Al Jackson's simple kick-drum part catches the upbeat to beat *three*. Adding to the funky fragrance are the ambiguous harmonies. While a traditional minor blues has minor I and IV chords and a dominant V chord, Booker T. has his own approach. When he lands on the IV chord he plays it as a major triad at first, before getting back to minor terrain on beat *three*. The V chord also gets dual treatment, as the bar moves from C to $E\flat$. This particularly adds to the stank in the bars where Cropper plays a $D\flat$ note against and in the same range as the D in Booker T.'s $B\flat$ triad. Keep that grease in mind if you play along, and focus on sitting in the middle of the pocket, because the tempo is on the bright side.

as if the words would come out wrong. It changed the whole direction of the music."

A lot of changes hit the MG's in 1968. Jones moved to California to begin a career as a producer. Stax pulled out of its long-time distribution deal with Atlantic. Sam & Dave split up. And Otis Redding—gone too soon in an airplane crash—posthumously achieved the biggest hit of his career. "I don't think Jim Stewart was too happy with 'Dock of the Bay' when Otis first sang it, because Jim always wanted him to stick to the big ballads," says Duck. "But I didn't think anything Otis did could be wrong; he had a great sense of what worked. It's hard to say how much we missed him."

As the '60s rolled into the '70s, soul music started carrying heavier messages, often delivered by such powerful personalities as Isaac Hayes—who recorded the pivotal *Hot Buttered Soul* at Stax. It was the era of a new groove, and it presented a challenge to Dunn. "I went through a period of doubt, wondering if I could uphold my reputation as the music changed. I probably pushed in some directions that didn't work well for me, but I learned a valuable lesson: to just figure out what it is you can do, and stick with it. I've been sticking with it a while now."

Ironically, it was the world of comedy that helped Duck to get back into a serious groove. He and Cropper were playing with Levon Helm's RCO All-Stars in 1977 when they got a call from John Belushi and Dan Aykroyd, asking them to join the Blues Brothers Band. With that unlikely group, Dunn toured, recorded three albums, and got to see himself on the big screen. "That may have started as a joke, but we got a really good band together, and it was nice to see how audiences appreciated the music. We got a lot of people interested in going back to the old records."

Live, Dunn used one of Jim Stewart's old Stax tricks to get the proper bass sound: playing with a lot of high end. "I always use a lot of highs. When I'm onstage, I hate what I call the 'roomful of boom,' where the low end is just roaring. I can hardly touch the strings when that happens; I feel as though everybody must be thinking, What's the damned bass player doing now? I've found that if you use a lot of highs onstage, the sound rounds off—just like it did at Stax."

Dunn says that after all these years, he couldn't imagine a better band to be working with than the MG's. "When I get a part just right with them, I can shut my eyes and just get lost in the music. It's a great feeling to be in the pocket of that groove. When I see Steve smiling, I know I've done my job—and when Booker looks around and you can see on his face that he likes what you're doing, it still feels like I'm hitting a grand slam."

★ DAVID HOOD WITH THE MUSCLE SHOALS RHYTHM SECTION BY RICHARD JOHNSTON ★

"This is a bass-intensive office," says David Hood, opening an envelope at a paper-cluttered desk amid instruments, amps, cardboard file boxes, photos, gold records, and assorted car magazines inside Alabama's storied Muscle Shoals Sound Studios. The envelope yields a check—payment for another round of "I'll Take You There" Chevy ads. "To use it on a commercial they have to pay the original musicians at current jingle scale—whether or not they cut it again. So far this year I've made $2,000 from it, and I didn't have to do anything."

Well, not exactly. David played the signature line and solo on the '72 Staple Singers classic, one in the decades-long parade of hits that stretches from his work with R&B/roots stars such as Aretha Franklin, Wilson Pickett, and Jimmy Cliff (including "Sitting in Limbo") to pop-rockers such as Boz Scaggs, Rod Stewart, Paul Simon, and Bob Seger. "I guess 'I'll Take You There' is my most famous line," David notes. "I got $71 for that session, and I probably did other songs that day."

Though he's punched the clock at Memphis and Nashville studios and logged a few road hours, David is best known for his workdays in northwest Alabama's Quad Cities area. (That's Muscle Shoals, Sheffield, Florence, and Tuscumbria, of course.) Born in Muscle Shoals in 1943, Hood studied piano early on and later took up trombone and then bass, which he played with a hard-working frat-party band called the Mystics. When the group broke up, David got a job at his father's tire store, right down the street from Rick Hall's Fame Studio. "I started hanging out there," Hood says. "The guy who was playing bass moved to guitar, and Rick Hall started bringing in Tommy Cogbill and later on Jerry Jemmott. I heard them and thought, Gosh, if I want to do this I've got to play like them. So I started working really hard."

David began doing demos at Fame, and in '66 he played on a Percy Sledge hit, "Warm and Tender Love." More and more work followed, and in '69 the rhythm section of Hood, drummer Roger Hawkins, guitarist Jimmy Johnson, and keyboardist Barry Beckett made the bold move of leaving Fame and buying their own studio. Working for producers such as Atlantic's legendary Jerry Wexler, the Muscle Shoals Rhythm Section created a sound and a body of music that defines the golden age of Southern R&B.

How many sessions do you think you've done?

Gosh, I don't know. Thousands. Sometimes we would cut 50 tracks in a week. The producer would run in these songwriters, we would record their track, they would leave and finish it, and we would never know what it was. Later on it would come out, and I'd say, "Is that us? It sounds familiar." For a while we were a track factory, and we were really good at it. We could make them all sound good and different enough. But it's hard over the long run. You start to burn out.

How do you keep up your concentration playing track after track?

I don't have a secret; I just have to shut out everything else and go into this state of mind where there's nothing but the music. When you're doing that and you're locked into a real good thing, it's almost like you're floating—your body's doing it without your having to think about it. That's a great thing, and I don't think it happens as much with rhythm sections that are thrown together.

A lot of players say it's easier to be spontaneous playing live than in the studio.

I'm sure that's true, because you don't have to do everything perfect. But I'm a shy person. I really don't care about having an audience. My audience is the speakers and the producer and the engineer. I don't get the satisfaction from playing live that I do from going into a control room and hearing a really good playback.

Do you remember your first session?

The band I played in booked the session—the lead singer's father put up the money. We rehearsed the song and just went in and played it. I wasn't scared or nervous, because I didn't know I should be. It was only after I started working for other people that I got nervous. Everybody else had been playing longer than me, and I always felt like I was a little behind. Back then it was all mono, so if you messed up it was stop and start all over again—there was no punching in. That was a bloodbath at first, because Rick Hall was a taskmaster who didn't mind embarrassing you in front of everybody. That's when I learned to just cancel my feelings and put everything out of my mind except the job at hand. I loved the job, though—I was learning new things and getting paid. Even though it wasn't a lot of money, it was better than working at the tire store.

What was it like working with Jerry Wexler?

He scared me to *death* when I first met him—this New York Yankee accent came over the talk-back in the studio: "David, would you come up here please?" "Oh, God, what does he want? He's gonna fire me!" We laugh about all this now, but in those days he was *really* a tough guy. Think about it: He produced Ray Charles on "What'd I Say?" He produced records I listened to before I even thought about being a musician. He's not a musician at all, but he's got the ultimate taste and ears.

It was tough being his bass player, because he had the best ones working for him before me. I came in after Tommy Cogbill and Jerry Jemmott on the Aretha stuff, and I was scared to death. But I just had to psyche that fear out of my head and work. He was from such a different culture, and even the words he used were funny. We would say, "Play *da da da da*." But he would say, "Davey, play *gi gi gon gon*." We'd go, "*Gi gi gon gon?* What's that mean?" But he has great intuition and depth of knowledge. If I wasn't getting something quite right, he would *make* it work. He could tell me where to accent and where to push, and he knew that when something is in the pocket, it can be one click faster or slower and it won't work. He could tell when it was *there*.

Do you and Roger Hawkins have any particular routine for working out parts?

Sometimes we work out some little pattern ahead of time, and other times we just start playing and fit together somehow without saying anything. For me that's because I was the last one to come into the scene, and I had to listen to everybody and make sure I was doing the right thing. I had to learn to lock in rather than to lead, because I was the new guy.

Most of the drummers I've worked with say they like working with me because I don't fight with them. So if I'm working with a good drummer I sound good, and if I'm working with a bad drummer I sound bad.

Have you been in many sessions where something just doesn't work?

Yeah, a lot—and I hate it. It's your whole soul on the line. Plus after all these years I have a reputation to live up to. But I've learned you can't force things; if it's not working one way you just try something else. Usually it helps to simplify. I'm not a real technical player anyway, so I'm more comfortable playing less. Having a good sound and playing in tune and in time is *much* more important than chops. You're not playing for yourself or for other bass players—you're playing to make a song come out. It's not brain surgery. It's all about *entertainment*. If you're not pleasing someone, you're wasting your time.

Don't get me wrong, though—I love for somebody to give me a challenging line. Even if I don't nail it exactly, it's fun to do my version of it. I get tired of sessions where *nobody* has any suggestions; that's not any fun. I know what *I* know, so it's fun to get outside ideas.

I get the feeling you don't get into a lot of arguments during sessions.

Sometimes we argue among ourselves in the rhythm section, because we don't beat around the bush. Roger might say, "Hey, do this," and I say, "Look, you play the drums and I'll play the bass." It's funny to us, but other people think, Shit, they're gonna get into a fight. But you have to do that. As a rhythm section we've been together over 30 years, and we don't mind saying, "That don't work, try something else." You can't have an ego about it, because you're all working toward making the song sound good. It's not just about the drums or the bass.

Did you ever feel starstruck working with some people?

In the beginning I did, and Aretha Franklin was one of them. I had a record of hers called *Trouble in Mind* that I thought was wonderful, and when they said they were bringing her here I said, "Hot dog! I'm going to get to work with her." On those first sessions I played trombone, but later I got to play bass with her, and that was fun. She's such a great vocalist and piano player that you can just pattern your part after what she's doing.

Any great sessions stand out for you?

I loved all the Staple Singers and Stax stuff, and there have been some great Atlantic things produced by Jerry Wexler as well as Arif Mardin and Tom Dowd. I enjoyed working with Phil Ramone, and I got to work with Otis Redding when he was producing. He taught me a lot of things about rhythm and feel, like playing on the upbeat when you would normally be playing on the downbeat. His feel was so good, and you can hear it in all of his records—horn lines and everything. You can tell Otis had a hand in that. I've been privileged to work with a lot of other great people. Some of the early Bob Seger stuff was fun, and so was Paul Simon, though he got kind of weird toward the end. He had heard "I'll Take You There," so he called Stax and said, "Who are those Jamaican musicians?" They told him, "Those are some white boys from Alabama."

★ DEEP CUTS: DAVID HOOD ★

Often hinging on two-bar riffs, David Hood's lines have provided the foundation for scores of gospel, rock, blues, country, and R&B tracks. Whatever the session, David always brings along solid timing, unshakably consistent phrasing, and an unerring ear for the groove.

The Staple Singers' "Respect Yourself" and "I'll Take You There." Both Hood and drummer Roger Hawkins cite their tracks with the Staples Singers as among their favorites of the thousands they've recorded. David's swaying two-bar lines give the juice to the grooves while Hawkins buttons up the pocket with a surprisingly light touch. On "Respect Yourself," David's syncopated riff varies slightly bar-to-bar, but he keeps the pulse steady by landing emphatically on the repeated *B*'s. Space and steady eighth-notes are the keys to "I'll Take You There." Note how the kick-drum syncopations move in and out of the bass figure. (Ska historians will recognize a similar groove in the 1969 Harry J. Allstars tune "The Liquidator.")

Paul Simon's "Love Me Like a Rock." For the song's gospel feel, Hood lays down a relaxed two-beat. The secret? His percussive attack lands squarely with the kick drum, while his precise release makes each note sound buoyant.

Wilson Pickett's "Don't Knock My Love." One of Jerry Wexler's inspired pairings was combining Pickett's combustible soul with the Muscle Shoals section's laid-back grooves. David drives his Dorian figure through to the end of each two-bar phrase, mirroring the intensity of the Wicked One's vocal.

Bobby Womack's "Woman's Gotta Have It." David's smooth quarter-note arch and bubbling descending line put the slink under Womack's sexy soul stylings.

★ LEROY HODGES AT HI RECORDS WITH THE REVEREND AL GREEN BY RICHARD JOHNSTON ★

In the '60s and '70s, while Duck Dunn and company were making Southern soul history at Stax Records, another Memphis studio boasted its own hard-grooving, hit-making rhythm section. At Hi Records, three Memphis-grown brothers—bassist Leroy Hodges, guitarist Mabon "Teenie" Hodges, and keyboardist Charles Hodges—and drummer Howard Grimes were laying down tracks for producer Willie Mitchell and a stable of soul stylists that included O. V. Wright, Syl Johnson, Ann Peebles, and the great Al Green. On chart-busters such as "Let's Stay Together," Leroy anchored Green's emotion-laden vocal pyrotechnics with laid-back, melodic riffs that gradually built to 16th-note syncopations and fills, recalling the style of Motown's James Jamerson.

How did you and your brothers become the Hi Records rhythm section?

We were Willie Mitchell's road band, and in the mid '60s we met Al Green and played behind him in Texas before he went to Memphis. I recorded with Willie first, though; I cut his *Sunrise Serenade* album in the early '60s, when I was still in high school. Willie didn't really give me any advice for playing in the studio; he just threw me in there. It was great experience.

How did you work up your parts for Al Green's hits?

We would all stand around the piano, and Willie would play a song over and over so everybody could get the picture. If Al wrote the song he would be there, too.

Did Mitchell make suggestions about your bass lines?

If we were playing a song and he didn't like the line, he'd let me know. But basically he gave me free rein.

Your bass has a big, round tone on those records.

The room itself had a good sound—it was an old movie theater with a high ceiling. Everybody played together on the floor, and that helped. We had all the amps baffled off, and you could sit out in the middle with your earphones on and see the other people playing. The drummer was in a booth by himself, and my amp was sitting next to the drum booth. Then Teenie's amp, and keyboards down on the other end.

In the early Al Green sessions, did the vocals and instruments all track together?

Yeah. We could only record four tracks at a time. Willie had one track for the vocals, and he put the bass on one track, the drums on one track, and the keyboards and the guitar together on one track. It was great—we did a lot of stuff that way. The only thing is, if the guitar or the keyboards messed up, you had to start all over! But I miss those days. It seems like everybody was closer together.

★ **DEEP CUT: LEROY HODGES** ★

Ann Peebles's "I Can't Stand the Rain." On this 1973 hit, Ann Peebles's reading of the verse lists toward the back half of each bar, allowing Leroy Hodges's bluesy two-beat eighth-note figure to drift to the forefront. Leroy keeps all the non-tied eighth-notes clipped, employing an especially staccato touch after the 16th notes to give the phrase a push-and-pull feel.

★ THE BAR-KAYS' JAMES ALEXANDER BY E. E. BRADMAN ★

James Alexander remembers his first big break like it was yesterday: He was 17 years old and playing with the Bar-Kays at the Hippodrome on Beale Street. Across town, some of the great soul stars of the day—including Wilson Pickett, Edwin Starr, the Manhattans, and Otis Redding—finished a show and headed to the Hippodrome to relax. They ended up sitting in. "We were all pretty young, and they were amazed how well we knew their songs, even though we had never rehearsed with them," James laughs. "Otis was so taken by the whole situation that he fired his regular band and gave us the gig." In the spring of '67, on the day they graduated from high school, the Bar-Kays left Memphis for a ten-day run at the Apollo Theatre. "We were country bumpkins who hadn't been outside a 50-mile radius of Memphis, and the first place we go is New York City to play with Otis Redding!"

Since those auspicious beginnings, Alexander's full, round P-Bass tone and deep pocket have graced dozens of classic Southern soul albums by the Bar-Kays and an impressive list of Stax/Volt labelmates, including Albert King, the Staple Singers, Rufus Thomas, and Johnnie Taylor. He's especially proud of his work on several Isaac Hayes albums, including the original *Shaft* soundtrack. The Bar-Kays scored their first hit for Stax, "Soul Finger," just before Redding and most of the band died in a December '67 plane crash. Alexander assembled a new group, which has toured and recorded frequently since the late '60s; his gritty lines are key ingredients in the band's dance-floor anthems ("Shake Your Rump to the Funk," "Freakshow on the Dance Floor"), slow burners ("Deliver Us," "Anticipation"), and gospel-flavored funk favorites ("Holy Ghost"). Columbia's *Wattstax*, filmed in Los Angeles at the 1972 Watts Summer Festival, captured an electrifying Bar-Kays live set—including a burning version of their "Son of Shaft"—and by this time, they had also become Stax session pros, second only to Booker T. & the MG's.

"They were the primary house band, but as time went on, there was just too much work. That's where the Bar-Kays came in," Alexander says. "We were young, we weren't set in our ways, and we weren't afraid to try stuff. The producers liked that." He also formed a friendship with MG's bassist Donald "Duck"

Dunn, and they shared credits on several albums. "Duck is about ten years older than me; we used to trade licks, and trade basses, too," he laughs. "One day you had to be in the frame of mind to play behind, say, Carla Thomas. The next day you had to back up Albert King, and the next day, Isaac Hayes. Playing behind such a diversity of artists gave us a lot of experience, and we're grateful for that. It came in handy."

Alexander played tuba in Tennessee's all-state high school band before acquiring a Harmony H22 bass in late '62. In addition to upright lessons, he picked up tips from a guitarist friend, Jimmy King. When King's bass player missed a rehearsal, James stepped in. That group would eventually become the Bar-Kays' first incarnation. "When we realized we were going to be a band, we all transferred to the same high school. The band director gave us a key, and we would get to school at 7 each morning and practice until 8:30. We got tighter and tighter. We developed a popularity around the Memphis area, and we went on from there."

As a young player, Alexander gravitated toward James Jamerson and blues session bassist Phil Upchurch. "The Motown sound was just becoming popular. I studied the bass lines on as many albums as I could afford—the old traditional way, just backing records up, over and over again. I was in awe of Jamerson because he was

> **"We were young, we weren't set in our ways, and we weren't afraid to try stuff."**

not a traditional bassist—he played melodies and other things on bass. He took bass to another level." These days, James admires his contemporaries Robert "Kool" Bell of Kool & the Gang, the Gap Band's Robert Wilson ("he's got a unique sound"), and Larry Graham. "He's loud, but he's playing so good and thumpin' so hard you forget how loud it is!" James also speaks highly of Marcus Miller. "He's one of the most versatile bass players out there. I like his sound, his attitude, and the way he attacks the bass—he's so tasty!"

Four decades after a traveling soul revue changed his life, Alexander has continued to tour with the United We Funk All-Stars, featuring members of the Bar-Kays, the Gap Band, Dazz Band, S.O.S. Band, and Con Funk Shun. Alexander jokingly attributes the Bar-Kays' longevity to their disdain for the 40-hour workweek. "Our fear of having desk jobs has kept the band together," he laughs. "Seriously, we've developed a camaraderie—it's like family. If you love what you do, you'll never work another day in your life. And we definitely have a passion for what we do."

★ DEEP CUTS: JAMES ALEXANDER ★

As the man who put the Bar-Kays back together, James Alexander served as the bedrock of the band and barometer of the times. Listening through the Bar-Kays' catalog reveals a band and a bassist who at different periods inspired—and perhaps were influenced by—contemporaries such as Cameo, P-Funk, and Earth, Wind & Fire.

Rufus Thomas's "Funky Chicken" and "Sixty Minute Man." Alexander's simple, bluesy pattern kicked off his Stax session career and helped "Funky Chicken" reach No. 5 on the R&B charts in 1970. Also from *Do the Funky Chicken*, "Sixty Minute Man" features Alexander in the intro; he holds the three-octave *E* line for the duration. "Rufus had a real knack for coming up with bass lines and parts. He gave me that one."

The Bar-Kays' "Soul Finger." Over the years, the self-described "country bumpkins from Memphis" have built upon the foundation laid by '67's classic "Soul Finger," whose catchy groove neatly supports the horn parts and doubles them at the climax of the chorus.

Isaac Hayes' "Theme from Shaft." The '71 Stax soundtrack to the film *Shaft* was a No. 1 hit, and the title song garnered composer/arranger/producer Isaac Hayes an Oscar. About two minutes into that famous *wocka-wocka* guitar comp, the unison line bubbles like brown sugar, only to give way to Alexander's emphatic verse groove. Canyadigit?

The Bar-Kays "I'll Dance" and "Shine." James and the Bar-Kays showed serious P-Funk affinity on "I'll Dance," a Top-40 hit from 1978. Its slippery, Parliament-style use of space contrasts neatly with Alexander's "Shine," also from *Light of Life*, an on-top groove that recalls the Brothers Johnson.

The Bar-Kays' "Freakshow on the Dance Floor." James attributes the seductive pulse of this 1984 No. 2 R&B hit to the perfect mix of his staccato pattern, keyboardist Winston Stewart's synth-bass part, and drummer Michael Beard's kick drum.

5

CHUCK RAINEY: STUDIO GROOVE MASTER

★ GROOVE SUMMIT: WILL LEE INTERVIEWS
CHUCK RAINEY BY CHRIS JISI ★

Chuck Rainey is among an elite few who virtually defined the role of the electric bass in pop music. He spent the '60s as *the* first-call bassist in the Big Apple, earning legendary status by playing with everyone from Louis Armstrong to Aretha Franklin. After moving to Los Angeles in 1972, he rapidly ascended to first-call status while compiling a résumé that rivaled his New York output. His gold-record-inducing lines graced albums by Steely Dan, Quincy Jones, the Jackson 5, and Rickie Lee Jones, and he appeared on numerous TV and film soundtracks.

Will Lee, who worked his way up to first-call New York studio bassist beginning in the '70s, and is one of late-night TV's most recognizable musicians, jumped at the chance to join me in interviewing Rainey, one of his bass heroes. "Chuck is my idol. Paul McCartney and James Jamerson were huge influences, but when I first heard Chuck, that was it for me. His touch, his sound, his feel—he had the whole package. He's the Godfather of the Groove."

Like Will, you've been able to sustain a studio career for decades. How do you stay in demand?

To start with, I'm a player, and I have been my whole life. I love to play and I need to play; the only music I don't like playing is music that isn't organized, and I encounter very little of that. I also realize what may be a good idea today isn't necessarily going to be happening a month or a year from now. I'm amazed how many of my peers still play the way they did 20 or 30 years ago; they act like it's the cutting edge, but it just sounds old-fashioned to me. I come more from the Miles Davis mentality: what's past is done, so let's move on to something new.

Will Lee: You've said the only way to create something new today is to know what happened yesterday. With that in mind, let's trace your roots. Where were you raised, and what are your earliest musical memories?

I was born on June 17, 1940, in Cleveland, Ohio, and raised in nearby Youngstown. My mother and father were amateur musicians, so music was always in the house. My father was a Fats Waller/Art Tatum-style stride pianist, and my mom played piano and flute. In addition to hearing them, I heard the early jazz, Dixieland, and ragtime records they would play, by people like Louis Armstrong, Earl "Fatha" Hines, and Ma Rainey. I also loved listening to our church choir.

Will Lee: I know you played trumpet before you played bass, as I did. When did your love affair with bass begin?

Being a bass player was always in my spirit; it just took me a while to pick up on it. My sister and I took a few piano lessons, and then I played violin and viola, and started playing trumpet in the sixth grade. I had good teachers, a strict father who made sure I practiced, and a wonderful musical environment surrounding me—so I ended up in all the local marching and drum-corps bands, both in and out of school.

I had also briefly played upright bass in high school, sang bass in a vocal group, and when I got to college, I joined the brass ensemble on baritone horn. Finally, while on duty in the military reserves, I learned how to play guitar.

Will Lee: How did you acquire your first electric bass?

I had seen an electric at a Hank Ballard & the Midnighters dance, and a local gospel group had one—but it really didn't register until I saw a bass in the movie *Rock, Rock, Rock*. Shortly after that, my mother and I went over to a local music store that had a '57 P-Bass in the window. This was 1961, and the owner was elated because it had been hanging there for four years. I got the bass and a 50-watt Fender Bassman 2x12 amp, all for $375.

From that point, the sky opened up. I was the only guy in the area with a Fender bass, so I became very busy. Between the sound and the look, the bass gave a lot of attention to bands I played in; people would come by just to see it. And when acts from Detroit or Chicago came through town and needed someone to play it, everyone would steer them to me. That's how I landed my first major gig with [saxophonist] Big Jay McNeely. Someone told him about me, and I didn't have a phone, so he came and knocked on my door. Up until that point, I had been using a pick—but I wasn't able to play some of the things I was hearing, so I threw it away and switched to plucking with my thumb. But I had trouble swinging with my thumb; I couldn't get the accents on my walking lines, and I couldn't play descending triplets—so I switched to my index finger.

Will Lee: Who were your early bass influences?

I had heard a number of blues artists, like Elmore James and Muddy Waters, and they would always have a second guitar sort of playing a bass line. When Jimmy Smith's *The Sermon* came out in 1958, I listened to it over and over because his organ bass lines were so clear and strong. I was also checking out great upright bassists, like Keter Betts, Ray Brown, and Percy Heath.

Everything changed when I heard Motown on the radio. In terms of me playing bass, Jamerson gave me the keys to get into the house. In those days, I had to play a lot of Top-40 music, which meant a lot of Motown—and every time I had to learn one of James's bass lines, it would kick me in the butt and open my eyes a little wider. That really motivated me to study and evaluate what could be done with the instrument. Even though later events contributed to my approach on the instrument, I would certainly describe myself as a Jamerson-type bassist. I have a lot of his motion and sound in my style.

Will Lee: Did you ever get to know Jamerson?

I knew who he was as far back as 1959, because the Motown acts used to tour all around the Great Lakes area. We first met at a huge concert in Ohio in the early '60s; I was playing with Big Jay McNeely and he was with the Miracles. Someone in the previous band had borrowed my amp and blown the speakers—so I plugged in and just pretended to play. Afterwards, James came up and told me I should have plugged into his amp, which was right next to mine. I appreciated that, and since then I've done the same for other bassists.

We kept in touch over the years, although we didn't get to hang out regularly until we both lived in L.A. in the early '70s. When I'd go to his house, he'd always be cooking something and we would talk shop. In retrospect, when he left Detroit he might have been better off going to New York or Philly, where a lot of his crew of musicians and arrangers ended up. He never quite seemed to fit in with the L.A. crowd.

James was headstrong, but I admired him for it. He felt the upright was the *real* bass. I remember bringing him to B.I.T. for an electric bass clinic, and he promptly told the audience to forget the electric and learn the upright. I knew him too well to be offended, though! He also felt there would be no Fender bass if it weren't for him, and if you consider his accomplishments at Motown, he was probably right.

How did you get to New York?

While I was playing with Big Jay, another saxophonist/bandleader named Sil Austin came through town looking for an electric bassist, and I was recommended. He was going to Canada and then New York, and that was all I needed to hear—anyone who was going to New York had me! Unfortunately, he lied about the stability of the band; when we got to New York in 1962, the band broke up, and I got stranded. Sil's guitarist, Lester Young, lived uptown and let me move in with him. Lester played a lot of hotel gigs all over the city, and eventually I became his bassist. At that time [saxophonist] King Curtis was very prominent on the scene, and he was the kind of guy who knew all the musicians—especially the new ones in town. I used to go see his band and daydream about being the bassist. One night, I was playing a supper club with Lester, and Curtis walked past me and said, "Yeah—Chuck Rainey." Lester turned to me and said, "He wants you in his band." Sure enough, on the next break Curtis asked Lester about me, and they ended up switching bassists.

I can now state unequivocally that my stay with King Curtis was the greatest musical experience of my career. He was the ultimate leader and showman, and the baddest tenor player of them all. And his band was revered wherever we went. Although we played mostly Top 40, we also covered everything from the blues to Ornette Coleman, and we *never* had an off night.

Will Lee: One of your more notable King Curtis gigs was a cross-country tour with the Beatles in 1965. What was that like?

Unbelievable! Curtis was hired to open the shows with a couple of songs and then back up about six artists; then there were two English bands, including the Hollies, and the Beatles would play the last hour. Initially we weren't familiar with the Beatles, so we had no idea of their magnitude until the first show in front of a packed house of screaming fans at Shea Stadium. From there it snowballed. We had a police escort all the way down to the Spectrum in Philadelphia. Then we started flying on special chartered jets, and wherever we landed there were thousands of people waiting. I remember the plane once screeching to a halt and everyone being thrown forward, because the crowd had broken down the fence and was attacking the plane! Anytime we would pass a part of the audience on our way to the stage, people would be scratching at us, pulling our hair, tearing off pieces of clothing—and we were just the opening band! It became routine to see hundreds of passed-out girls laid out in designated areas.

> "You've got to play with an attitude, because everybody's listening to the bass—and I dare anyone to challenge me on that."
>
> —CHUCK RAINEY

How did you get into the studio scene?

After the Beatles tour, King Curtis broke up the band for personal reasons. I got a road gig with Sam Cooke, and Eric Gale was the guitarist. Eric and I hit it off, and when we got back to New York he told me if I had a consistent phone number he would call me for studio dates. He was contracting a lot of sessions, and he often played guitar and bass to earn double scale—but he preferred to play just guitar with a live rhythm section instead of overdubbing it. Eric also felt there were too many older musicians in the studios; he and [drummer] Bernard Purdie were younger and played with more energy, and they wanted to bring in more younger players. At age 26, I fit the bill.

Eric started me on demos so the other musicians could get used to me; from there, I started doing actual record dates, including a lot of singles. I couldn't even tell you the first hit record I played on, because we were churning out so many singles. I came in at the end of the vocal-group era, with artists like the Four

Seasons, the Ronettes, and the Shirelles.

Will Lee: You gave R&B, and groove playing in general, a fresh sound—and an approach on which I've humbly based my entire career. Would you say your style came together in New York?

Without a doubt. In New York, the drummers were playing with a 16th-note feel; that awakened a similar rhythmic sense in me, rooted in both my drum and bugle-corps background and my exposure to rag music early on. I hear all the stuff *between* the notes when I play—like the tuba's funky two-feel in a Dixieland brass band, or the high-tom parts in a drum corps. All those in-between rhythms and ghost notes provide the nuances that give a groove that swinging, push-pull feel. In Detroit, Benny Benjamin and Pistol Allen weren't playing as busily as the New York drummers—so I was able to clearly hear all of those rhythms coming from Jamerson.

I've always described myself as a busy player, but not "busy" as in playing a lot of notes. I'm rhythmically active—almost like a drummer playing bass.

Is this also the period when you developed your back-and-forth plucking technique with your right index finger?

Yes—that evolved from doing long sessions at Atlantic Studios. We would work to the point where my finger would get tired and stiffen up; I couldn't stop playing, so I started moving my finger back and forth on the strings to keep up. Eventually I got good at it, and a successful style developed.

It never occurred to me to use two fingers until the early '80s, when I worked that into my playing as well. Similarly, before I started slapping with my thumb the conventional way, I would pat the strings with my right-hand palm for the same effect. The '60s was also when I really got my reading together. The two things that kicked my butt the most were sight-reading high ledger-line passages, and Latin bass lines written in cut time.

Will Lee: I've always wanted to ask you about the chordal stuff you play in the upper register, like your classic tritone lick on Roberta Flack's "Reverend Lee."

I got that from a bassist named Mervin Brunson, who followed me in King Curtis's band and who later worked with Larry Coryell. I walked into Small's in Harlem one night while Don Gardner and DeeDee Ford were singing a ballad, and Mervin threw in a riff that ended with a high *G* and *B* against his open *A* string, for an *Am9*-type chord. That slayed me! I immediately split and went back to my room, grabbed my bass, and worked it out; from there, I started figuring out all the other chordal possibilities. The hardest part about using chords was learning when *not* to play them!

What was your favorite rhythm section in New York?

I did the most sessions—literally thousands—with Bernard, Eric, keyboardist

Paul Griffin, and Carl Lynch on second guitar; that would sometimes be altered to include Jimmy Johnson on drums or Richard Tee on piano. My first-call subs were Jerry Jemmott and Gordon Edwards, who were great bassists in their own right, of course.

Will Lee: That section became legendary as Aretha Franklin's recording and touring band. What stands out about that period?

Aretha's brilliant singing, as well as the band's ability to thoroughly kick ass every time we played. The tours in the early '70s were some of the most exciting times of my life. What I'll always remember are the opening moments of those shows: The house would be dark while the sound system blared the theme from *2001: A Space Odyssey*. Then Aretha would walk out onstage in her gown and furs, and we would play the first few notes of "Rock Steady." The crowd would go insane, and I would feel the blood rushing to my head!

Will Lee: On the first session I ever did with Bernard Purdie, I noticed he listened to the song and let the melody and lyrics dictate his drum part, as opposed to just bashing away. That forever changed the way I approached my role. Is that how the two of you came up with your grooves?

Absolutely—it was all based on the song and the artist. We would try to create a groove that would both complement and serve the melody and the lyric. I wouldn't just try to lock into Bernard's kick pattern; I'd listen to the rhythm of his whole kit, and I'd find something to play off of. Fortunately, we had a special chemistry, so everything would fall into place pretty easily. Back in those days, an artist would sing the song as many times as was needed to get a take. Sometimes Bernard would ask for a certain section to be sung over and over until we all felt comfortable with our parts.

What led you to move to Los Angeles?

The first time I ever saw L.A. was at the end of the Beatles tour; I was captivated by the lifestyle, and I knew I'd live there someday. What set everything into motion in 1972 was a call Quincy Jones made to me and Eric Gale. We had just recorded *Walking in Space* with him, and he was putting together a 24-piece jazz band in L.A. I began by commuting to rehearsals, and each week I'd end up staying a little longer before returning to New York. Finally, in June 1972, I gave up my Manhattan apartment and moved to L.A. permanently.

I started doing sessions for Quincy, and because of that, a lot of producers and contractors began calling me. Motown called with work as well, since many of the artists and musicians knew me from back in the Great Lakes area, and they had two studios going around the clock. On top of that there was the weather, the beaches, the convenience of driving right to a session and parking my car, and— of course—the fact that I was getting double and triple scale.

Will Lee: How did the L.A. session scene differ from New York's?

A lot of the bassists played with a pick, so they had a clicky, twangier sound. I switched to roundwound strings, and I even had a DeArmond pickup installed by the bridge of my P-Bass for a while to get more of that snappy tone. But it wasn't just the bass players; the whole sound coming off the board was much brighter than in New York. On the business side, there were a few ploys I didn't care for. If someone wanted you on a record date and another person on the project wanted a different bassist, sometimes that person would call and book you on a bogus session that took place at the same time. Then, when he got the player he wanted, he'd cancel you on the fake session, and you would end up with nothing. The other hassle I ran into was bassists—and I mean *notable* bassists—taking credit for something I had played on. I was sort of a maverick in town, because I worked as an independent contractor, and I refused to be pushed into any cliques. Overall, though, I have fond memories of my time in L.A. The only downside was that my chops suffered, because I wasn't working as much or enjoying the playing as much as I did in New York.

I had the honor of playing with many great drummers in L.A., such as Earl Palmer, Hal Blaine, and Johnny Guerin. Probably my favorite experiences were working with Jeff Porcaro and Bernard Purdie; the two of them were perfect. Some drummers were stiff and played in a way that demanded you follow them, but Jeff and Bernard were loose, and they played with nuance. They went with the flow and never forced you to play in a certain way. I got to work with both of them on the Steely Dan albums.

Will Lee: How did you like working with Steely Dan's Walter Becker and Donald Fagen?

Overall, it was quite pleasurable. They had great budgets, which meant they paid well and always had great musicians and sound people involved. They never kept you more than six hours, and half the time you did nothing. On top of that, they're great writers, so the music was always interesting. As for the bass lines, Walter would either write parts or have ideas for most of the songs, but he and Donald always gave me plenty of creative freedom. An example would be "Peg" [on *Aja*]: Walter came up with the verse bass line, but the introduction and chorus parts were mine. Looking back on their albums, I liked the first two [*Pretzel Logic* and *Katy Lied*] the least; I enjoyed *The Royal Scam* and *Gaucho*, but my favorite was *Aja*.

Is there an intangible aspect to studio players that separates them from other great musicians, or were they just in the right place at the right time?

I think studio work is a highly specialized job; not everyone can do it. In addition to having your musicianship together, having a great feel, and being extremely versatile, you have to alter your concept of sound and get used to hearing the bass small. Then there's the whole non-musical side of it: being on time, having the proper decorum, and being able to relate to people. On the other hand, I'm certain there were bassists around who were just as qualified or even more qualified than I was, but for whatever reason they were unable to crack the scene.

Whatever the situation or level you're playing at, my feeling is you've got to be a *strong* player. Bass is a strong instrument; you can't allow yourself to play it weakly, with no authority. You've got to play with an attitude, because everybody's listening to the bass—and I dare anyone to challenge me on that. When you listen to a record, the melody and lyrics may be obvious, but what you really hear the most is the bass.

Will Lee: Who are your favorite bassists?

There are so many I admire, but the three who stand out for me are Jamerson, Buster Williams—my all-time favorite upright bassist—and Paul Jackson. Paul is probably the baddest cat I've ever seen on the electric, and he sings as well as anyone out there. People associate him with the Headhunters, but that wasn't the true Paul; I heard him prior to that in his native Oakland. The bass players from there—Larry Graham and Rocco Prestia, to name a couple—have a special approach to music.

★ DEEP CUTS: CHUCK RAINEY WITH ARETHA FRANKLIN AND STEELY DAN ★

Chuck Rainey sees his groundbreaking, groundshaking approach to bass in basic terms: "My concept is two-dimensional. First, I think rhythm before notes; I decide on the rhythmic phrases of my lines, and then I match them with note choices. I also play my fills like a drummer, and I use my James Jamerson influence to come up with the melodic content. Second, when it comes to melody, I keep it simple; I'm busy rhythmically but not melodically. Usually, I'll grab a root-5th-octave shape and work around that, maybe adding notes like the 3rd, 7th, 6th, or 9th for color. My patterns are very defined in that I've been playing the same thing on everyone's records for over 30 years—just like Jamerson." Close examination reveals the numerous stylistic devices that give Rainey's parts their personality: slides, slurs, ghost notes, chords, raked arpeggios, multi-layered feels, right-hand pats, and back-and-forth index-finger plucks.

Aretha Franklin's "Rock Steady." There are few funkier sub-hooks than the part Chuck Rainey created for Aretha Franklin's 1971 Top-Ten single "Rock Steady," which Rainey and the Atlantic Records rhythm team cut in Miami with the Queen of Soul in the fall of 1970. At the top are Rainey's percussive slides up the *G* string, often mistaken for organ or percussion. Then there's Rainey's massively funky A section lick, fortified and funkified with right-hand pats. Note how the part keeps beats *three* and *four* as the repeated motif—albeit with extra rhythmic tension added by occasionally anticipating beat *three*—while the first two beats are more loosely improvised with occasional upper-register fills. On the bridges, Rainey switches to back-and-forth index-finger plucking with Jamerson-like drops and chromatic lines, topped only by his own octave-bouncing syncopated climbs. Bernard Purdie's nasty drum breakdown is an all-time classic groove moment.

Aretha Franklin's "Until You Come Back to Me (That's What I'm Gonna Do)." This sweet, mid-tempo tune presents many of the signature elements of Rainey's style. While the melody quickly establishes an eighth-note-based feel, there's a subtle, swinging shuffle implied by both Franklin's vocals and Purdie's drums. "Both Aretha and Bernard had that shuffle nuance in everything they sang and played, so I developed it too. I would say that subtle shuffle and the kickback motion of my index finger are the main differences between my style and Jamerson's." Like the Motown master, though, Rainey continually develops his part as a song progresses. While his notes and rhythms change slightly from verse to verse, he liberally decorates the song with upper-register arpeggios, drum-like fills, and combinations of chordal and slurred ideas high on the neck for some of the part's most exciting moments. "The trick is to be subtle," he says. "I try to create little 'ear kisses' with the chord shapes."

Steely Dan's "Peg." Rainey added his upper-register flourish to the intro's descending chords, but then followed the verse's arranged part fairly closely, adding percolating variations on Becker's written theme. Check the rhythm-shifted two-bar verse tag. "I played it the way Walter hummed it, complete with the slides," says Rainey. "I admit I had difficulty getting that because it's so odd." The slapped choruses are all Rainey, who got the idea from his friend, drummer Jeff Porcaro. "Walter and Donald were clear that they didn't want any slapping; I think they were thinking of that nasal, Louis Johnson kind of sound that was on so many records at the time. Finally I turned my body, adjusted my music stand, and moved one of the gobos so they couldn't see what I was playing. They were unaware I was slapping, but when they listened back, that was the sound they liked the most."

Steely Dan's "Kid Charlemagne." "On those early Steely Dan sessions, I remember playing everything that I knew—everything I had ever come across," laughs Rainey. "'Kid Charlemagne' is one of my most prized accomplishments as a recording bassist making up bass patterns." Indeed, "Kid Charlemagne" is chock-full of groovy ghost notes, savory syncopations, slick double-stop slides, and open-string passing tones. Still, with its super-tight groove and careful balance of long and short tones as well as low and high registers, not a note seems out of place. It's a testament to the ability of a great bassist to transform a good song into a brilliant work of art.

BOB BABBITT
(© CARY HAMMOUND/REDFERNS)

6.
BOB BABBITT

★ BOB BABBITT: MOTOWN AND BEYOND
BY ALLAN "DR. LICKS" SLUTSKY ★

Detroit, 1967: Bob Babbitt receives a call from the local record company that exports the city's second-most-famous product. Their celebrated house bassist is having "personal problems," and they want Bob to pinch-hit for him on a session. In an atmosphere that could be described as cliquish and skeptical at best, the producer, the arranger, and the rest of the musicians descend upon Babbitt with a litany of instructions on how to sound and play like their missing comrade. Nobody in the room says it, but they all expect him to fall short.

A decade later, Bob finds himself in New York City, where he has been called in to cut an album of traditional Italian songs produced by a famous Mafia don. In addition to being told how and what to play, he's been given more instructions: "Wear a suit, don't make any mistakes, smile, and most of all, don't even *think* about walking into the control booth"—where the don is holding court.

Now Bob's playing bass for a Gladys Knight & the Pips project. The rhythm section is huge. There are just too many instruments and too many written notes on his chart, and about 20 takes in, rigor mortis has begun to set in on the groove. The producer's solution? Asking Bob, "Can you try to play something like Chuck Rainey would play?"

Gladys's producer eventually came to his senses, sent half the rhythm section home, tore up the charts, and told Bob to play whatever he felt against the chord changes. The result was a double-platinum, Grammy-winning No. 1 pop hit called "Midnight Train to Georgia."

Bob's long journey didn't start in New York, Detroit, Los Angeles, or any other of the studio-rich cities where he's earned more than 25 gold and platinum records. It began in Pittsburgh, Pennsylvania, a town renowned more for its steelmaking than its hitmaking. Born Robert Kreiner to Hungarian parents, Bob received classical training on upright bass, although he says the gypsy music to which his family exposed him at a young age was far more influential. At 15, inspired by early rhythm & blues hits like Bill Doggett's "Honky Tonkin'" and Red Prysock's "Hand Clappin'," he began performing in local nightclubs. Two years later, after hearing his first electric bass in a local club, Bob traded his upright for a '60 Jazz Bass, using the 1–2–4 classical fingering system on his new instrument until he could figure out how to work in his 3rd finger.

In 1961, because of limited job opportunities and low wages in Pittsburgh,

Babbitt turned down a music scholarship and moved to Detroit, where he worked on construction crews during the day and played clubs at night. Within a year he had joined a local band, the Royaltones, that provided his initiation into Detroit's blossoming studio scene. He charted seven or eight records with the Royaltones, including a Top-Ten hit called "Flamingo Express." The group caught the attention of singer-guitarist Del Shannon, and they became his touring and recording band through 1965.

As Bob's reputation grew, so did his recording schedule. One frequent employer was local R&B producer Ed Wingate, who owned Golden World studio. During this period Babbitt first came into contact with some of Motown's moonlighting musicians, including keyboardists Joe Hunter and Johnny Griffith, guitarist Eddie Willis, drummer Benny Benjamin, and—most important—bassist James Jamerson, the troubled genius whose career would crisscross with Bob's for the next seven years. "On my first Wingate session," Babbitt recalls, "I saw a list of musicians posted on a wall. It had the names of Jamerson and eight other bassists. I said to myself, Man, I'm never gonna work here—but I wound up doing so much work there they had a cot brought in for me."

By 1967 Bob was on a roll, as the word spread among Detroit's producers that there was another bassist in town besides Jamerson who could make some magic in the bottom end. The three or four dates a month Babbitt had been happy to get a few years earlier quickly turned into seven or eight long sessions a week. In addition to steady work at Golden World, he was busy at United Sound, Tera Shirma, and just about every other studio of any consequence in the Detroit area—except for Motown, which was still Jamerson's realm. Babbitt played on some classic R&B tunes during this period, including "I Just Wanna Testify" by the Parliaments, "Love Makes the World Go Round" by Dion Jackson, and "Cool Jerk" by the Capitols.

"I'll always remember the 'Cool Jerk' session," Babbitt states proudly. "It was the first date I played on when I instantly knew it was a hit. It also stuck out in my mind because the Capitols were actually there, which was rare for a Detroit session. In New York, the artists were always at the date, doing reference vocals with the rhythm section so you knew what the song sounded like. In Detroit, you never knew what the song was about until you heard it on the radio. The Detroit producers usually just cut a rhythm track and then wrote a song to it.

"George Clinton worked like that, too. He was one of my favorite guys to record with, although I have to admit I wasn't quite ready for his transformation [from doo-wop with the Parliaments to eccentric leader of Parliament/Funkadelic]. George was one of the cleanest cats around—he always had on a suit and a pressed white shirt. About two years after I had cut 'Testify' with him, I got called for another Parliaments session, and I saw this guy who looked like he had taken a piece of canvas or burlap, thrown paint on it, and cut a hole in the middle for his head to go through. His hair was pointing straight up. Somebody said, 'That's George Clinton.' I said, 'You gotta be kidding me!'

"Edwin Starr's 'Agent Double O Soul' was another great date, because it was my first contact with Jamerson. We were doing a two-bass session at Golden World, and I was kind of nervous because all of the top Motown guys were there—Jamerson, [drummer] Uriel Jones, and I think either [keyboardist] Earl Van Dyke or Johnny Griffith. I had cut the original part, but they decided to redo the tune. James and I divided up the bass part; one of us played an eighth-note pedal and the other played a figure on top. As it turned out, they used the original track anyway."

Being part of Hitsville's staff was the dream of every musician in Detroit—and Babbitt was no exception. He had tried to break into Motown in 1965, by auditioning for the Supremes' road band, but Ed Wingate talked him out of it. Two years later, a second opportunity presented itself when company founder Berry Gordy tried to eliminate all competition in Detroit by buying out Golden World.

Bob had been playing some live dates with Stevie Wonder, so Gordy's move left him perched right on Hitsville's doorstep. "My first Motown date was a Stevie Wonder song called 'We Can Work It Out.' My immediate impression of Studio A was how good they made the bass sound. It made you feel as if you could do no wrong. In terms of practical matters, like working with producers and engineers, those were the best music lessons I ever had. For one thing, I learned that most of the time when people say, 'You sound great,' they're not talking about your technique or the notes you're playing. They really mean the *sound* itself. I also learned that if the music doesn't feel right, the first thing they're gonna do is blame the bassist or the drummer, so feel is more important than the notes."

Because of the overwhelming presence of James Jamerson within the company, Babbitt soon found that working in Studio A was a bit more complicated than just showing up, plugging in, and cutting a hit. "Working at Motown was the hardest thing I ever did, because I always felt like I was in the hot seat," he sighs. "I cut 'Touch Me in the Morning,' 'Signed, Sealed, Delivered,' 'Smiling Faces,' 'War,' 'Tears of a Clown,' and a lot of other hits for the company, but I never felt really secure. I always felt I had so much to live up to, because of Jamerson. On a lot of those sessions, I knew that the producer and the rest of the musicians wanted James, but he was going through a lot because of his drinking problems. To make matters worse, sometimes he'd come into a session where I was subbing for him and watch.

"One time they called and told me to get right over to the studio. Everyone was in the middle of a session, but James was messing up so we both played. One of the guys was bustin' on him, saying, 'You gonna let this white guy run all over you?' But it wasn't malicious. Eventually, I became good friends with all those guys and was accepted into that circle. They just wanted to kick James in the ass and snap him out of it. Everybody wanted to see him do well.

"He was a great guy, but if you hung around him you had to run into a problem sooner or later. One time, the Platters hired Jamerson and some of the other Funk Brothers to play some live gigs around the Detroit-Dearborn area. James was packing a gun, because Dearborn was pretty hairy back then. At the same time, Luther Dixon, who produced the Platters, hired me to cut 'With This Ring' and 'I Love You 1000 Times.' When I walked into the studio, there was James sitting at the organ. He said, 'I'm playing the session tonight,' and when he leaned back I could see the gun in his waistband. So I laughed and said, 'Well, I guess you are,' and turned around to leave. Luther stopped me and told me not to worry about it. Eventually, James just left.

> "Working at Motown was the hardest thing I ever did, because I always felt like I was in the hot seat."

"But we genuinely liked each other. James didn't hold grudges. A few days after that incident, I was in Golden World and James came in with his bass, kicked everybody out of the room, and said, 'Come on, Bob, let's go!' We played for hours. Boy, I wish there had been a tape recorder running, because there was some serious stuff bouncing off those walls."

Between 1970 and 1972, Babbitt, like Motown, was going through a transition period. Work had slowed down, and he was involved with a lot of unfocused and unfinished projects. Jeff Beck and drummer Cozy Powell came into Hitsville to record with Bob and some of the other musicians, but nothing ever came of those sessions. And Beck's offer to take Bob back to London with him as part of his band was blocked by Motown, because he was under contract. A company-sanctioned Babbitt solo record never got off the ground; neither did an album project with a group called Scorpion, of which Bob was a member. To supplement his income, Babbitt became a professional wrestler for six months.

In 1972, just as everything seemed to be falling apart with the imminent departure of Motown to the West Coast, Bob got the opportunity to make a once-in-a-lifetime artistic statement on Marvin Gaye's *What's Going On*. "Marvin and [arranger] Dave Van dePitte basically left us wide open to create," recalls Bob. "'Mercy Mercy Me' was just a chord chart. 'Inner City Blues' had a written figure, but I was told to improvise off it. We all knew we were going into uncharted territory, but the album became Motown's all-time biggest seller."

Bob has kept his lengthy studio career alive by knowing when it's time to move on. When Arif Mardin and other New York arrangers and producers began trying to convince him to relocate to the East Coast, that was his cue. Bob moved to New York in 1973, and his first dates included Mardin projects for Bette Midler and Barry Manilow. Within a short time, Babbitt and drummer Andrew Smith—another Motown refugee—became one of the hottest new rhythm sections in town; producers recruited them to record with everyone from Stephanie Mills, Jim Croce, and Bonnie Raitt to Engelbert Humperdinck and Frank Sinatra. Philadelphia International Records also took notice of their work, and it wasn't long before Bob was commuting back and forth to Philly to work with legendary producer Thom Bell on such Spinners classics as "Then Came You," "Games People Play," and "Rubber Band Man."

By the late '70s, Bob's workload reached critical mass. "I was recording with so many different artists in so many different styles, I didn't know which end was up. I remember cutting three complete albums in three weeks at one point. The first was with the Spinners out in L.A.; then came an Alice Cooper record in Toronto; then I did Sinatra in New York. I didn't just have to play differently on each session—I had to *dress* differently."

When things began to slow down in the early '80s, Bob moved away from album projects, cutting jingles and filling up the rest of his schedule with a foray into jazz, touring, and recording with flutist Herbie Mann and saxophonist Stanley Turrentine. As the mid-'80s approached, the golden era of the studio bassist was coming to an uneventful end. Adjusting to the new realities of the session scene, some hitmakers landed lucrative touring gigs, while others faded away into club dates and teaching. Babbitt, like Willie Weeks, David Hungate, and other studio veterans, opted to head for what has become the last safe haven of real bass recording: Nashville.

"It was the most logical move for me because a lot of R&B influences were creeping into the traditional country scene. There's also a busy gospel market in Nashville, and that's right up my alley. Even so, my first few years were kind of dry. There was a lot of demo work, and a few sessions, but I learned Nashville isn't an easy town to break into. They don't care about what you did before. Most of the bigger sessions I was getting were out of town." As for absorbing the necessary stylistic and technological changes, Bob has a simple answer: "I always seem to play with younger guys, and that keeps me current. It wasn't easy to learn to slap after 20 years of trying to perfect another style, but the younger guys helped me to adapt."

Unfortunately, no one has been able to help Bob deal with the same kind of typecasting Jamerson had to endure. "To this day, no matter what I do, no matter how many hits I've had away from Detroit, all anybody ever asks me is about Motown," he laments. "Even though the most important hits I did were at Motown, they never gave out gold records. I have more than 25 of them, and none are from Motown."

★ DEEPER CUTS: BOB BABBITT ON MARVIN GAYE'S "INNER CITY BLUES (MAKE ME WANNA HOLLER)" BY CHRIS JISI ★

Bob Babbitt was one weary Funk Brother in 1971. Motown sessions were running at 7 am, 11 am, and 3 pm, while the production team of Holland-Dozier-Holland, who had gone off on their own, held 7 pm, 11 pm, and 3 am calls. Little did Babbitt know, however, that his finger fatigue would play a key role in one of the classic sub-hooks of the '70s.

But first, the backstory: In January '71, Marvin Gaye began recording his masterpiece, *What's Going On*. Politically charged and groundbreaking both musically and socially, the work has since been hailed as arguably the finest soul record ever made, and it's even been listed as one of the top five all-time albums in any genre. The disc's nine songs were recorded in order, with James Jamerson appearing on the first five cuts (including his legendary title-track performance, purported to have been overdubbed while he was flat on his back, on the studio floor). Sadly, Jamerson's demons had started to affect his consistency, so Babbitt was summoned for the final four tracks, including "Mercy Mercy Me (The Ecology)" and the brooding "Inner City Blues (Makes Me Wanna Holler)."

The latter was the album's final single, reaching No. 1 on the R&B Singles chart and No. 9 on the pop chart. The backbone of the tune is a two-bar call-and-response bass phrase that Babbitt more than made his own. He remembers, "When I got to the session, I saw that it was out of the ordinary: Marvin was playing piano, and there were some outside musicians. Over the next few days, as we ran down the music, you could sense Marvin was going someplace new; there were tempo changes, transitions, and exciting chord progressions unlike anything we had ever played. He was reaching and experimenting, but he knew what he wanted."

On the "Inner City" session, in Hitsville's Studio A, Gaye played piano without providing a scratch vocal. Babbitt sat on a stool in the curve of the grand piano, plucking his '65 Fender P-Bass, which had La Bella medium flatwounds and a dampened household sponge placed under the strings by the bridge. He recorded direct only, with the sound coming out of the studio's big monitor speaker. Bob recalls the part being notated to some extent, with a few run-throughs occurring before the take, and no punches or fixes afterward.

As it turned out, the line he cut that day was only a portion of the final bass picture. Babbitt was called in to record a repeated one-bar phrase throughout all of the song's verses. He surmises, "The main part went pretty high up the fingerboard, and Marvin was used to hearing Jamerson, who generally played on the lower part of the bass, rarely venturing above high *C* or *D*. I think he had me overdub the second part to fill out the bottom." Additionally, there were some sonic problems with the original bass track, leading Babbitt to be brought back to recut the original part in the booth, with an important twist. He relates, "It was late at night and I was really tired, so instead of reaching up for the high 3rd (*G♭*) on the *G* string, as I had on the original version, I slid up to it, and Marvin went, 'Yeah!' That led me to gliss into the note every time."

In the first verse, Babbitt tends to fill in the back half of the two-bar phrase. "The pickup fills, that occasional *G♭*, and the slides are my main contributions to the written two-bar bass line. And remember, I didn't have a scratch vocal going; if I did, I might not have filled as often."

On the B section, Bob was given the chord changes and the freedom to come up with his own part. "I recall wanting to play the section differently each time, to contrast the repetitive A-section figure. For the first one, I stayed mainly on the root and varied the rhythms. This was something I was doing a lot of at that point; you can hear the same approach on 'Mercy Mercy Me.'" For the second B section, Bob moves away from his root-only approach to play a melodic figure on the downbeat. "Really, most of those note choices come from my left-hand fingering of index and pinkie."

Babbitt plucked the part using mostly his middle finger (supported by his index finger behind it), with the occasional index pluck. As for the rhythmic feel, he notes, "You would think with the swing feel, the part sits behind, but it's pretty much square on the beat." He reflects, "Hearing it again after all these years took me right back to the session, but my overall feeling is how fortunate I was to have played on an album that had such a huge impact on both musicians and society at large."

★ WHO PLAYED BASS? BY BOB BABBITT ★

James Jamerson and I were once hanging out in a bar across the street from where the Capitols' "Cool Jerk" was recorded: Golden World Studio, which later became

Motown Studio B. The bar had this great-sounding bubble jukebox, which started playing "Cool Jerk." Jamerson walked over to it, leaned down, and waved me
over next to him. "Listen to that bass," he said.

"Yeah, what about it?"

He stood up, pounded his hands on his chest, and said, "*Moi*. Me. That's me."

I said, "*Nooooo* . . . that's *me*."

"They must have recut the record."

It's not uncommon for session musicians to list certain songs on their résumé
while someone else lays claim to playing on one or more of them. Why does this
happen? There are several possibilities. The first one could be that the résumé is a
lie! I know one musician who, when confronted about songs he claimed credit for,
replied, "I would do or say anything to put food on the table for my kids." Second,
a lot of albums were released with no credits, and since many sessions didn't go
through the union, there were no contracts that would have listed the players.
Another possibility is that the part was overdubbed, or the entire song was re-
recorded at another time.

When you constantly play sessions day after day for years, it can be hard to
remember everything you played on. In Detroit, it got to be like a factory job.
Through the years I have heard other musicians talking about playing on records
I know they did not play on. Some people may believe them.

One reason musician credits can be confusing is the session contracts—or
lack of them. One ex-employee of the Detroit musicians union claims that at
some point in the late '70s or early '80s, they shredded the contracts because they
were running out of room! Then, when the movie and TV industry started using
the songs as background music, the film studios needed to see copies of the contracts before they would pay anyone residuals. So in Detroit they made up mock
contracts for sessions, assuming certain players had played on certain records. In
the case of Motown they often figured it was James Jamerson who had played bass,
so they put his name on the mock contracts, then submitted them to the film
companies and put them on file. I played on Marvin Gaye's "Mercy Mercy Me
(the Ecology)" from *What's Going On*, which was used in several films and commercials. But Jamerson's name was on the mock contract, so he got the residuals.
In another example, I played on Edwin Starr's hit song "War," which has been
used in six or seven movies and was the theme song for a popular TV show. I was-
n't getting any residuals, so I called the union. There were two contracts for that
title, and neither listed the artist. It turned out they had been paying residuals
based on the session contract for the Temptations' version, which had the same
personnel except for Jamerson on bass instead of me. I have also worked for producers and arrangers who were so busy or so into drugs that there was a definite

possibility they forgot who actually played on the records they produced.

Often a session would be recut, or someone would be called in to overdub and play the exact same part but perhaps with better feel or execution. If the arranger or producer didn't like the overdub, they might have gotten a third player to overdub, or they might have gone back to the original. This also happens at times with recutting the whole track. If the new player's sound was close to yours, it may be hard to tell whether or not it's you on the track—but I think every player can tell their own sound and recognize their signature licks. For Rare Earth I did an album cut and the single "Losing You." The group's bass player got credit instead. There were similar situations with the first Funkadelic album, with the Flaming Embers, and with Wilson Pickett's "Don't Knock My Love." Sometimes the producers didn't even tell the group.

Now, I want to say that every record I have claimed to play on I really feel in my heart and soul that I played on. When I hear these songs I can visualize the session and remember certain things that happened in the studio. I did only a couple of sessions for Smokey Robinson and I remember "Tears of a Clown" as being one of them, yet Jamerson gets credit. The record "Touch Me in the Morning" by Diana Ross was one I had overdubbed at Motown Studio B. Yet, on a Diana Ross greatest hits album they credited a Los Angeles bassist because the original track was cut in L.A. If there was a contract filed, it probably would have the L.A. bass player's name on it—but I remember that overdub because it was the first time I took my wife to the studio. When that record became a hit I wanted her to come to all of my sessions because I thought she was a good luck charm!

It is hard when you hear that other bass players are getting credit for some of your work. But, if those few songs in question were recuts or overdubs, I guess I'll have to live with that. The fact that there were no credits on those records hurt everyone. But as a New York bassist once said to me, "I know what records *I* played on."

7.
LARRY GRAHAM AND
THE INVENTION OF SLAP BASS

★ LARRY GRAHAM: THE SLY & THE FAMILY
STONE YEARS BY JIMMY LESLIE ★

Larry Graham doesn't just play bass—he thumps it until the earth trembles. And when he sings, he's no mere baritone; he's James Earl Jones with a knack for melody. Larry Graham's bass presence is so powerful, his history so sanctified, his groove so infectious, that he can summon even the most jaded spirits to the dance floor, where all will testify: Larry Graham's whole soul resonates *deep*.

As a kid, Larry tried piano, clarinet, saxophone, drums, and guitar before finding his true calling. His multi-instrumental background and open mind

ultimately led him to create an entirely original electric bass style. Some call it slap and pop—Larry calls it "thumpin' and pluckin'"—and it's arguably the single most innovative and influential technique in the history of bass. Even players who consciously steer clear of its now-ubiquitous presence need to at least have a handle on the technique just to get through a typical wedding set. Larry Graham's funky creation is a lasting one.

Graham found the ideal outfit for his then-bizarre chops and robust vocal resonance during his celebrated tenure in Sly & the Family Stone, the multicultural ensemble that sprung up from the same San Francisco Summer of Love scene that produced the Grateful Dead and Santana. Yet, even during the countercultural heyday of the late '60s and early '70s, Sly & the Family Stone was different. It was the first major act to include both black and white members as well as men and women. It was also the first to mix R&B with psychedelia, funk, and pop. No group before or since—with the possible exception of Prince—has had such success crossing funk grooves and pop melodies the way Sly and his band did on tracks such as "Stand!" and "You Can Make It If You Try." The brilliant group vocal arrangements and socially conscious lyrics of songs like "Everyday People" and "Everybody Is a Star" made the music universally appealing—at once of its time, and timeless.

Graham has rarely strayed far or long from the limelight since he left the Family fold in 1972. His band Graham Central Station reeled off a string of impressive bass-driven albums for the remainder of the '70s, with incredible thump-led tunes like "Hair" and "The Jam." Graham's vocal-oriented solo material made him a star all over again in the '80s, with ballads like "One in a Million You" and "Just Be My Lady." Since the late '90s, he's been living in Minnesota, collaborating with and spiritually counseling Prince.

What are your favorite Sly & the Family Stone bass lines?

"Dance to the Music" stands out because bass players weren't using effects up until that point, and that opened the door. "Everyday People" is unique because I'm just thumpin' one note with the same rhythm for the whole song. I'd never heard that before. That's simple as I could ever play. "Thank You (Falettinme Be Mice Elf Again)" features my thumpin' and pluckin' prominently. It's the foundation of the song, so I'm happy about that.

> "I wasn't interested in learning the so-called 'correct' overhand style of playing bass, because in my head I was going back to guitar, anyway."

You planted a thump-and-pluck flag on "Thank You." How did you feel when everybody started picking up on the technique?

I always took the fact that they were imitating my playing style as a compliment. Most bass players come up and compliment me and thank me. I'm still overjoyed to this day because now it's a part of how you play.

A lot of people that love my thumpin' and pluckin' style don't know where it originated. Their favorite bass player listened to me, but they only know that bass player in that band. I'm not seeking credit, but it makes me feel good when bassists like Verdine White, Stanley Clarke, Flea, Bootsy Collins, or Victor Wooten talk about me being an influence on their bass playing. It means the most to know that I was able to contribute something to the world of music that is ongoing and will probably be around forever.

How did you and Greg Errico work together in the Family Stone rhythm section?

Fortunately, Greg had a drumming style that really complemented what I was doing. We never had any collisions! It wouldn't have worked if he filled up a lot of space, which is what everybody else was doing at the time. He found a way to complement the song and the bass line by being creative and open.

Can you describe how you both approached the beat in terms of feel?

Greg plays on the money; he doesn't rush or lag. I can play on the money, but I can also lay back, depending on the song. You can hear me deliberately laying back on "Just Like a Baby" [*There's a Riot Goin' On*], "Que Sera, Sera" [*Fresh*], and "Sex Machine" [*Stand*]. The actual bass line to "Dance to the Music" [*Dance to the Music*] is an example of being on it. The fuzz track is a little more laid back. I laid it down after the regular part. "Thank You (Falettinme Be Mice Elf Again)" [on *Greatest Hits*] had to be on the money because the bass line sets the pattern, and lot of stuff was built on it.

How did you record your lines?

A lot of stuff was cut live, so we miked the amp in the control room and ran a direct line as well. We didn't do anything fancy. The most important thing was making it sound right in the room by capturing what was coming out of the instrument, strings, pedals, and amp—like a concert—as opposed to trying to create something different.

How were the arrangements created?

One of the elements that contributed to the band's success was that folks were allowed freedom of expression to a great degree. Sly would lay out the song and the pattern—the basic course that we were to follow—but everyone was allowed to contribute, especially the rhythm section. We would do extended versions of songs in concert. We'd start by playing the song pretty much like the record, and then we'd run through it a second time when you had the freedom to do whatever you wanted. Some of those licks and concepts would end up being new songs.

Did you ever write lyrics or share a songwriting credit?

No, but I played whatever I wanted to play. Nobody else in the band is credited with writing or co-writing any of the songs, although by today's standards we would all be viewed differently, and some would probably be credited differently. We're making no claims or complaining about credit. I'm happy for the success we had, and that it proved to be a springboard for me.

What was your first major musical moment?

My father gave me his guitar when I was 11 because he decided he wasn't going to play anymore. I taught myself to play it, and one of the songs I learned was Clarence Gatemouth Brown's "Okie Dokie Stomp." A mutual friend told Ike and Tina Turner that I could play it well, and they brought me onstage with their band at the Fillmore West. That night was a big deal to me because it was my first experience on a big stage. The crowd went crazy watching this little 13-year-old guy playing that song note for note.

How did you follow that up?

I continued playing gigs with my band, the Five Riffs, and then when I was 15 my mother and I started playing all over the San Francisco Bay Area as the Dell Graham Trio. She played piano and sang, I played guitar and sang. Reuben Kerr, from my old band, played drums; then it was a guy named Pinky, and after him, my mother decided we would just be a duo. We were working at the Escort Club in Redwood City. They had an organ, and I would play the bass pedals with my foot while I played the guitar. We were used to having bottom, so when that organ broke I rented a St. George bass from Music Unlimited in San Leandro, which is still there. I was renting the bass until the organ could be repaired, but they could-n't find parts, so I got stuck on the bass [*laughs*].

Did you start thumpin' and pluckin' straight away?

I started thumpin' and pluckin' from the first time I played bass because I played guitar with my fingers—not a pick. I would thump the strings with my thumb to make up for the bass drum, and pluck the strings with my fingers to make up for the backbeat snare drum. It made sense to me because I had been a drummer in the school band. I wasn't interested in learning the so-called "correct" overhand style of playing bass, because in my head I was going back to guitar, any-way. Then I realized, Hey—this is pretty cool. I would imagine that some folks thought my playing was a little strange. You know, like, 'You're not supposed to play the bass like that—that's not correct!' The only reason I didn't trip on that is that I was constantly thinking, I'm going back to guitar, so I don't care what any-body thinks.

What were you doing just before you joined the Family Stone?

I went straight from playing with my mother to Sly. We were playing at Relax with Yvonne near the corner of Haight and Ashbury when Sly came and told me about this band he was starting. With my mother's blessing, I went to a rehearsal at Sly's house, and we all hit it off right from the jump. He was origi-nally going to be the bass player, but he jumped to keyboards, and we started playing gigs around the Bay. Most people think I play on every song, but Sly is an excellent bass player. He sometimes used a pick, so if you're really trippin' on the sound and style, you can hear that and tell it's him. My favorite line of his "You Can Make It If You Try."

What were the circumstances when you left the Family Stone in 1972?

Sometimes in a family, it comes time to go. Nothing is specifically wrong; at some point you leave home, and you aren't mad. You still love your parents and your brothers and sisters, but you leave. Everything is still cool. A number of us have worked and toured together since then. Greg Errico is on my instructional video. At one show, I had everybody from the original band onstage at the same time with the exception of Sly and [guitarist] Freddie Stone.

What was it like to assume the reins in Graham Central Station?

My mother and Sly were both great bandleaders, and I learned from them. Sly & the Family Stone was an appropriate name because the whole band ran like a family unit. You always felt secure and protected, and that the direction given was reliable. I brought that vibe to my band, and it reflected in the music, espe-cially during live performance.

Were you able to do more of the things you wanted on bass?

Sure—I was able to feature my bass more, and my singing, too. In Sly & the

Family Stone I mostly sang parts, but with GCS I sang a lot of lead.

Did your bass approach change at all due to increased songwriting, vocals, and showmanship duties?

I changed more as a singer, especially by the time we got to *One in a Million You*, because for the first time in my career the focus was more on my vocals. *Million* was my biggest record, so it kind of overshadowed my bass playing. Some folks didn't know my funky history with Sly & the Family Stone and GCS. Seeing me walk onstage with a bass was a surprise to the suit-and-tie crowd that started showing up at concerts. I'd go from "One in a Million You" to "The Jam," and they were like, "Oh, *that* guy!" [*Laughs.*]

How do you feel about the band's legacy?

I think we made a major contribution to the music world. We influenced so many groups, who in turn influenced other musicians. We were like a massive tree with multiple branches that provided comforting shade to keep a lot of people cool.

★ LARRY GRAHAM: HIS PLAYING STYLE WITH SLY & THE FAMILY STONE BY BILL LEIGH WITH BOBBY VEGA ★

When you think of Larry Graham's bass playing with Sly & the Family Stone, what naturally comes to mind? Could it be that persistently swinging, short-long pulse, exemplified by the thumb-thumping, fuzz-bass-doubled line of "Dance to the Music"? Could it be the one-note thump genius of "Everyday People"? Or the spanky octave slap from "Thank You Falettinme (Be Mice Elf)"?

When Larry himself thinks of his bass work with Sly, only one thing comes to mind: "My mother, Dell Graham. I hadn't listened to any bass players when I took up bass with her when I was about 15, and I went straight from playing with her to playing with Sly. My heroes were Clarence 'Gatemouth' Brown, Chuck Berry, and B. B. King—and I always thought I'd go back to guitar. So my only real bass influence was the way my mother carried bass lines with her left hand on the piano. A lot of things she played went into my ear and my heart, and influenced me later as a bass player."

There's much more to his lines than straightforward thumb-slaps, though. For example, when Larry employed octaves on "Fun"—presaging a technique that would soon became a disco mainstay—he wasn't 'thumpin' and pluckin'" per se; instead, he was using his thumb and finger to stroke the strings like the fingerstyle guitarist he once was. And when he played octaves on parts like the main verse line of "Are You Ready," he'd slide into both octave notes together, then maintain a bottom pulse while plucking syncopated finger-popped accents. "It's like two lines coming into one," says Larry. "That's the kind of thing you have to do as a drummer to keep the bass drum going with the snare. Remember, I played drums before I played guitar." Still, on the quick-tempo track "Underdog," one of the Family's first singles, Larry showed just how dexterous he could be with that thumb. Larry's busy line cruises through the lively verse changes, in pointed contrast to the chorus's long-held dribble-fingered tremolo notes.

"I Wanna Take You Higher" has all the elements of a great Sly & the Family Stone song—high-energy rhythm, a recognizable riff, and vocal shout-outs from various band members—but it also encapsulates the quintessential elements of Larry's style. After the intro riff—where Larry's snarling fuzztone gives apt voice to a sneering flatted 5th—the line goes into a short-long pulse. But first, the rhythm gets weird, as anyone who's ever tried to work this line out knows. The secret's in bar 3's skipped beat, and knowing where to expect the vocals to come in—on the very next downbeat. How did the band come up with that? "Sometimes when you play live, things happen," Larry laughs. After the chorus, when most of the band drops out to sing "Boom-shaka-laka-laka," Larry reduces the short-long pulse to a 1-string, ghost-filled bounce that perfectly matches Greg Errico's up-down drumming. Listen closely and you'll hear multiple bass tracks in the recording, including the chorus's fuzz-bass swoops up to the ♭7. The longer album version has an offbeat bass solo—one of the few things Larry says he played fingerstyle—which comes in around 4:17 over a rocking bed of fuzz bass.

What does Larry think when he listens to these albums now? "They sound just like yesterday to me. We try to keep this music alive, too. It's a part of me, and I love them just as much now as I did then."

PART II:
FUNKY BASS FLOURISHES

As the turbulence and tension of the '60s spilled over into the '70s, funky music became the perfect release. From the lush, soulful arrangements of Philadelphia International Records to the freaky frontiers of Parliament/Funkadelic, funky music flourished throughout the decade and into the '80s, with numerous bands creating their own original take on funk, and a new generation of session players embracing the genre's techniques.

Acts likes Earth, Wind & Fire, Tower of Power, and the Brothers Johnson introduced towering bassists with strong, influential playing styles. Established jazz artists like Miles Davis and Herbie Hancock started to explore seriously funky rhythms, in the process helping create a new jazz fusion alongside groups like Weather Report and Return to Forever. And the disco craze helped bring funky bass to the forefront of mainstream culture.

ROCCO PRESTIA
(PHOTO BY PAUL HAGGARD)

8

ROCCO PRESTIA WITH TOWER OF POWER

★ ROCCO: TOWER OF POWER'S FINGERFUNK
JUGGERNAUT BY CHRIS JISI ★

From his obscured spot behind the five-horn front line of Tower of Power, Francis Rocco Prestia established himself as an all-time bass stylist and funk institution. Prestia is best known for his innovative, fleet-fingered, 16th-note-based grooves. "Without his motion on the bass," notes drummer Herman Matthews, "we would be just another horn band."

Growing up, Francis Rocco Prestia was less than enthusiastic about the lessons his mother encouraged him to take on the Sears Silvertone guitar and amp he received for his tenth Christmas. Born on March 7, 1951, in Sonora, California, Rocco lost his father five years later. By the time his mother remarried and settled in Fremont (just south of Oakland), Rocco and his two brothers and sister had become aware of rock & roll. "I remember hearing and liking early rock on the radio and TV," he says. "What I didn't like was being told to practice guitar. In retrospect, I think my problem was that I wasn't very good; it just never clicked for me." Nevertheless, Rocco stuck with the instrument long enough to audition for classmate Emilio Castillo's band at age 14. Prestia smiles, "I could play only I–IV–V, but I got in because I had good hair." A short time later, Castillo's father hired a jazz guitarist named Terry Saunders to guide the band. "Terry surveyed our instrumentation—and my guitar abilities—and said to me, 'You need to play bass.' We all went, 'What's a bass?' The next day we headed over to the music store where Terry worked, and he put a white P-Bass copy in my hands. The only thing I knew about the bass was it was bigger than me!"

Saunders began teaching the band members how to play their parts for cover versions of tunes by the likes of the Beatles, the Animals, and Paul Revere & the Raiders. "Terry gave me a felt pick, which I tried for a week," recalls Rocco. "But it wasn't working, so I switched to my two fingers. Before long, tenor saxophonist Castillo got hip to soul music through an East Bay horn band called the Spiders. He immediately added horns to his group, and the band began covering R&B tunes by James Brown, Sam & Dave, Wilson Pickett, the Temptations, and Booker T. & the MG's. Of his own evolution during this period, Rocco says, "My influences were *sounds* more than specific bassists: Motown, Memphis, Muscle Shoals, Atlantic, and James Brown. It wasn't until later that I became aware of names like James Jamerson, Duck Dunn, Chuck Rainey, and Jerry Jemmott. Even back then, though, I wasn't into learning lines note-for-note. It was always more about copping the feels; that, along with being in a unique band and the freedom I was given with my parts, is the reason I was eventually able to develop my own style."

With the horn section having swelled to five and the band having become a fixture at local clubs and dances, Castillo and Kupka (who came up with the name Tower of Power) began writing originals. The final piece fell into place with the addition of drummer Dave Garibaldi in 1969. Reports Rocco, "With Dave, it was magic right from the gate. Basically, he and I were good for each other because he was really busy, and I came from a more simple, laid-back, R&B bag. We met in the middle and refined our concept from there. But I have to give him a lot of credit for opening me up rhythmically. I found myself adding notes and accents and playing with more propulsion. He was so crafty and clever, too—dropping beats or moving everything over by an eighth- or a 16th-note to create turned-around feels. He could make things sit where you wouldn't think they would sit. The ideas started flowing like crazy between him and Emilio, and they would help me or make suggestions for the bass parts."

After a successful TOP performance at the Fillmore Auditorium in San Francisco, legendary rock impresario Bill Graham signed the band to his management company and released their first recording, *East Bay Grease*, on his San Francisco Records label in 1971. The raw but critically acclaimed album resulted in a deal with Warner Bros. in 1972. TOP soon hit its stride, driven by the subdivision like-mindedness of Prestia, Garibaldi, Thompson, and Conte in the rhythm section. The subsequent albums *Bump City*, *Tower of Power*, *Back to Oakland*, and *Urban Renewal* yielded such classic tracks as "You're Still a Young Man," You Got to Funkifize," "Soul Vaccination," "Squib Cakes," "Oakland Stroke," "Don't Change Horses (in the Middle of a Stream)," "Down to the Nightclub," "Can't You See," "Only So Much Oil in the Ground," and—of course—the quintessential funk anthem, "What Is Hip?"

Though TOP followed *Urban Renewal* with two more albums for Warner Bros. and three for Columbia through 1979, they failed to match the group's early '70s peak. The band continued its heavy touring pace, but substance abuse began to take a toll on personnel. Rocco acknowledges, "We were right there during the hard-drug scene that followed the '60s, and although we may have experimented innocently, we all developed addictions." A faction of the band decided the best approach to sobriety included making an example of someone. That and other factors led to Prestia's firing in 1977. Initially, this turn of events resulted in further substance problems for Rocco, as well as the end of his first marriage. However, he soon began his comeback with bass in hand. He toured with a Bay Area blues band headed by guitarist Bobby Murray and vocalist Frankie Lee, and he anchored jams with Alberts King and Collins. Following a stint with a Top-40 band, in 1983 an old drummer friend got Rocco a Las Vegas audition in with Lola Falana. He explains, "I was hired because Frank Fiore, the conductor, was a big TOP fan. He knew I couldn't read, and he was nice enough to take me under his wing and teach me the parts."

Over the years, Prestia ran into various TOP members and even sat in with the band on a number of occasions while Victor Conte and then Vito San Filippo filled the bass chair. "I had accepted the situation and I was no longer bitter," he assures. "It wasn't like I was expecting to get my gig back." In fact, a 1984 call from Castillo with an invitation to rejoin the band took Rocco by complete surprise. After briefly weighing his options and obligations in Vegas, he consented. "It was a very natural reunion; I felt like I'd returned home." Actually, the band soon relocated from the Bay Area to Los Angeles. In 1987, they released *Power*, which produced the instant TOP classic (and the band's lone video) "Credit," a half-time shuffle driven by Rocco's ridiculous double-time bass line.

The late '80s also marked a high point for the band's horn section, which became an in-demand session crew and touring unit with Huey Lewis & the News. Rocco confides, "It was a difficult time for the rhythm section. The horns were getting twice the money and recognition, and the rest of us were struggling to survive. The silver lining was that it led me to explore the L.A. scene for the first time. I met and played with other musicians, and I even had my own club band, called Flexx, for a while." He continues, "It also got me to focus on my career separate from TOP, which later made it possible to do other projects and to work on my instructional video."

Did your muting style evolve as a result of needing to get more separation between notes in rapid-fire grooves?

I'm more of a rhythmic player, and I guess at some point I realized that more staccato and percussive playing seemed to lock better with the drums. I played longer tones early on—and I'm playing more long tones lately—but short tones are still the way I hear the groove.

As for technique, I usually play with my left hand in one position, no matter where I am on the neck. I fret the notes mainly with my index and middle fingers, and occasionally with my 3rd and 4th fingers. My whole hand lies across the fingerboard, and the fingers that aren't fretting are the ones that mute the strings. Some muting also comes from the way I attack the strings with my right hand, too, so it's a combination of right- and left-hand touch. In the right hand, I alternate my index and middle fingers to pluck the strings—usually at the halfway point between the neck and the bridge—while my thumb anchors on the pickup or the *E* string.

Were you tempted to try slapping, having grown up near Larry Graham?

First of all, Sly Stone was a huge influence on our band. We all saw him play when we were still in school. Larry was there, and his slap style was amazing; I tried it, but it wasn't natural for me. Then Dave started jamming a lot with the late Dougie Rauch, a great bassist and slapper who was with Santana, so Dave would encourage me to slap—but my hands just didn't work that way. In truth, I would credit Larry and Paul Jackson, who became friends of mine on the club scene, with inspiring me to really zero in on my own style, because they both had such strong individual voices on the instrument.

You've said practice for you consists of shows, recordings, and rehearsals. Does your right hand ever cramp up or get tired during sets, especially after a long layoff from playing?

It happens occasionally. There was a period when my hands would get numb on me, which was probably a circulation problem. I do warm up before a set by playing up and down the neck—slowly at first—to loosen up the muscles in both hands. I also try to relax as much as possible during the show, so that if my hand does cramp up, I can shake it off and keep going. Sometimes it'll hurt for a minute—but I can't stop playing, because that's my job.

How has your style evolved over the years?

It hasn't! [*Laughs.*] Truthfully, I had always been a little afraid of stifling my playing by thinking about it too much, but working on my instructional video changed all that. It made me figure out and understand what it is I do, and because of that, I've been able to refine my playing. Like most musicians, I think maturity has economized my playing, as have the kinds of songs TOP is writing now. I still like to get "stoopid" at times, but in a different way; maybe with fewer notes. I've come to realize the one criterion I have is that I need to make a part my own. I'll play a given line from somebody's demo, and as long as it feels good, I don't care how few notes there are. But I have to be able to put my spin on it, or else I might as well not bother. Even if it's one little note or rhythm every 16 bars, and I'm the only one who knows about it, that can be enough to make it mine.

The more I learn about my style, the more I realize it's not that big a deal [*laughs*]. I like doing things like using 3rds up high on the neck and then dropping down for contrast, but anyone who can play can do what I do. I just approach it with a certain feel, and I guess that's what makes me unique. Overall, I try to be spontaneous with my parts, but I have my clichés like all players do. I get locked into certain things that feel good for a while and I'll play around with variations of them, and then I'll come up with something new and go there for a while.

How has the TOP drum chair changed over the years?

Obviously, Dave was *so* pivotal early on. Each drummer who followed him had something unique to offer, but the best ones understood the requirements of the gig while bringing their own styles to the music, rather than trying to be Dave clones. That's what keeps the music fresh for everyone else. Someone will come in with a new concept, and it's like, *Boom!* I'll think, I've been playing this song for

20 years, and I never thought about it from *that* slant.

Herman Matthews is special. He's got a natural, raw thing going on in his playing—a real gut-bucket hump. We're always coming up with new kicks and talking about tempos or where we want to sit in the pocket on different tunes. I find that because we're driving ten pieces, and due to the nature of the music, the band seems to sound best when he and I play a little more on the edge and push things along. That's essentially the East Bay sound; it's soul music with a different bump to it—a rhythm that's played slightly on top.

What was it like reuniting with Dave?

It was great. Other than when he subbed with TOP very briefly in the early '90s, I hadn't played with him since the '70s. We've grown in different directions over the years, but the magic came back immediately. Not long after, I brought in Dave, Chester, and Bruce for my album, which was also very comfortable. Everybody was on the same page musically, and we laughed, hung out, and talked. I think it was something the four of us had wanted to do for a long time, but we didn't have the right vehicle. In fact, the way everybody's schedules coincided, it was like it was finally meant to be.

How aware are you of your influence on other bassists?

I never would have believed some of the compliments I've gotten from bass players had they not expressed them to me in person. I always feel very uncomfortable when I'm put in the category of such innovators as James Jamerson or Jaco Pastorius, because there are people out there who play *my* shit better than I do! Obviously, no one is going to play *you* better than you, but I've heard my style played at all levels, and it's very flattering.

I love what I do, and I've been fortunate enough to do it in a great band. Tower has always had the ability, no matter what the circumstances, to pull it all together once we take the stage. When the whole band hits on all cylinders and starts grooving, there's no feeling like it. That's the point I strive to get to, because it's the only place I know that's mine; no one can touch me there. I think every musician lives for those magic moments in the zone where playing, energy, and emotion all meet and elevate you to a higher level.

★ THE FEEL FACTOR BY CHRIS JISI ★

It remains one of the great mysteries in all of bassdom: How can Francis Rocco Prestia play such busy parts, yet fit so seamlessly into the groove and so tastefully within a ten-piece band? The answer, according to fans Will Lee and Jeff Berlin, is *feel*. Rocco notes, "The key to being able to play as busily as you want without getting in the way is to lay it in the groove. You can have all of the chops in the world—but if you don't have a feel and a concept, it doesn't matter. It's got to come from the heart." On the technical side, Lee and Berlin point to several other factors: Prestia's preference for creating and developing patterns in a single root-5th-octave position, as opposed to playing moving lines all over the neck; his application of muted notes, which lock with the drums more efficiently than long tones; and his use of space to break up steady 16th-note patterns.

★ DEEPER CUTS: ROCCO PRESTIA ON TOWER OF POWER'S "WHAT IS HIP?"
BY CHRIS JISI ★

In addition to being TOP's "greatest hit," "What Is Hip?" is the song most associated with Rocco and Dave Garibaldi's 16th-note approach. "'What Is Hip?' was a specific concept Dave came up with," says Rocco. "He had the bass playing steady 16ths on one note, with accents in various places." Rocco recalls recording direct, using the modified '60s P-Bass Paul Jackson gave him. "I recently learned that the only reason the bass line is so prominent is it wasn't mixed correctly," he explains. "They never got around to fixing it."

At the top of the track, as guitarist Bruce Conte solos over the eight-bar intro, Rocco's steady *E*s (played on the 7th fret of the *A* string) are interrupted only by the octave *E*s and *B*-and-*E* pushes at the end of every two-bar phrase. Prestia alters the steady *E*s with an *E7*-flavored line during a mid-verse break in the vocal melody. The entire band plays unison kicks during the lead-in to Chester Thompson's organ solo, and as a new groove is set up, Rocco keeps up the steady 16th motif while matching the trio of accented notes with Garibaldi and Conte. Rocco's advice for those who might attempt to play along? "Don't worry so much about the notes. Just be sure to cop the feel."

★ BOBBY VEGA: SUBBING FOR ROCCO WITH
TOWER OF POWER BY E. E. BRADMAN ★

Northern California bassist Bobby Vega had played with plenty of icons in his three-decade career, including Booker T. & the MG's, Sly & the Family Stone, Crosby, Stills & Nash, Etta James, Joan Baez, and Santana. But none of these gigs were as challenging or affirming as his stint with Tower of Power. When Rocco Prestia was first diagnosed with hepatitis in 2002, keyboardist Roger Smith filled in on left-hand bass until TOP leaned on three San Francisco Bay Area pros—Mark Van Wagenen, Darryl Anders, and Vega—to fill in for the gigs. Of the three, Vega stayed the longest, putting the bottom under 35 Tower shows across the U.S. and Canada. And for Vega, a huge Tower fan who named his son Rocco, it was a dream come true.

Vega was given a week's notice to audition with three songs of his choice. After choosing "Soul With a Capital S," "Can't You See (You're Doing Me Wrong)," and "What Is Hip?," he immediately set out to extract each song's nuances and feels, and to decide which versions to learn. "I knew the songs, of course, but I had never taken them apart," says Vega, who spent four 12-hour days to prepare. "I asked myself all sorts of questions: Do you learn the stuff off the record, or do you learn the live stuff? How much can you embellish and still sound like Tower of Power?" Vega learned the parts the hard way: playing and rewinding every bar until he had it right. Most difficult of all, he constantly walked the tightrope of playing Rocco's masterfully percolating funk lines without sounding like a technician or a clone. "I can't play the lines note for note; I don't think anyone can. But the trick is, the band as a whole has to sound good. So when you play the lines, the band has to sound like Tower of Power. It's not like you just have to sound like Rocco."

Live, Tower of Power is a knockout. After a four-beat count-off, the band rips right into a ferocious excerpt of "Soul Vaccination" that twists, turns, and finally settles on the rhythmic hits that lead to "Soul with a Capital 'S.'" The band is razor-sharp precise; each hit is clean, each fill meticulously executed. "It's one thing to learn a song, but it's a whole other thing to stand up there and play it with them. They count it off, and *bam!*—it's on." No medleys here: During each show, more than a dozen TOP gems—from "Can't You See (You're Doing Me Wrong)" to crowd favorites "Diggin' on James Brown" and "You've Got to Funkifize"—are given their full due. Everything is set in stone; little improvisation happens. Bobby watched Garibaldi closely, and when he walked off stage 90 minutes later, he often felt like a boxer after 15 rounds. "I can barely talk," he gasped, after one typically intense show. "I need a standing eight count."

Vega carefully tailored his approach according to feedback from band members who noticed even slight deviations from Rocco's parts. Even as his run came to a close, Vega continued to work on the songs for two hours a day, discovering new fingerings and subtle Rocco-isms that helped give the songs just the right feel. "You can't be overconfident, because you have to change if the band changes. Anything can happen, and you have to be able to catch it."

Known for his funkified pick playing, Bobby conquered most of the tunes with pick in hand, but he played fingerstyle on "You're Still a Young Man," "Willing to Learn," "This Time It's Real," and "And You Know It." He slapped on "To Say the Least You're the Most." He also laid down a funky pick solo on "Knock Yourself Out." "No one can play exactly like Rocco. But my job was to bring Rocco's feel to the songs. I was like the rental car you drive while the regular car is getting fixed." So what was special about Bobby's approach? "I'm willing to adapt—just give into it so the music happens. I've learned that good don't get the gig; you've got to aim so high that even if you hit low, you're still better than everybody. If you know you can do a better job and you don't do it, you're selling yourself short, and you're selling all the people you're working with short. That's part of playing—whether you step up or not."

9.
VERDINE WHITE WITH EARTH, WIND & FIRE

Onstage with Earth, Wind & Fire, Verdine White cuts a wide swath. His dapper threads and flowing locks react to his kinetic dance steps like visual backbeats, while his buoyant bass lines bound off the kick and snare. On vinyl, of course, White is even more imposing, having forged a legacy as an all-time bass stylist with what many contend to be the greatest band—R&B or otherwise—in pop history. While EWF was unifying listeners across musical and global boundaries with spiritually uplifting hits like "Shining Star," "September," "Getaway," "Fantasy," and "After the Love Has Gone," White was busy down below redefining the 16th note with soulful syncopations and melodic, pocket-perfect pickups that have since become an indelible part of the bass lexis.

Yet, while he may stand shoulder to lofty shoulder with such funk figureheads as Larry Graham, Bootsy Collins, the Meters' George Porter, and Tower of Power's Rocco Prestia—as well as with single-band innovators like the Who's John Entwistle and Yes's Chris Squire—Verdine White is a down-to-earth delight. Exuberant and gracious, Verdine White always seems to have a smile as wide as his groove.

White's musical training ground was rife with veteran leadership. Born in Chicago on July 25, 1951, Verdine was raised on the recordings of Miles Davis, John Coltrane, and other jazz greats, spun by his dad, Verdine Sr., a doctor who also played saxophone. White found additional musical stimuli through the radio sounds of Motown and the Beatles, as well as through two brothers who were drummers. At age 15, he spotted an upright bass in his high school orchestra class. "It just spoke to me," he recalls. "So I chose bass. Soon after, I got a red electric bass, too. My dad and Maurice suggested I take private lessons and really learn the instruments." White studied the Bille double bass method with Radi Velah of the Chicago Symphony Orchestra, and on weekends he took electric bass lessons with Chess Records session bassist and trombonist Louis Satterfield, who would later become a member of Earth, Wind & Fire's famed horn section, the Phenix Horns. Gravitating more toward his newly bought Fender Telecaster Bass than the upright, Verdine began working the local club scene with bands like the True Sounds, and made his first recording with Kitty Haywood, "Mama's Baby Ain't a Baby No More." Meanwhile, brother Maurice, who was a session drummer at Chess and a member of pianist Ramsey Lewis's trio, had formed the Salty Peppers, scoring a local hit that caught the ears of Capitol Records. In early 1970 Maurice moved to Los Angeles, hoping to record the group, which he had renamed Earth,

Wind & Fire. Seeking to expand the band and abolish the borders between musical genres, Maurice soon summoned Verdine to fill the bass chair. On June 6, 1970, White arrived in Los Angeles, in no way aware that he was about to help make musical and bass history.

What were some early bass influences that helped form your style?

Well, I was way hip to James Jamerson and Paul McCartney, and on the classical side, Gary Karr—I saw him on a TV show in duet with Richard Davis. The local upright player I checked out in a big way was Cleveland Eaton. But everything I learned and know on the bass guitar is from the late Louis Satterfield. I wouldn't be here if it wasn't for Satt. He played bass on a lot of Chess recordings with Maurice, like "Rescue Me" by Fontella Bass, and he had a style all his own from being a jazz trombonist. I would describe it as almost like a lead bass, but always holding the groove. Satt taught me scales and modes, 6/8 and 7/4 time—all kinds of stuff that opened up my mind. He played a Fender Telecaster Bass and an Ampeg B-15, so that's exactly what I bought. And, of course, Maurice had a huge influence on my playing, being a great session drummer.

When do you feel your style first locked in?

My style came together much faster than it probably would have, right from our first record [1971's *Earth, Wind & Fire*], because of Maurice. His ears are huge—he hears everything—so he would say, take this out there or play this here. And 'Rice is very spontaneous, so whatever we used to rehearse, when we got to the studio, he would totally change it! I learned to think on my feet quickly and to not get attached to any rehearsed parts. That said, we had the time to be indulgent; we were recording 12 hours a day, so I was able to try different ideas and be relaxed—there was no "red light syndrome."

A key element to your style is your use of pickups, with melodic or chromatic passing tones.

For me, it's like dancing on the bass. You want to dance up to the one, or to the next downbeat—or even *on* the next downbeat. And I always like to be aware of the chord qualities and the progression, so I can pick certain notes out of the chord or find an interesting way to get to the next chord. To be honest, my training was so concentrated early on that it occurs naturally for me now; I don't think about it. But if I look back, I can credit moves that Satt gave me, hearing upright jazz bassists, and coaching from Maurice and [EWF co-producer/arranger] Charles Stepney.

How would you say your style has evolved?

Early on, in the band, I just wanted to hear bass, bass, bass—the perils of youth! But as I began to admire and appreciate vocalists and songwriting, my playing became more focused and melodic. More important, I progressed as a musician and a listener. Once I realized the song was king, I didn't worry so much about the bass notes.

How do you come up with your bass parts?

As I said, I'm fortunate to have always been in a special situation: playing great songs, with plenty of time to prepare and record. Generally, I get the songs in advance, so I can listen while I'm shaving or driving around. Listening first—that's the key. When I get to the studio, I like to do five to ten different takes and keep them all, because even if a take isn't happening, it may have some magic in it. From there, I'll pick out sections from each take to form the final part, or I'll record some more parts incorporating what I liked from those takes. To me, recording is all about space, and I think what made the classic EWF albums successful is we each found our place in those songs—where to shine and where to lay back. Beyond that, I always try to find the center of the track: that certain space among all the other instruments and vocals where I can grab on and hold it all together. If you play off center, or play too many notes, it all falls apart and you don't even hear the bass anymore.

> "Once I realized the song was king, I didn't worry so much about the bass notes."

Can you discuss your technique?

Playing with precision, so you can really hear the notes, is important to me. I pluck with my index and middle fingers alternating, digging in with a heavy touch. I also use a lot of index pops or hard plucks, but I rarely use any thumb slaps. I do grab octaves or chords by plucking with my thumb and index fingers, and I like to use harmonics. I mute notes with a combination of my right and left hands. Generally, I've found that live, you have more freedom to try out different techniques, but in the studio you have to find the best way to cut through sonically, which can mean, say, plucking a double-stop instead of strumming it.

What's your approach to the groove and playing with drummers?

My first commandment is to hold the groove; you have to hold it down. I normally play on top of the beat, so I'm always conscious—particularly in this era of hip-hop tempos and feels—of trying to lay back and sit down a bit. Drum-wise, the snare and the kick are most important for me. Obviously my earliest hookup was with Maurice, whose feel is right down the middle. Beginning in the mid '70s, my brother Fred came aboard for a dozen years, with a similar feel. The great Sonny Emory stayed ten years, then Gordon Campbell for a year, and since 2001 we've had John Paris, who reminds me a lot of Fred. John sings, and that's key; I think drummers who sing are better drummers for it, because they learn how to play behind a singer.

What are your reflections on the period when EWF did elaborate concerts with magic tricks and special effects?

It was exhausting but effective, because it really helped establish us as we hit our heyday, and it earned us a reputation as top-flight entertainers. The cool part was when I would have a costume change or was involved in an illusion, Louis Satterfield would switch over and cover for me on bass.

Dancing is still a big part of your stage role. Does it hinder or help you to play the groove?

To be honest, one has no bearing on the other. They're totally separate. The dancing comes from studying with the legendary African-American choreographer George Faison, when we first got to L.A. We took dancing, acting, and signing lessons; it was all part of Maurice's concept to be the best band we could be.

When it comes to longevity and success as a career bassist in one band, you've cornered the market. Any other itches to scratch?

Not really; the range of styles we cover has always been musically fulfilling, and I never look ahead that much—the future is now. My focus is still on doing what I do with as much truth and integrity as I can. I go out and work hard every night, because I'm constantly aware there may be some young bass player in the audience who is hearing me for the first time, and I owe him or her my very best.

★ DEEP CUTS: VERDINE WHITE ON TEN CLASSIC EARTH, WIND & FIRE BASS LINES ★

"Shining Star" and "Getaway." "'Shining Star' was straight from the minds of Maurice, Philip Bailey, and Larry Dunn. I suggested a second bass part that sort of answered the vocals. I recorded two bass tracks on 'Getaway,' too, but what I remember is how difficult it was and how long it took to record. The result, though, was one of the most challenging, 'different' songs ever on pop radio."

"Can't Hide Love" and "That's the Way of the World." "Those were the genius of the late, great [producer/arranger] Charles Stepney. Had he lived, he would have been the next Quincy Jones. Charles gave me the opening chromatic lick in 'Can't

Hide,' from $B\flat$ to F, which I played in the 1st position on the A and D strings, with an open D in there. Then he told me to come up with the rest of the part myself, so I just followed the changes. When we performed the tune live years later, I was playing the opening wrong, so I had to go back and re-learn it from the record."

Verdine delivers serious groove and delicious fills throughout "That's The Way of the World." The song is in $D\flat$, a flat-heavy key more comfortable for horn players and pianists than bassists, for whom every open string is out of the scale. Still, Verdine liberally bounces off open strings, in the style of Motown's James Jamerson and other upright-trained electric players, and though it works, he further departs from strict harmonic allegiance by playing quick $\flat7$'s under *major 7* chords. "At the time I broke a lot of rules, because I was still learning about harmony," he says. "I probably wouldn't do that now."

"Got to Get You into My Life." "We got a call from George Martin to do the song for the *Sgt. Pepper*'s movie, so we went to Sam Goody's on the way to the airport and got the sheet music. Maurice came up with the concept of doing it as a Chicago-style shuffle on the plane. We recorded in a small, funky studio in Denver, in a day; Ralph Johnson played drums. The session was loose, and you can hear me freeing up and adding things as the track goes along. Will Lee always tells me it's his favorite track, and it's still one of the biggest tunes in our shows."

"September." "We actually cut the track at Hollywood Sound in September, the year before the song came out. We did it in one take, with my brother Fred on drums, David Foster on keyboards, and Al McKay on guitar."

"Fantasy." "We cut it first with just Maurice on drums, myself, and Larry Dunn on keyboards; it was such a complicated song we couldn't do it with a lot of people. It's one of my favorite bass lines. I don't know how I came up with it; doing the session was like floating in space. That album, *All 'N All*, was probably the hardest and most intense we've ever done; it was our first without Charles Stepney and, consequently, the one where we all grew up a great deal."

"In the Stone" and "After the Love Is Gone." "Those were two of the all-time greatest songs, from a great song period for us. When David Foster laid them on us it was magnificent, and they just played themselves—especially 'After the Love.'" All I had to do was play simply and not add a lot of bass chatter."

"Boogie Wonderland." "That was cut in the middle of the *I Am* album. We had from noon to 6 pm on a Saturday to record it, but we had been in the studio all night Friday working on another song, so by the time we returned and got ready to go on Saturday, it was 5 pm! Somehow we were able to come up with our parts and finish the track in an hour. In the middle of one of the verses you can hear me going up instead of down; I had gotten lost and was trying to find my place again!"

★ DEEPER CUTS: VERDINE WHITE ON EARTH, WIND & FIRE'S "SHINING STAR" BY CHRIS JISI ★

Among bassists, White's most famous performance is his two-bass foundation beneath the No. 1 hit "Shining Star," from EWF's 1975 breakout album, *That's the Way of the World*. "We recorded the album over two months at Caribou Studios in Colorado, so it was very relaxed. The band would record all day with plenty of breaks, and on off days, Charles Stepney would work with us individually to clean up and overdub parts." For "Shining Star," the rhythm section went in first with no charts, giving Verdine his usual freedom to create his own part. He plugged his roundwound-strung Fender Telecaster Bass into a miked Ampeg B-15. His overdubs were recorded direct.

As the song begins, Verdine doubles the walking guitar part in the song's opening two bars. When the verse groove kicks in, listen for two bass parts: Verdine's on-the-*one* root hits and the syncopated fills he overdubbed. "Maurice reminded me to leave space for the vocals, horns, and anything else we'd come up with later—so I just laid down those low *E*'s. When I went back in with Stepney I suggested we add another bass part. The inspiration for those fills came from hearing Stanley Clarke's solo albums—especially *School Days*, which had just come out." As cover-band bassists have known for years, White grins, "Playing the two parts live is no problem because of the way they're spaced."

For the chorus, Verdine played his signature ear-grabbing tenths on the original rhythm track, though he may have made some overdub fixes. He explains, "The groove was so happening I just tried to find something new and different to add, and I'd been experimenting with octaves and tenths using my right-hand thumb and index finger."

The second extended verse has more interesting overdubbed fills. Dig Verdine's preference for open strings, as well as his use of ghost notes—especially in the bass fills in every fourth bar of the verses. For the out-chorus White sets up a cool four-bar, tenth-laden phrase that resolves first downward then upward, alternating every other two-bar phrase. As the track ends, the rest of the band has been faded out, leaving only Verdine's on-the-*one* bass part against the syncopated vocal chant.

10.
FUNKY FUSION

★ STANLEY CLARKE: FUSION BASS VANGUARD BY KARL CORYAT ★

Stanley Clarke is among the most elite of bassists: his name is a household word. But unlike Sting and Paul McCartney, whose fame rose out of the popularity of their hit bands, Clarke got to where he is the hard way—with only his hands and his instrument. He made important contributions to the world of bass with Return to Forever and in guest appearances with such artists as Al Di Meola and John McLaughlin, being the first jazzer to lean heavily on the slap-and-pop techniques pioneered by Larry Graham and Louis Johnson. But Stanley's biggest claim to fame has been his solo career, which began when jazz-rock fusion was in full swing. He struck paydirt when his 1976 effort *School Days* became a crossover hit,

the title track snaring listeners with its unforgettable parallel-fifths bass hook. At that point, Stanley Clarke became almost synonymous with bass virtuosity.

In recent years, Clarke has divided his time between his solo work and a successful career writing film and TV soundtracks. He has left his musical mark on such major motion pictures as *Boyz N the Hood*, *Passenger 57*, *What's Love Got to Do with It*, *The Transporter*, and *Romeo Must Die*, as well as the Showtime series *Soul Food*. He's also continued to produce solo albums, and in 2008 he reunited with Return to Forever for a world tour.

Stanley Clarke was born in North Philadelphia on June 30, 1951, the son of Blanche and Marvin Clarke. His first exposure to music was through his mother, who sang opera. After a brief and "embarrassing" period on accordion, Stanley switched to violin—but as he grew and grew and grew (he's now 6'4"), he graduated to cello and then to string bass. Formally trained from the beginning, Clarke began to hone his bass chops on the Simandl method, and by the time he reached the 12th grade, he had become a *very* serious student. "I locked myself up," he remembers. "It was almost sickening how serious I was about it—eight hours a day, bleeding fingers, everything. At the time, I was in some *very* avant-garde groups that played music by strange composers, like John Cage. We didn't really play what I would call music; it was more like noise. My parents thought I was nuts!"

At 16, when the "conventional" after-school jobs he was holding down weren't quite working out, Clarke decided to try playing music for money. The first thing he did was buy an electric bass. "It was a Kent hollowbody that cost $29," he remembers. "I didn't even have a case; I used to put it in a bag." The bassist joined a blues combo, a country outfit, and then a Top-40 band, jumping headfirst into the Holiday Inn circuit. Along the way, he picked up ideas from guitarists Jimi Hendrix, Jeff Beck, and Eric Clapton as well as bassists Jack Bruce and Noel Redding.

Meanwhile, Stanley's classical education continued. "I was like Dr. Jekyll and Mr. Hyde," he says. "One minute I'd be listening to Hendrix, and then it was Bach, Beethoven, and Wagner. I also started getting into jazz, and I started to check out bassists like Charles Mingus, Scott LaFaro, and Paul Chambers. I was heavily into rock, classical, *and* jazz—all three." He attended the Philadelphia Academy of Music for three-and-a-half years, studying string bass and composition, but he soon got the itch to leave Philly for New York. Realizing a diploma wasn't going to do him any good anyway, he dropped out. "Leaving Philadelphia was a decision that was absolutely correct," he says.

Alone in the Big Apple with just his Gibson EB-2 and some clothes, Stanley began to root out work. He gigged with pianist Horace Silver, played on TV-commercial dates, and landed some sessions with Aretha Franklin, Carlos Santana, Stan Getz, and Art Blakey. The young bassist was well on his way.

The first major turning point in Clarke's career came in 1971, with the birth of Return to Forever. Stanley had worked with drummer Lenny White and was an acquaintance of Chick Corea, who had just left Miles Davis's group. Corea decided to put together an electric band, and he found instant chemistry with Clarke and White. RTF quickly became one of the flagships of a rapidly growing new genre, jazz-rock fusion. After their first couple of records struggled in the stores, the band regrouped and made a string of influential and critically acclaimed records, beginning with the highly successful *Hymn of the Seventh Galaxy* in 1972.

Clarke is often credited with introducing electric slap-bass to jazz. Surprisingly, his introduction to the technique came not from Larry Graham but from Lenny White, who had modified Graham's approach. "Lenny didn't really know what he was doing on the bass, but he had great rhythm, says Stanley. "Since I learned from him, my slapping was a little different." But while Graham and his contemporaries stuck mostly to the key of *E*, Clarke was the first to transpose the technique to other keys. "Chick wrote tunes in *A♭*, *C♯*, everything. I didn't get a chance to slap in *E* until I did my solo stuff, and that was like a release—*whew!*—because it was so much easier."

Another important turning point happened in 1973. "We were playing at a club in San Francisco, and this guy came up to me and said my playing was great but my sound was atrocious. It was Rick Turner, who was with Alembic. He had a bass with him, so I tried it out. It was like a new bass player was born that night—suddenly, I could play anything I heard in my head." That was the beginning of a long relationship with Alembic, one that continues today; Clarke's current collection of Alembics is so big he doesn't know how many he owns. Stanley Clarke and the Alembic bass will forever be linked.

In the mid-'70s, Clarke came into his own as a solo artist. Although he had released a 1972 solo album on which he played acoustic exclusively (*Children of Forever*), 1975's *Stanley Clarke* was the first record he considered truly *his*. With a strong backing band, including drummer Tony Williams and keyboardist Jan Hammer, *Stanley Clarke* established the bassist as a serious contender on the fusion scene. With the smash success of *School Days*, there was little doubt Clarke had arrived. He continued to put out solo albums throughout the '70s and '80s and participated in numerous ensembles, including forays into pop with the Clarke/Duke Project (with keyboardist George Duke) and Animal Logic, a rock group with drummer Stewart Copeland and vocalist/keyboardist Deborah Holland. On all of the records he's graced, Stanley's trademark staccato soloing and popping can be heard. It's a sound that has shaken the bass world and inspired players of many different styles, from Michael Manring to Les Claypool to practically anyone else who's laid thumb to string.

When asked about his goals, Clarke emphasizes that impressing listeners is his *last* priority. "I think the older I get, the more I learn to put everything into proper perspective. When I recorded my first couple of records, I would worry about what people thought. It's not that I don't care anymore, but after getting many good reviews and many bad reviews, I guess I've become jaded. I appreciate that people have opinions, but I've learned you simply can't control human thought. There are people out there who like what I do, and there are people who hate it—but after all I've been through, I'd be a dead man if I thought too much about it."

⋆ PAUL JACKSON: HEADHUNTER BY MIKAEL JANSSON AND CHRIS JISI ⋆

Of all the ingredients that made up the gourmet stew known as '70s funk, the spiciest was Herbie Hancock's Headhunters. The exploratory grit-'n'-grease quintet, featuring keyboardist Hancock, saxophonist Bennie Maupin, percussionist Bill Summers, drummer Mike Clark (Harvey Mason played on the band's self-titled 1973 debut), and Oakland ostinato monster Paul Jackson, was essentially together for just three Columbia albums: *Head Hunters*, *Thrust*, and *Flood*, a live recording. The band's uniquely perfect blend of funk and jazz established a cornerstone sound for the genres. A key was Jackson, whose edgy, vibrato-laced Fender Telecaster Bass served as a seminal influence for scores of younger players—from Marcus Miller and "Ready" Freddie Washington to Meshell Ndegeocello and Raphael Saadiq. While "Chameleon" and Hancock's updated version of "Cantaloupe Island" were accessible Headhunters hits, it was the more ambitious "Actual Proof" (from 1974's *Thrust*) that became an all-time bass groove classic, hoisting Jackson into a Mount Rushmore-like position with his fellow Bay Area bass brothers Larry Graham and Rocco Prestia.

Paul Jackson's interest in the bass came from his musical family. His father was an amateur piano player, and at age eight the young bassist-to-be was struck by Paul Chambers's playing with the Miles Davis Quintet. As he started learning to master the big bass, he came to even further revelations.

You started on acoustic as a kid. When did you make the transition to electric?

I worked in a music store, and I brought home a Harmony bass that had sat there for a long time; I picked it up and played it one day, and that was pretty much it. I played it like I play the upright: *hard*. My whole electric approach is based on the way I play the upright; I used to play in an 18-piece big band through a little amplifier, so I had to play real hard to be heard.

My playing tends to rely more on my hands than on any kind of trick. I never tried to play thumbstyle or anything like that. It's not that I don't like it; I just enjoy the way I play—fingerpickin'—and I can get a lot of sounds that way.

How did you hook up with Herbie Hancock?

I got a call to play a session with the Pointer Sisters, and at that time Herbie and the Pointer Sisters had the same manager; he asked me to audition for Herbie. I was called back after about three weeks—a lot of bass players wanted the job—and I just played the way I play.

I like to listen to other musicians; the bass player has to guide the group some-times, find subtle ways of leading it. He isn't responsible for keeping time, but he more or less guides the flow. I like doing that—that's what the bass does for me.

Who are your favorite bassists?

Oh, I have to go all the way back to Oscar Pettiford, Sam Jones, Ray Brown. Of course Paul Chambers, who made me pick up the bass in the first place—his tone was *so* sweet! Chuck, Stanley, Jaco—I'm probably one of the few people who's been in a two-bassist thing with Jaco; we used to hang out. Then there's Rocco and Larry Graham. I particularly like bass players I can listen to on record and say, "Oh, that's *him*!" That's what I really like about other players—when they're con-fident in their own personality. There are lots of younger musicians with different experiences who have developed a sound of their own, too. I really like Victor Wooten; because of his approach, you can always tell when he's playing on any-thing. Also, Meshell NdegeOcello does some very impressive things.

These days, music has been compartmentalized to the point where people believe they have to sound a certain way to sell a record or get a job. That's never been a factor for me. I feel very good sounding like Paul Jackson. I like the way I sound! I try to get out of the bass what I feel; I try to get out a part of myself. Gettin' out the right note in the right place!

★ JACKSON/CLARK: PORTRAIT OF A RHYTHM SECTION ★

Like Prestia and Garibaldi, Dunn and Jackson, and Porter and Modeliste, Paul Jackson and Mike Clark comprise one of the all-time classic rhythm teams: one that knows how to put a groove in the pocket and keep it there. The dynamic duo met at a 1968 organ-trio jazz gig Clark was playing. "Paul came in, sat in the audience, and smoked cigarettes and looked cool, so I figured he was a musician," Mike laughs. "When I walked off the stage I was going to approach him, but he walked out—he just dissed me! So I followed him all the way to the parking lot and asked him, 'Are you a musician?' He said yeah, and I said, 'Will you come back in and play with me?' and he said, 'Yeah!' He told me he played bass but also B-3 [Hammond organ], and we struck up such a hell of a groove we were dying of laughter. We've been playing together ever since."

After getting ditched by their respective girlfriends on the same day, Paul and Mike moved into an apartment together, which became a jamming place for the two and their friends. There was a B-3 in the house, along with a bunch of amps and Mike's three drum kits. "That's where we engineered a lot of the grooves we later played with Herbie," Clark recalls. "When Paul first brought home a bass, it sat on the floor for about two weeks. Then one day he took it out of the box, plugged it in, and just started playing exactly the way he plays now. I began playing right along. It wasn't like we discussed it first; we just looked at each other and started blowing—and we're still there! We had gigs every night and played all day, too. It was a fantastic time!"

Their alliance has had a huge impact on Jackson over the years. "Mike affected the way I listen to how drummers play," Paul points out. "It's probably close to the way a drummer listens to himself."

★ DEEP CUTS: PAUL JACKSON ★

"Watermelon Man." The 1973 re-arrangement of Herbie Hancock's 1962 composition on *Head Hunters* saw the band chop the original tempo almost in half and funkify it with a 16th-note groove. For his part, Jackson employed 10ths to build one of the most recognizable sub-hooks in jazz. The blues form's triple turnaround, which turns it from a 12-bar blues into a 16-bar blues, sees Jackson sticking with the double-stop motif before delivering some devastatingly funky fills.

"Actual Proof." Nathan East, who stayed close to Jackson's original 1974 part during a 2006–2007 tour with Hancock, says, "Paul's part is incredible and indelible. The groove is a combination of funk and samba, and the most important parts are the two opening and two closing measures. Probably the biggest challenge bass-wise is counting and landing on your feet!"

★ MICHAEL HENDERSON: FROM STEVIE TO MILES AND BEYOND
BY CHRIS JISI WITH NEIL STUBENHAUS ★

It would seem difficult to attach the word "unsung" to a career that includes locking down Miles Davis's landmark leap into electric jazz and going on to sell over a million albums as a bass-playing, soul-singing solo artist. Yet somehow, Michael Henderson is rarely mentioned among such heavies as Larry Graham, Bootsy Collins, Verdine White, and Paul Jackson. No doubt, some of the blame can be placed on the numerous jazzheads who abandoned Miles when he concocted his forward-thinking brand of voodoo funk in the late '60s and early '70s. And it appears plenty of Miles-liberated electric bassists were too blinded by Stanley's and Jaco's emergence to notice Henderson's unabashed bass work—which ranged from Jamerson-like finger funk to fretless ballads to slapped instrumentals—beneath his smooth vocals on eight solo albums. One bassist who did notice is first-call L.A. sessioneer Neil Stubenhaus, who jumped at the chance to help us interview one of his heroes. "Michael elevated the meaning of groove to a level that was completely off the charts," says Neil. "He's an all-time master of instinct and a king of feel."

> **"I knew a lot of Detroit musicians who died broke from not writing any songs or having any publishing, so I made up my mind early on to do both."**
>
> —MICHAEL HENDERSON

An only child born in Yazoo City, Mississippi, on July 7, 1951, Michael Henderson sang along with pop, rock, and blues records as a tyke. He later messed around with his stepdad's acoustic guitar and tried a few piano lessons. When the family moved to Detroit in 1959, his interest picked up from the surrounding musical activity. "I went to see a Motortown Revue show when I was 11," he recalls. "Tony Newton was playing Fender bass, and the low end caught my ear. Plus, he was flashy; he had curly hair and a nice suit, and he was playing his butt off." Michael's mom soon bought him a Crestwood bass and a Silvertone amp. A quick learner, he began taping the Motown sounds of James Jamerson from the radio and playing along, as well as jamming in basements with a drummer pal. Henderson soon went from sneaking into clubs and hanging around the studios of Golden World and Ric-Tic Records to playing and recording with such local artists as the Fantastic Four, and—at age 13—becoming a member of the Twenty Grand Club house band.

His big break came a year later, when he replaced the Detroit Emeralds' bassist Ray Tillman, who couldn't get off work to do a gig. The underage Michael soon found himself on the road at theaters like the Apollo in Harlem and the Regal in Chicago, where he saw Stevie Wonder warming up behind the closed curtain. "I ran and got my bass, plugged in, and started playing with him. He asked his conductor to get my number, and a short time later he called, and I joined his band." Henderson filled the remainder of his schedule performing live with the rest of Motown's roster, while his growing reputation also led to the bass chair in Aretha Franklin's band. But it would be a raspy-voiced man with a horn who would historically alter Michael's career path in 1970—a role he was ready for, thanks to the tutelage of Jamerson and Wonder.

Neil: When did you first meet James Jamerson, and how did he impact your style?

Michael: When I was 14, at the Twenty Grand Club. I was working there with Rudy Robinson, and he walked in and wanted to sit in. He came up and played the heck out of my Jazz Bass, and then I had to go back and play while he listened and watched me with those penetrating green eyes! He influenced me several ways. First was attitude—every note had that aggressive, play-to-win, take-over-a-song intensity. Next, he was all about syncopation; he could keep a syncopation going until the cows came home, patting his foot in the weirdest off-time places. I also emulated how he kept his strings up high and pulled at them with just his index finger. When you do that, you can hurt somebody with a note!

What did you learn from your time with Stevie Wonder?

Michael: The main lesson was how to play with feeling and expression. Shortly after I joined his band, he got the very first Clavinet. He'd come up with an altered bass line in the middle of a song and say, "Play this with me." So his left-hand work—which, of course, was inspired by Jamerson—had a huge influence on me.

Neil: How did you hook up with Miles Davis in spring 1970?

Michael: [Miles's wife, soul singer] Betty Davis brought him to a Stevie show at the Copacabana in New York. When he walked into the dressing room, I noticed that everyone stopped and stared at him, but I had no idea who he was. He told Stevie, [*in raspy voice*] "I'm takin' your fuckin' bass player." Stevie said nothing; he just moved his head side to side, smiling. Then he came to our rehearsal next door to the Apollo, gave me his number, and said, "I want you to play for me. I'll pay you good and take good care of you." I'm not sure how he heard about me, but I called up [Motown bandleader] Hamilton Bohannon and told him this dude named Miles wanted me to join his band, and he said, "Man— you'd better run and get that gig!"

Neil: What was the first playing experience like?

Michael: It was a rehearsal at Miles's brownstone for a session the next day that would become "Right Off," from *Jack Johnson*. Billy Cobham, Herbie Hancock, John McLaughlin, Keith Jarrett, and Airto [Moreira] were there, and I think Jack DeJohnette was, too. We didn't do much playing; we just talked and felt each other out, and Miles showed us a few things on keyboard. The next day we didn't even play what we'd worked on. John started a shuffle groove while we were waiting around in the studio, we all joined in, and that ended up being the session.

Did Miles specify your role?

Michael: Oh, yeah—at the brownstone. He told me he wanted me to hold the band down, to hold it all together. He said, "I know I got these motherfuckers playin' that jazz shit, but I want you to play what you play. Don't change it, no matter how hard they try to make you move." He'd show me lines along the way, but he always said, "Do what you do." Basically, he wanted me to stank it up—make it funky and keep it there. So that became my mission.

Neil: When you joined the live band soon afterward, what was your reaction to playing with a jazz drummer like DeJohnette, or to what Jarrett was throwing at you?

Michael: It was a little intimidating, but it was the most fantastic stuff I'd ever heard. For some reason, when Jack messed with the beat, I instinctively knew what he was doing and where the time was. I can't tell you how; it just felt natural. It was probably because of all the syncopation I learned from Jamerson—who was, after all, a jazz musician.

Neil: Describe the transition to the second phase of Miles's electric band, with people like Pete Cosey, Al Foster, [percussionist] Mtume, and [rhythm guitarist] Reggie Lucas.

Michael: Pete was a brilliant voice on guitar, but the key for me was having Al on drums; we hit a special note together. He and Mtume and Reggie really held down those African-rooted grooves, which freed me up to try different things. I started extending my lines, or I'd tune down my *E* string in the middle of the song; we were all reaching and exploring and following each other. That period, culminating with *Dark Magus*, was the pinnacle of my Miles stay.

How did your time with Miles end?

Michael: By 1975 he was quite ill. He was missing some shows, and others were canceling. After the last concert at Central Park that September, I wasn't told anything. Then I heard he was forming a new band with his nephew Vince Wilburn and Pete Cosey, which never happened. I never spoke with him again, although I tried unsuccessfully to visit him in the hospital before he died. He knew I was doing okay, though, because his manager became my manager. In all the time I played with him, we never had an angry word. We had a great, father-and-son-like relationship I'll forever cherish.

Neil: How did you make the transition to being an R&B-singing solo artist?

Michael: It was pretty much by accident. In the first place, I knew a lot of Detroit musicians who died broke from not writing any songs or having any publishing, so I made up my mind early on to do both. I had already put together a track for Bill Cosby, and I had co-written an album's worth of material with Marvin Gaye and other members of Hamilton Bohannon's band around 1972—some of which was only recently released. With Miles's gigs cutting back in '75, we all started to work with other people. Norman Connors was a fan of the band, and after asking to hear some of my songs, he wanted "Valentine Love." I brought it to him and sang on the demo; he ended up keeping my track, added [singer] Jean Carne, and it became a big hit. For his next album I wrote and sang "You Are My Starship" and "We Both Need Each Other," which also became hits. So his label, Buddah, signed me, and I started recording my own albums. Around the same time I wrote "Be My Girl" and several other songs for the Dramatics.

Had you been singing all along?

Michael: I sang as a kid, but not much at all after I joined Stevie. Vocally I absorbed a lot from him, Aretha, Marvin Gaye, and the Dramatics' Ron Banks. I also loved Jackie Wilson, Frankie Lymon, Nat "King" Cole, and Frank Sinatra.

Although your vocals were the focus of your albums, your bass playing is equally impressive.

Michael: Much of the credit goes to Miles. He made me confident about who I was and helped me discover the hidden stuff inside, which became the singing and playing on those albums. The fretless tracks were inspired by Jamerson's early Motown work on upright and my own flirtation with cello in junior high. "Happy" [1978's *In the Night-Time*] was a nod to the amazing playing of Larry Graham and Bootsy Collins. And I used synth bass on my biggest hit, "Wide Receiver," inspired by Bernie Worrell with P-Funk—they were recording next door at the time.

Neil: How did your solo career get off course?

Michael: I'd had Top-Ten hits plus increased sales with each of my first three albums. Then, for 1980's *Wide Receiver*, I decided to change to a more funky, fun approach. Even though the album and title song were hits, Arista, which had taken over as my label, didn't like my new direction. They wanted me to stay in the romantic loverboy vein. I managed two more albums with them, but I was getting fed up with fighting over creative decisions and advance money. I did one more album, with a new label—but I wasn't being true to myself. I was just going along making money. When the label's president was arrested for racketeering in the mid-'80s payola scandal, my album was pulled, and I knew it was time for me to step away.

What did you do between dropping off the scene in 1986 and now?

Michael: I stayed in L.A. at first, doing a few behind-the-scenes projects. In 1994, I moved my family to Phoenix to distance myself from the industry and focus on raising my kids. Then a miracle happened. The rappers started calling: they all wanted to license the bass line from "Starship" or "Let Me Love You." Other artists were covering my songs as well. With that good fortune, we moved to Las Vegas in 1998.

Neil: What led you to decide to get back into performing?

Michael: After moving to Vegas, I went to visit friends in Detroit. I ended up in the basement of the Hitsville museum, where they have a movable wall featuring the names of all of the Motown musicians. I looked under "bass" and saw a list of names headed by three in big print at the top: James Jamerson, Bob Babbitt, and Michael Henderson. Seeing that made something in me click. I realized how fortunate I was to have learned my craft from a lot of very talented people who are not here anymore. I decided I owed it to them, and I owed it to myself, to carry on the tradition as a bassist, vocalist, and writer, and to try to reach my full potential.

★ DEEP CUTS: MICHAEL HENDERSON ★

Whether Michael Henderson is playing the filthy funk figure that runs in various effected forms throughout Miles Davis's *On the Corner*, or the flowing fretless lines on romantic solo ballads like "I'll Be Understanding" or "Am I Special," one ingredient stands out: his in-your-face conviction.

Miles Davis's "What I Say" from *Live-Evil* and "Rated X" from *In Concert*. The two-bar bass line on "What I Say" runs through the 21-minute track, while a one-bar ostinato holds together "Rated X." "A lot of people asked if I went insane playing those figures over and over," says Henderson. "But it wasn't about repeating a line—it was about creating a feeling or energy that set the piece's mood."

Norman Connors's "You Are My Starship." Henderson's bass line is ear-catching and in your face, in a way that makes this slow jam groove hard. Marcus Miller calls the bass breakdown at the end of the chorus, "The illest bass break ever!"

Marvin Gaye's "You're the Man." Available on the Deluxe Edition of *Let's Get It On*, this circa-'72 track features a funky opening groove by Henderson as well as some whole notes and slides, played by Jamerson and dubbed in by Gaye.

★ ALPHONSO JOHNSON: FUSION REVOLUTIONARY BY CHRIS JISI ★

In most musical circles, the '60s are remembered as an era of great freedom, experimentation, and diversity. However, with the exception of such trailblazers as James Jamerson, Paul McCartney, and Jack Bruce, it wasn't until the onset of the fusion movement in the '70s that the electric bass fully shed its support shackles and claimed a share of the spotlight. One of the key players in this "Bass Revolution" was Alphonso Johnson.

Johnson rose to prominence as a member of the mid-'70s edition of Weather Report and through his solo albums, which climbed the jazz charts alongside the efforts of fellow revolutionaries Jaco Pastorius (who succeeded him in Weather Report) and Stanley Clarke. Since then, Alphonso has kept a relatively low profile, deploying his smooth, melodic sound chiefly as a sideman, to the benefit of dozens of artists in a wide range of styles including jazz, funk, rock, R&B, Brazilian, and Latin.

Johnson was born in Philadelphia on February 2, 1951, and raised in the city's South End. As the tallest nine-year-old in his elementary school music class, he was directed to the acoustic bass. Subsequent exposure to classical music, jazz, and '60s rock and R&B, coupled with the acquisition of his first electric bass, soon led to numerous gigs. After stints with vocalists Ronnie Dyson and Billy Paul as well as work with a Philly fusion outfit called Catalyst, Alphonso hit the road as a member of Woody Herman's Young Thundering Herd. In 1973, Herd drummer Joe LaBarbera brought his rhythm-section-mate along when he joined the Chuck Mangione Quartet, and it wasn't long before Johnson laid down the famous $B\flat$ ostinato that anchored the gold-selling "Land of Make Believe."

When the Mangione Quartet opened for Weather Report, Johnson's nimble fretless caught the ear of saxophonist/co-leader Wayne Shorter. It wasn't long before Alphonso was invited to join the seminal fusion band, and he spent the next two years touring and recording three albums: *Mysterious Traveller*, *Tale Spinnin'*, and *Black Market*. Although his contributions were somewhat overshadowed by Jaco's subsequent outburst, Johnson crafted memorable lines on such Weather Report anthems as "Mysterious Traveller," "Nubian Sundance" (both from *Mysterious Traveller*), and "Black Market" (*Black Market*), and also chipped in several fine compositions, including his 4-string classic, "Cucumber Slumber" (*Mysterious Traveller*).

While working with Weather Report, Alphonso relocated to Los Angeles; by late 1975, he was doing sessions with keyboardist George Duke (including the critically acclaimed George Duke/Billy Cobham Band), the Crusaders, guitarists Allan Holdsworth and Lee Ritenour, and many others. Then, adding the Chapman Stick to his bass arsenal, Johnson recorded three solo albums in three years: *Moonshadows* (1976), *Yesterday's Dreams* (1977), and *Spellbound* (1978).

After fusion ran out of steam in the early '80s, Johnson applied his virtuosity to the pop world, adding fretted and fretless punch to albums by Phil Collins, Bob Weir's Bobby & the Midnites, Jeffrey Osborne, Bob Dylan, and the

Whispers, to name a few. Coming off a seven-year, three-record stay with guitar legend Carlos Santana, he recorded a live album with Tony Williams and Herbie Hancock and then made his debut as a producer for Dutch R&B/pop artist Mildred Douglas. Alphonso has also been a member of a supergroup known as the Meeting, with Patrice Rushen on keyboards, Ernie Watts on saxophones, and Leon "Ndugu" Chancler behind the drums. He has remained active playing sessions and performing fusion covers of Grateful Dead tunes in Jazz Is Dead.

Philadelphia has blessed the bass world with Stanley Clarke, Nathan East, Jamaaladeen Tacuma, Victor Bailey, Gerald Veasley, and you—to name a few. Is there something in the drinking water there?

I don't know about that, but it might have something to do with the living conditions. A lot of us came from ghetto areas where being the very best you could be at music, or whatever you did, meant the difference between getting out of that environment or getting buried under it. From the time I began to play string bass in elementary school, I was fortunate to have positive reinforcement from strong role models both inside and outside the home. When I was 15, a city social worker named Joe Faulk, who helped to keep young kids off the streets and who had taken a special interest in my musical abilities, bought me my first electric bass with $85 of his own money. And my classical upright studies led me to a wonderful teacher who became my mentor, George Allen. He not only pushed me to go beyond the instrument to learn theory and harmony but kept me out of trouble through junior high and high school.

Who were some of your other influences on bass?

The first bass line I learned note-for-note was from my parents' recording of "Summertime" by a singer named Billy Stewart. Through their collection, I was exposed to bassists like Jimmy Blanton, Paul Chambers, Ray Brown, and Ron Carter. Then I began to notice what my brothers and sisters were listening to, and people like James Jamerson, [Philly session ace] Ron Baker, and Paul McCartney became huge influences. Another important thing was hearing Noel Redding with Jimi Hendrix. What impressed me was that he was a guitarist who had converted to bass, which meant he was stepping out of the traditional role and bringing along a lot of chops and chord knowledge. That inspired me to be more than "just a bassist" playing ordinary bass lines.

When did you put the acoustic aside and begin playing the electric bass exclusively?

I've never stopped playing the upright. To this day, I'll use it on certain things with my band. But because I picked up the electric later, during my developmental years, and was self-taught on it, it's the instrument on which I did all my experimenting and growing. Also, most of my early gigs were on electric.

When did you begin playing fretless?

In 1971. I asked the manager of a club band I was in for an advance so I could buy my first really good bass, and when I was shopping I came across a fretless Fender Precision that blew me away. It was a new concept: an electric neck without frets or fret lines. I figured since I already played upright I would have some affinity for it, but the main reason I bought it was because no one else I knew of was playing one—sort of the novelty of it. Because the club-band gigs involved a lot of reading, I had to woodshed around the clock to get my intonation together without looking at the neck.

From a bass point of view, the demise of fusion in the early '80s was something of a relief. Too many bass players had gotten so far away from the traditional role that the keyboardists had to fill out the bottom end. Then a lot of fusion bassists, including yourself, began to pare down their styles and step into rock, pop, and R&B situations. How were you able to make that transition?

Like any trend, fusion ran its course. There were some great fusion groups, though, and I think the music we made in the '70s will stand with the music of any other era. Unfortunately, it seems that when you label a style of music, you're giving it the kiss of death. If you listen closely, *most* music is a fusion of styles—bands like the Police and Genesis have so-called "fusion" elements. The music didn't die, it just went on to other levels.

It is true that after disco came in and took the focus away from the musicians, my playing become economized. I didn't make a conscious effort to do so; my style just evolved. Listen to how many notes Wayne Shorter was playing back in the '60s with Miles, and then listen to how few he plays nowadays. As you mature, you learn to say more with less. I don't think I'm playing any less in terms of *quality*, I've simply learned to say as much or more with fewer notes.

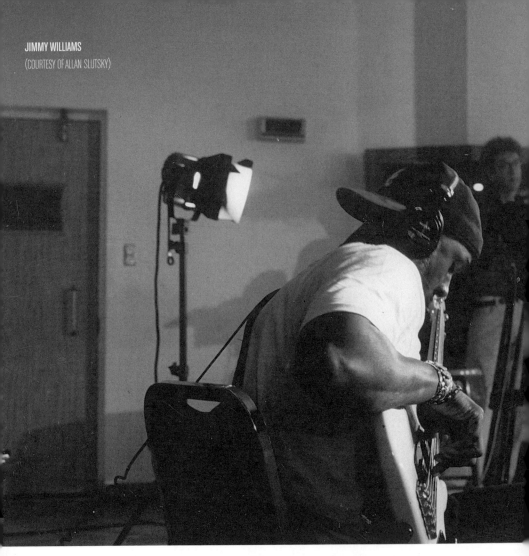

11.
THE BASSISTS OF PHILLY SOUL

★ BROTHERLY GROOVES: THE BASS PLAYERS OF THE PHILADELPHIA SOUND BY ALLAN "DR. LICKS" SLUTSKY ★

Even though Philadelphia was also the home of John Coltrane, McCoy Tyner, and Philly Joe Jones, Philadelphia's most celebrated musical export was not jazz—it was R&B, especially as embodied in the highly influential "Philly Sound" of the mid '60s through the early '80s. That sound reached its zenith in the form of Kenny Gamble and Leon Huff's Philadelphia International Records (often referred to as PIR) and the various independent productions and labels affiliated with their songwriting and producing careers. PIR artists like the O'Jays, the Intruders, the Delfonics, Billy Paul, the Stylistics, the Spinners, and Harold

Melvin & the Blue Notes monopolized the radio waves and record charts in a manner that hadn't been seen since Motown's golden era. And like James Jamerson's seminal work on countless Motown hits, the Philly bass greats ended up having a monumental impact on generations of bassists, spanning numerous genres and styles.

THE WIN WILFORD YEARS: 1964-68

Before Kenny Gamble and Leon Huff became record moguls, they worked at Philadelphia's Cameo-Parkway Records, a label that pumped out songs of youthful angst by Bobby Rydell and other teen idols. Gamble was a freelance songwriter, and Huff was a work-for-hire session pianist. Songwriter/arranger/producer Thom Bell also was on staff, and Joe Tarsia—the founder of famed Sigma Sound Studios and the Philly Sound's sonic architect—was originally Cameo's head engineer. (Gamble & Huff would eventually buy out Cameo's recording facility and office complex.)

Some historians say the Philly Sound began in 1964, the year Barbara Mason's bittersweet soul classic "Yes I'm Ready" was recorded and became the prototype for the lush string arrangements that would define the genre. At Frank Virtue's recording studio on North Broad, a rhythm section consisting of bassist Ronnie Baker, guitarist Norman Harris, and drummer Earl Young (who collectively came to be known as Baker, Harris & Young), along with guitarist Bobby Eli, were handling most of the recording work, including all of Barbara Mason's records.

Also in '64, a second significant rhythm section evolved out of Cameo's belated recognition of the growing market for black music. The label's halfhearted attempt at producing R&B hits necessitated an all-black rhythm section, enabling bassist Win Wilford, drummer Karl Chambers, and guitarist Roland Chambers to get their foot in the door for a handful of recording sessions. They had been playing around town as the backup band for Kenny Gamble's doo-wop group, the

Romeos—so when Gamble wrote a faux-Motown dance track for Candy & the Kisses called "The 81," he brought in his rhythm section to record it.

For the next three years Win Wilford, along with Karl and Roland Chambers, gigged around town, occasionally landing a recording session at Cameo or Frank Virtue's facility—but it wasn't until 1966 that they began to hit their stride. Gamble & Huff started a new label called Gamble Records and bet the house on the Intruders, a vocal quartet. Wilford and the Chambers Brothers played on all the early Intruders hits, including "United" (1966) and the bombastic, horn-driven "Together" ('67)—but they also cut records for other labels, like the Showstoppers' raucous 1967 hit "Ain't Nothing but a House Party."

"I loved Winny's playing," recalls Joe Tarsia. "He had a very distinctive, hollow tone. He played one of those basses with the scroll head [an Ampeg AEB-1], and he had a simple, fundamental style that fit the music Kenny and Leon were coming up with at the time. But he was gone by the end of '67. He was a good-looking guy, and he moved to New York to pursue a modeling career." After he left Philadelphia, Win wound up marrying world-renowned dancer Debbie Allen.

THE RONNIE BAKER ERA (1968–75)

With the eventual breakup of the Romeos and Wilford's departure, Karl and Roland Chambers continued to record for numerous Gamble & Huff productions—but Baker, Harris & Young, along with the ever-present Bobby Eli, became Philly's dominant rhythm section. "We'd been playing together in the streets for years," recalls Earl Young. "We played for everybody who came into town: B. B. King, Jackie Wilson, and all the stars who played at the Uptown Theater, where we were part of the house band. We were close. When you booked any one of us, you got all three."

Playing on 1968 hits like the Intruders' "Cowboys to Girls," Jerry Butler's "Hey Western Union Man," and the Delfonics' "La La Means I Love You," Ronnie Baker wasted no time in establishing the formula that would define bass playing within the Philly groove for the next eight years: a sunburst pre-CBS Fender Precision; heavy-gauge flatwound strings (deadened at the bridge with masking tape or paper towels); a lot of open strings;, and above all, proximity and eye contact with not just the drummer but the drummer's kick-drum pedal. "Baker would watch my feet," explains Earl Young. "He sat on my left side, and he'd copy whatever my foot was doing. We had the artists stand in front and sing, and we'd play with them like it was a live show. Then, once we got a feel for where the song was going, we'd kick them out. We never knew what we'd do that day. A lot of times, we'd just jam and they'd write a song to it. Like [Harold Melvin & the Blue Notes'] 'Bad Luck'—Ronnie came up with that bass line in the intro, which is almost a scale exercise. The same thing with 'The Love I Lost.' That was originally a ballad, but we changed it up. The engineers and producers would just try to capture it all on tape before it went away."

However, not every session was as free and creative for Baker as those two Melvin dates. When Thom Bell produced, he was interested only in what was on the paper; he wanted musicians to just read the ink and keep their creative ideas to themselves. For example, Bell wrote out almost every note Baker played on Stylistics tunes like "You Make Me Feel Brand New" or the Spinners' "I'll Be Around." But it worked—for two reasons: Baker was a good reader, and Thom's bass writing was first-rate. If it wasn't, he would have had had a problem. "Baker had a bit of an attitude," points out Bobby Eli. "If Ronnie didn't like a producer or an arranger, he wouldn't play well." Joe Tarsia concurs: "Baker was a little rough around the edges. I used to try to make the recording process as invisible as possible to make everyone comfortable. Nobody used headphones, because they wanted to feel each other. Bassists plugged into an Ampeg B-15 just so they could hear themselves, and we took a direct box off it. Sometimes Baker would give me a bad sound to mess with me. I would go crazy repatching everything, thinking the amp or the direct box was bad. And then he'd just smile and say, 'Oh, is *this* what you want?,' and the sound would be perfect. I'd just walk away muttering to myself."

Baker's sound could be summed up in three words: dead, deader, and deadest. Keeping his strings from having any ring to them was an obsession. "He wanted his notes to be short and staccato," recalls Tarsia. "He never changed the strings. His playing was also a little loose, particularly on ballads, where he lay way behind the beat—but that was part of his playing's charm. His real talent was in making his bass lines an important melodic element of the song—not just a support kind of thing."

In 1971 Gamble & Huff allied themselves with Columbia Records, part of the CBS conglomerate. Philadelphia International Records was now on the map, and the added financial muscle was instantly apparent. Recording sessions went on around the clock at both Sigma Sound and Cameo's old facility at 309 South Broad. Over the next five years, the label's studio band, now known as MFSB (Mother, Father, Sister, Brother), unleashed a torrent of hits on the airwaves—and Ronnie Baker was on almost every one of them.

Heavily influenced by both Motown's James Jamerson and Stax/Volt's Duck Dunn, Baker displayed an astonishing variety of feels, moods, and colors on Harold Melvin & the Blue Notes' "If You Don't Know Me By Now," the Stylistics' "Betcha By Golly, Wow," the Three Degrees' "When Will I See You Again," MFSB's "TSOP" (the *Soul Train* theme), and the O'Jays' "Back Stabbers," "Love Train," and "I Love Music." "Those cats up in Detroit and down in Memphis were like gods to us," explains Earl Young. "Whenever Ronnie, Norman, and I heard a hit record from those guys, we'd try to cop it and do something like it. We'd just party and jam. It was a fun thing."

As the '70s progressed, pop and R&B artists from all over the country flocked to Philadelphia in hopes of striking gold with the magical combination of Gamble, Huff, and their ass-kicking rhythm section. However, working with other labels' artists like Joe Simon, Wilson Pickett, Laura Nyro, and Dusty Springfield was no different to Baker, Harris & Young than any other PIR session. They had always augmented their Gamble & Huff dates with outside work. In 1967, they played on Cliff Noble's percolating dance instrumental "The Horse" as well as Eddie Holman's 1969 falsetto masterpiece "Hey There Lonely Girl." Bobby Eli recruited them on his 1974 and '75 productions of "Sideshow" for Blue Magic and Major Harris's "Love Won't Let Me Wait." But as the '70s continued, they were branching out into their own productions with the establishment of their publishing company, Golden Fleece. Away from PIR's staff of orchestrators, Ronnie Baker's little-recognized talents as a string and horn arranger were now a valuable asset. Many of the trio's efforts centered around Earl Young's band, the Trammps, which eventually scored mega-platinum status in 1977 with "Disco Inferno." But by the end of '75, Gamble & Huff were phasing out Baker, Harris & Young from their production schedule because of growing unavailability as well as the trio's ambitions to follow their own path.

THE SUGAR BEAR/JIMMY WILLIAMS YEARS (1975–82)

When Michael "Sugar Bear" Foreman graduated from West Philly's Overbrook High, the school's most famous alumnus was basketball great Wilt Chamberlain. While Sugar Bear never scored 100 points in a game like Wilt, he did accomplish something almost as impossible: He was the only bassist who ever got along with Ronnie Baker. That friendship landed him the PIR bass chair, as the mantle was passed on during two late '75 Sigma Sound recording sessions: the O'Jays' "Unity" and Harold Melvin & the Blue Notes' "Wake Up Everybody." As the Delfonics' bandleader for almost a decade, Sugar Bear had actually been on the scene's fringes for some years before he began recording for Gamble & Huff.

Foreman had a much stronger jazz background than Baker, which was evident whenever he had a session on which he had to play a walking bass line. His chops were a bit more precise than his predecessor, and he also broke the string of P-Bass-driven hits at PIR by playing a sunburst Fender Jazz Bass with round-wound strings. (Though he originally started out on an Ampeg scroll bass, like Winny Wilford, before switching over to a Jazz.)

While Sugar Bear's first two significant recording dates were with the O'Jays and Harold Melvin, most of his output involved drummer Charles Collins and guitarist Dennis Harris. This included the Jacksons' self-titled 1976 album, Lou Rawls's "You'll Never Find Another Love Like Mine" ('76) and "Lady Love" ('77), and Teddy Pendergrass's first two albums in '77 and '78. Sugar Bear also did some roadwork with Billy Paul, and Baker, Harris & Young used him on some of their productions. But by 1979, his studio workload had dwindled to almost nothing. Two years later in '81, he tragically died of a drug overdose.

Jimmy Williams was a late bloomer as a bassist. He was originally a vocalist in a South Jersey group called the Italics. After winning a recording contract at a local talent contest, his group received a visit at one of their rehearsals from Win Wilford and Thom Bell, who were both in the Romeos at the time and had an interest in producing the Italics. The Italics never went anywhere, but the meeting changed Jimmy's life. "Man, I was 17 and didn't even know what a bass was," laughs Williams. "Then here comes Winny walking in with that Ampeg scroll bass. I fell in love with it and said to myself, 'That's what I want to play right there.'"

Shortly afterward, Williams was working at the Campbell's Soup factory in his hometown of Camden, New Jersey, and he was picking up whatever he could on bass from records and some local teachers. More important, Leon Huff was seeing a girl right down the street from Jimmy's house, and Jimmy was all over him. "I'd be like, 'When you gonna give me a shot at doing some studio work?' And Leon would say, 'Just keep playing that bass.'

> "I learned to simplify and listen to the song and try to be an integral part of what was happening."
>
> —JIMMY WILLIAMS

So I started hanging out in the lobby of the Schubert Building on Broad Street, where they had an office, and they eventually allowed me to play on some writing sessions. Then one day, Huff told me to get with Ronnie Baker and learn a few things from him. I was naïve, so I called Baker. He just barked into the phone, 'I ain't got time,' and he hung up on me. He was a tough guy to get close to."

Jimmy was doing some roadwork with a PIR group called the Ebonys when his persistence paid off. In 1977, he was brought in to play on a Teddy Pendergrass tune called "The More I Get the More I Want," and the date became an important learning experience. "I came in there playing all this technical busy shit, trying to show them I could kick Ronnie Baker's ass, but they quickly let me know I'd better slow down and cut it in half or I wouldn't be working there no more. So I learned to simplify and listen to the song and try to be an integral part of what was happening." A year later, Jimmy played on Teddy Pendergrass's "Close the Door," his first PIR date that resulted in a major hit record. The economical, elegant bass part he laid down proved he'd learned his lesson well.

Williams also needed to get acclimated to his new rhythm section partners and the working styles of the various PIR producers. "The dates I played on had either Charles Collins, Quinton Joseph, or Keith Benson on drums and Dennis Harris on guitar, and most of the tunes were head charts. At best you'd get a sketch—not even a legitimate chord chart. Usually, they'd bring in a cassette with Kenny singing and Leon playing piano, and we'd start playing along. Then one of them might say, 'I want that right there,' so you'd go with it. Once I got the basic idea of what they wanted, I'd enhance it a bit more. That's the way Gamble & Huff's sessions went. Now with some of the other producers, they might have had more formal rhythm charts, but there was never heavy notation other than indicating rhythmic hits."

The peak years for Jimmy Williams were 1978 and '79, when he averaged ten dates a week between PIR and Golden Fleece, who also gave him work. But it was with the songwriting/production team of Gene McFadden and John Whitehead that Jimmy struck paydirt. "We were in Sigma's Studio B horsing around," says Jimmy. "There was a dance at the time called 'The Rock' where you swayed back and forth, and I came up with a bass line that had the same kind of movement. We were supposed to be working on another tune; McFadden & Whitehead weren't even in the studio at the time. When they came in and heard what we were doing, they freaked and screamed, 'Turn on the tape!' They added the lyrics and melody afterward. That song became "Ain't No Stoppin' Us Now."

Jimmy's playing at PIR looked both backwards and to the future. Being a devotee of James Jamerson, Willie Weeks, and Chuck Rainey, he reverted to the pre-CBS Fender Precision and flatwound-string approach that Ronnie Baker had brought to the Philly Sound a decade earlier. But his thirst for musical knowledge, as well as his studies with legendary Philadelphia jazz mentor Dennis Sandole, led him to bring new melodic and harmonic elements into his sessions. As with Ronnie Baker before him, Jimmy's reputation spread around town, causing other producers to seek him out to play on their projects. In addition to his PIR duties, Jimmy was working on album projects with artists like Edgar Winter, Grace Jones, Robert Palmer, the Manhattans, Gloria Gaynor, and Curtis Mayfield. His ability to lock onto a groove like a pitbull on a T-bone steak left him choking with work—but nothing lasts forever.

By the early '80s, activity at PIR began to slow down dramatically. Jimmy

Williams hit the road with the O'Jays, with whom he plays to this day. Baker, Harris & Young continued to work their own productions until 1987, when Norman Harris died of a heart attack. Three years later, Ronnie Baker passed away at age 50. He may have been tough on producers, engineers, and rival bassists, but he was deeply loved by his rhythm-section soulmate. "We were on a session and Ronnie kept saying the headphones were hurting his head," laments Earl Young. "He kept popping aspirins and had to lie down. He had lung cancer and it had gone to his brain. Later he told me, 'Look, Earl, I got the big C.' I didn't want to play no more after he died."

There were other bassists in the PIR story. Anthony Jackson played on Billy Paul's 1972 album *The 360 Degrees of Billy Paul*, which included the Grammy-winning single "Me and Mrs. Jones," and of course he created his own pick-and-phaser masterpiece on the O'Jays' "For the Love of Money." Bob Babbitt was recruited for some of Thom Bell's sessions, like the Spinners' "Rubber Band Man" and "Then Came You," and local Philly bassists Doug Grigsby and Steve Green also jumped onboard for some late-era sessions (notably Green's work on Patti LaBelle's 1983 hit "If Only You Knew").

Baker, Harris & Young finally got Philly's official recognition in 1995, when they were inducted into the Philadelphia Walk of Fame. Their plaque is embedded in Broad Street's sidewalk just a few blocks up from PIR's 309 recording complex and office facilities. Philly neo-soul stars like Jill Scott, Musiq, and the Roots have rediscovered and paid homage to the grooves that Win Wilford, Ronnie Baker, Sugar Bear Foreman, and Jimmy Williams helped to create—but the days when they swaggered down Broad Street in their platform shoes on their way to add another gem to the Philly Sound's storied catalog are long gone.

★ DEEP CUTS: TEN KEY MOMENTS IN PHILLY BASS RECORDINGS ★

Whether directly or indirectly, '60s and '70s Philadelphia bassists like Win Wilford, Ronnie Baker, Michael "Sugar Bear" Foreman, and Jimmy Williams had an indelible impact on almost all bass players who followed. Here's a look at ten of the Philly Sound's high-water marks in the low end.

The Intruders, "Together" (1967) is an excellent example of Win Wilford's straight up-and-down, root-5 style. This basic, foundational approach varies slightly in the form of a few passing tones and a few syncopated rhythmic hits played by the whole rhythm section. Note how he often avoids attacking in the same spots as guitarist Roland Chambers's backbeats, creating a bouncing rhythmic counterpoint.

The Intruders, "Cowboys to Girls" (1968). Ronnie Baker's more active, syncopated style had an instant impact on the Philly Sound. On "Cowboys to Girls," when the minor chord enters in the second half of the verses, Baker intensifies the tension with 16th-note pickups and tied notes across barlines. Gamble & Huff knew their productions were getting an infusion of rhythm and melody.

The O'Jays, "992 Arguments" (1972). Without a moment's hesitation, Joe Tarsia named this track when asked which PIR sessions stuck out in his mind. "They were so locked in, they must have played this tune for 20 minutes straight," says Tarsia. Being a Thom Bell arrangement, the bass line was probably written out. Dig the two-bar vamp that enters 2:47 into the LP version and continues unchanged for the next three-and-a-half minutes. Ronnie Baker's drive and conviction to the groove are what make this track so irresistible.

Blue Magic, "Sideshow" (1974). Ronnie Baker's playing could be very busy, but he also knew how to keep things simple when called for. On this Bobby Eli-composed and produced tune, Ronnie plays mainly chordal roots, with the exception of some 16th-note passing tones. That way he avoids doing anything that would jolt the listener out of the lush orchestration's hypnotic spell.

MFSB, "TSOP" (1974). Anthony Jackson cited this as "some of Ronnie Baker's finest work. It's a performance that shows a lot of the influences that Jamerson had on him." For example, listen for notes held across beats *two* and *three*, descending lines disguised by the insertion of quick upper notes, and "changing tones" (upper and lower neighbor tones leading back into the tonic of the next chord change). These types of devices impart a forward push or drive into the lines, which isn't resolved until the next chord change.

Harold Melvin & the Blue Notes, "Bad Luck" (1975). If ever a musical example made a case for practicing scale exercises, this is it. The simple *E* Mixolydian pattern at the beginning sets the table for everything to come in this recording—the groove, the arrangement, even the composition itself. "They didn't have no song when we started the session," recalls Earl Young. "Ronnie was messing around with that figure, and everything grew out of that." What follows the first four bars is Baker in his nastiest, take-no-prisoners mode. Can a root-5 figure get any funkier than what he lays down in the verses?

The Jacksons, "Enjoy Yourself" (1976). While Ronnie Baker had one foot in the past and one in the present, at the time "Enjoy Yourself" was recorded, Sugar Bear Foreman functioned more in the present and the future. One of the reasons is Sugar Bear's switch to roundwound strings after years of Philly bass flatwound dominance. His choice of fretted instead of open strings in this example is symptomatic of that transition, and it changes the resulting sound.

Teddy Pendergrass, "Close the Door" (1978). This is the first PIR session where

Jimmy Williams (in his own words) learned to "cut it in half." The 16th-note pick-ups into beat *three* are reminiscent of the Verdine White "Shining Star" type of rhythms that were riding the radio waves in the '70s. Jimmy was obviously reaching outside to bring fresh ideas into the Philly Sound.

Teddy Pendergrass, "Love T.K.O." (1980). Songwriter Dexter Wansel and producer Leon Huff added an octave box after the fact to Jimmy's performance on "Love T.K.O." "All kinds of other notes and overtones came out after they added that effect," explains Jimmy. The chorus's simple two-bar vamp is punctuated with 16th-note fills, some of which, according to Jimmy, were pretty tricky, as he played them high up on the neck and then had to leap back down to grab the next downbeat—and still make it sound smooth.

McFadden & Whitehead, "Ain't No Stoppin' Us Now" (1979). Like Anthony Jackson's signature bass line on "For the Love of Money," Jimmy Williams came up with a motif of such extraordinary originality that it became this song's single most important and identifiable melodic element: the two-bar vamp that occurs throughout the song. Part of the uniqueness of Jimmy's line is his half-step lead-in notes in the second bar of each repetition. Jimmy makes subtle variations on the motif throughout the recording but still stays fairly close to the original. When you have a mega-platinum bass line that ain't broke, don't try to fix it!

★ DEEPER CUTS: "BAD LUCK" BY HAROLD MELVIN & THE BLUE NOTES BY CHRIS JISI ★

Baker, Harris & Young played on a vast amount of hits for both PIR and non-label artists, with Young's drums the component everyone adhered to, especially Ron Baker. But Ronnie was equally revered for his creative, melodically potent, deep-pocketed lines. "When he was on, no one was better," offers Sigma Sound's Joe Tarsia. "The easiest way to sum up his playing was: He was a bass arranger."

This theory is best borne out in Baker's most propulsive and impressive bass part: Harold Melvin & the Blue Notes' spring '75 hit, "Bad Luck," from their gold-selling fourth album, *To Be True*. Young, with Baker at his side, had helped launch the disco era with his four-on-the-floor drumbeat on the Blue Notes' 1973 dance hit "The Love I Lost"; "Bad Luck" was their even more successful bookend. The single reached No. 15 on the Pop charts and No. 4 on R&B, but to this day it holds the record for the longest-running No. 1 Dance Club single, at 11 weeks.

"Bad Luck" was created out of good fortune during a typical daytime rhythm-section session at Sigma Sound. Co-writers McFadden & Whitehead had improvised a lyric to a Victor Carstarphen piano chord progression. As was usually the case, Gamble & Huff's MFSB team of session musicians was called and given chord charts. The artist would then sing the song in front of the group, while each musician came up with a part. Earl Young recalls Baker's intro figure being a spark plug for the whole track: "He played this scale-like riff, and that really got everyone going."

The song begins with that riff, doubled by guitar. For the first verse, Baker settles into a funky root-5-octave bounce, closely locked with Young's equally nasty foot and kit work. Says Earl, "Ron would always start with my kick-drum pattern, and then he'd add accents and upbeats, playing off and around it. We were so tight and similar in tone that it was difficult to hear the separation between bass and kick." Baker's verse pattern continues with subtle variations and Jamerson-like use of chromatic passing notes in the prechoruses. Notable is his fill on the last two beats before the first chorus, another Jamerson-like device that anticipates the coming tonic chord. At the chorus, Baker backs down a bit over the I and IV chords, picking up the intensity at the end of the chorus with what will become a signature descending line over the V chord, which also ties in nicely to his intro figure.

12

THE BASSISTS OF P-FUNK

★ THE BOMB: THE HISTORY OF P-FUNK BASS BY JIMMY LESLIE ★

Anyone who has played bass in a dance band is familiar with songs like Parliament's "Flashlight" and "Give Up the Funk (Tear the Roof off the Sucker)," Funkadelic's "One Nation Under a Groove" and "Cosmic Slop," and group leader George Clinton's solo smash "Atomic Dog"—classic funk tunes with widely divergent bass styles. Less commonly known are the bassists behind those styles, and how they influenced the sound and direction of the P-Funk collective over a history of nearly 40 years.

From the late 1950s doo-wop days in Clinton's Plainfield, New Jersey, barbershop, to the hip-hop leanings of the collective's more recent albums, the P-Funk story, and the story of its bassists, is complicated. For starters, the group's name has changed, often for legal reasons. They were the Parliaments, then Funkadelic, then Parliament *and* Funkadelic. By the mid '70s, Parliament/Funkadelic comprised a loose collection of musicians—including several bassists—whose abundant studio sessions ended up on albums by both bands, with Clinton often tending to put the more mainstream, horn-oriented tracks on Parliament records, while reserving the edgier, guitar-oriented tracks for Funkadelic. Then there were the offshoots: the Brides of Funkenstein, Parlet, Fred Wesley's Horny Horns, and bassist Bootsy Collins's Rubber Band.

On the surface, the group currently billed as George Clinton Presents the P-Funk Allstars is a traveling circus. As many as 30 musicians, dancers, and singers in such stagewear as bridal gowns, giant diapers, and prosthetic noses may grace the stage at any given time, with Clinton serving as ringleader during the marathon-length performances. Deeper still, the music, the show, and the band have a definite structure, with members old and new forming a distinct hierarchy based on tenure and talent.

Most bassists are aware of William "Bootsy" Collins, whose contributions to James Brown were as significant as those to P-Funk. Some may even be aware of Billy "Bass" Nelson, Cordell "Boogie" Mosson, Rodney "Skeet" Curtis, and Lige Curry. But few understand exactly how their arrivals and departures from Parliament/Funkadelic led to profound musical changes. It's an exercise in futility to try to mark every move, so what follows is a collection of recollections direct from the mouths of these principal players.

RICHARD BOYCE: PRE-FUNK

Tenure 1964–67
Style Gospel-infused R&B

Can be heard on Clinton's early demos
George Clinton says "Richard was a damn good player. I really liked him because he could play gospel music."

"I was George Clinton's first bass player, and my brother Frankie was his first guitar player. We backed up George's original doo-wop group, the Parliaments. Everyone would gather at George's barbershop to rehearse, party, and of course, get haircuts. When George moved the band to Detroit in 1967, we were asked to come with them, but we were busy recording our own material as the Admirations [not the Chicago-based band], so the Funk Brothers' Bob Babbitt played bass on the Parliaments' first hit, '(I Wanna) Testify.' Then my brother and I got drafted in 1968. They wouldn't send two brothers to fight at the same time, and Frankie volunteered to go because I had a wife and daughter. Frankie was killed in Vietnam, which made me quit playing music for a while, but I went on to tour with the Soul Seekers and the Manhattans. When I landed in Europe for the first time, I kissed the ground and told Frankie we'd made it."

BILLY "BASS" NELSON: FUNKADELIC FOUNDATION

Tenure 1967–71, 1994–2004
Style Raw and rockin' with a robust tone and a Motown influence
Can be heard on Funkadelic's *Free Your Mind . . . And Your Ass Will Follow*, *Funkadelic*, and *Maggot Brain*; Parliament's *Osmium*; "The Placebo," from *Funkentelechy Vs. the Placebo Syndrome*
George Clinton says "Billy set a high standard for everything that followed. His Funkadelic work is still among my all-time favorite stuff, because he had the Motown flavor with an aggressive rock attitude."

"I'd hung around George Clinton's barbershop since I was a little kid, and I started to work there when I was 15. Eddie Hazel inspired me to learn guitar, and when the Parliaments would go on the road, I would play rhythm guitar and work out the arrangements for the house-band rhythm section. We played mostly Motown hits. When we moved to Detroit, I met James Jamerson, who taught me how to play bass. 'Music for My Mother' is a good example of how he taught me to stay in the lower register. I used an Ampeg bass on that song. I was also really into the Beatles and the Jimi Hendrix Experience, so my style became a combination of those influences mixed with my natural tendency to aggressively attack every note and every show with 100 percent of my energy.

"George eventually assembled a backing band consisting of me on bass, Eddie Hazel on lead guitar, Lucius 'Tawl' Ross on rhythm guitar, Ramon 'Tiki' Fulwood on drums, and Bernie Worrell on keyboards. There was a definite rift between the vocalists and the backing band, and the *band* came up with that funky rock sound. One day, Eddie and I were tossing ideas back and forth when we came up with the name 'Funkadelic,' which perfectly fit the psychedelic funk music.

"I always played an assortment of basses. It surprises people to find out that I sometimes used a Hagstrom 8-string, which produces an almost synth-bass tone when played with a pick. You can hear it on 'I Got a Thing, You Got a Thing, Everybody's Got a Thing' and 'Free Your Mind . . . and Your Ass Will Follow.' We were touring primarily with Kustom amps until one very important gig opening for the Vanilla Fudge in 1968. We were forced to use their Marshall guitar amps and Ampeg SVT bass amps, and the sound was so *huge*. We already had the look and the material, but it was at that moment that the true Funkadelic sound was born.

"Due to credit, compensation, and various other issues, the entire band split in 1971. I'm very outspoken, so I was the most vocal about being unhappy. That's when George grabbed Bootsy Collins and his band to replace us, but the sound wasn't nearly the same, because those guys were from the James Brown funk school. They didn't take what we were doing seriously, especially the look, and they lasted on the road for only about seven months before George wisely began to split the thing into Parliament and Funkadelic.

"I moved on to play with Ruth Copeland. We spent almost two years opening for Sly & the Family Stone, so I picked up a lot from Larry Graham, as he did from me. I freaked him out because instead of slap-and-pop, my technique is more like 'hit-and-pinch,' where I use my thumb or index finger to hit the low note, and then use my thumb and index finger to pinch. The attack is more aggressive that way. I did session work for Motown, too, and you can hear me using that technique on the Temptations' hit 'Shakey Ground' from *A Song for You*.

"I sat in with P-Funk when they came to Pittsburgh in 1994. George really dug having me play on the old tunes and asked me to come on the road, which I did for ten years. I'm not a happy P-Funk camper right now because of monetary and credit issues, and because I'm disappointed it became a settle-for-less organization. Despite the shortcomings, I really enjoyed coming back and working with the band again. I have more confidence in my abilities as a professional bass player than ever before."

CORDELL "BOOGIE" MOSSON: THE OLD G

Tenure 1972–78 on bass, 1979–present on guitar

Style Simple, laid-back, funky, and versatile

Can be heard on Funkadelic's *America Eats Its Young*, *Cosmic Slop*, *Standing on the Verge of Getting It On*, *Let's Take It to the Stage*, and *Hardcore Jollies*, and Parliament's *Live: P-Funk Earth Tour*

George Clinton says "Boogie's bass style lies somewhere between Billy Nelson's raw Funkadelic groove and Bootsy Collins's Parliament funk, which made him the perfect guy to play all the material live, or on either bands' recordings."

"I've known George since I was a kid, because my cousins Richard and Frankie Boyce played with the original Parliaments. Richard inspired me to play bass, and I also learned to play my brother's drums. When Funkadelic came together, my old friend Billy Nelson was the bass player, and I would go on the road and play with them for fun before I was officially in the band or even old enough to be in the clubs. After George and Billy ran into some issues, guitarist Garry Shider and I—who were playing in a band called United Soul—got called to meet George in Detroit in 1972. Funkadelic was recording *America Eats Its Young*, and I played all the bass tracks except a few, with Bootsy Collins and Prakash John splitting the others. From that point on, I played some bass on just about every Parliament or Funkadelic record.

"The band didn't really make a distinction between Parliament and Funkadelic; we just played whatever fit the music when we were in the studio. Bootsy did play a lot of what wound up being the Parliament stuff, but not all of it. I remember playing bass on 'Mr. Wiggles,' 'Testify,' 'Handcuffs,' 'Funkin' for Fun,' and 'I've Been Watching You (Move Your Sexy Body).' Sometimes Eddie Hazel or Garry Shider played bass. Eddie taught me a lot on guitar, and sometimes I'd play that. I played almost all the bass on some Funkadelic albums, including *Standing on the Verge of Getting It On* and *Cosmic Slop*.

"Playing live was another matter. The name on the marquee was Parliament/Funkadelic, and I'd play bass on all of it. Bootsy did play live with Parliament/Funkadelic at one point, but if Bootsy was on the road, his Rubber Band would usually open the show. Then we'd go out and play, and he would come back out for the encores, which we'd all play together. I would stand back, play solid funk bass like I'd normally play, and let him go, because he's Bootsy, the star bass player with all the gadgets who has to be out front. When I was the only bassist, I wouldn't try to play exactly like Bootsy, because by the time I wasted that energy, I'd lose the band. Instead I put my thing on what he did. I know how to slap and pop, but I really don't like it. I can beat you up with my fingers, and I do play with a pick sometimes if I want to get a more flamboyant sound, play faster, or pick while muting with the edge of my right hand. Honestly, I'm not a very forward person, but I've got your back. I play bass the way Eddie Hazel played guitar: fluent, funky, and slick. My style is much more relaxed and laid back in the pocket—but I'll be back there hurtin' you.

"The best thing George taught me was to relax and pay attention to where I put the note. He might want it on the *one*, behind the *one*, or in front of the *one* to put a little edge on it. Just because you're a bit ahead of time doesn't make it out of time, but mostly I put it in the middle. The most important thing is to lay back and pay attention. If you hear a player make a move, you can follow him and still be on time if you're laid back.

"By the late '70s, I needed a break and took a hiatus from the band. When I returned I switched over to rhythm guitar and vocals, which is still my role. I'm an older dog in the game now, and I will do it until the end. Dig a deep hole and throw me down in there with my amp and my bass—leave the cord plugged in, because I've got to have a connection—and you'll hear from me. I ain't bullshitting. You'll hear from me."

WILLIAM "BOOTSY" COLLINS: SPACE BASS STAR

Tenure 1972, 1974–82, ongoing guest appearances
Style Flamboyant and aggressive, often with envelope-filter effects
Can be heard on Parliament's *Up for the Down Stroke, Chocolate City, Mothership Connection, Funkentelechy Vs. the Placebo Syndrome, Motor Booty Affair, Gloryhallastoopid,* and *Trombipulation;* Funkadelic's *Lets Take It to the Stage, Hardcore Jollies, Tales of Kidd Funkadelic, Once Nation Under a Groove, Uncle Jam Wants You;* Bootsy's Rubber Band's *Stretchin' Out in Bootsy's Rubber Band, Ahh . . . the Name's Bootsy, Baby! Bootsy? Player of the Year,* and *This Boot Is Made for Fonk-N.*
George Clinton says "Bootsy was particularly good playing at slower tempos. I built Parliament's dance sound off Bootsy's bass lines—or sometimes Bernie Worrell's synth bass, like on 'Flashlight' and 'Aqua Boogie'—and then added the horns. Sometimes I'd use a Bootsy track for Funkadelic, like 'Be My Beach,' but I mainly used his recordings for Parliament because they were less rock and more funk."

"I first met George Clinton in Detroit after my crew had split from James Brown and the original Funkadelic group was done with George. My band, the House Guests, was playing at the Love Club, where I met a girl who told me I had to connect with George because we dressed and sounded similar. She took me to George's house where he was sitting in the Buddha pose wearing a sheet and looking crazy and all spaced out on acid. I was like, 'Wow! This is the cat I want to be with,' because that was the kind of freedom I wanted.

"He was attracted to my persona, and I think he knew he could do something great with me as a separate act, but neither of us really had it figured out. We made an arrangement that the House Guests would be assimilated into his new Funkadelic road show, but we were supposed to retain our own name—like Funkadelic & the House Guests—and George was supposed to get us our own record deal. We didn't really want to be Funkadelic, which was more about funk rock, whereas we brought a James Brown-style funk groove, where everything was on the *one*. We started working on *America Eats Its Young*—that's us on 'Philmore'—but we wound up quitting. George brought in Cordell Mosson and Garry Shider, who were much more in the vein of Billy Nelson and Eddie Hazel and sounded more like Funkadelic.

"I went home to Cincinnati for a while, but I kept thinking about how well George and I clicked as writers, so I went back to Detroit by myself to see if we could create something new. Cordell and Billy Bass hipped me to a new slap-and-pop technique that Larry Graham was using, but none of us really knew it was going to be the next big thing in bass. I started working it into my approach, using my thumb for the thump, pulling with my 1st finger for the snap, and slapping with my whole hand the way you might slap a baby's bottom—or a chick's bottom [*laughs*]. I think the fact that I didn't really know the proper technique made me come up with a unique version, but I was still searching for a way to make the *sound* different. Once I discovered the Mu-Tron it was happening, because the envelope effect made it so I could almost *talk* through my instrument, instead of sounding like a regular bass being popped and pulled. We wrote 'Up for the Down Stroke' and 'Chocolate City,' and I think that's when the idea clicked in George's head to start a new version of Parliament based on that style, while placing the other stuff with Funkadelic.

> "From the beginning, George and I had an understanding that I would help him do his thing, and that he would help me do my thing."
>
> —BOOTSY COLLINS

"I'd moved from playing a Fender Jazz with James Brown, to a Fender Precision Bass through a Kustom with the House Guests, Funkadelic, and early Parliament. Then I had the first Space Bass built and got an Alembic preamp. That happened sometime during the recording of *Chocolate City*, and by the *Mothership Connection* record, it was on!

"From the beginning, George and I had an understanding that I would help him do his thing, and that he would help me do my thing. We started doing Bootsy's Rubber Band once the Parliament thing was really kickin', but I've kept in touch and been involved in whatever George and the guys were doing ever since. I sat in with them just a couple of weeks ago when they came through town. I played 'Cosmic Slop,' which is actually based on a riff we would open our House Guest shows with; George lifted it from us. It's funny how things come back around."

RODNEY "SKEET" CURTIS: THE JAZZY FUNKATEER

Tenure 1977–79, 1981, 1983–85, 1989, 1994–98
Style Slick and jazzy, with frequent slapping and popping
Can be heard on Funkadelic's "Grooveallegiance" and "Who Says a Funk Band Can't Play Rock?" from *One Nation Under a Groove*; "Oh, I" from *The Electric Spanking of War Babies*
George Clinton says "I'd direct Skeet a little more onstage than in the studio, because if it got too artsy-fartsy we couldn't dance to it. But I'd let him record more in his own style, because it was good as hell and we built a lot of stuff around it. Skeet did some great work on the Bernie Worrell album, *All the Woo in the World*, which is so smooth.

"I hooked up with P-Funk through my old friend Gary 'Mudbone' Cooper. He got the job singing with Bootsy's Rubber Band, and he called me in 1977 to say that George needed a bassist for some Brides of Funkenstein and Parlet sessions in Detroit. George liked the way I played and asked me to come on the road with Parliament/Funkadelic. Cordell Mosson and I shared the bass chair at that time. I primarily played the newer Parliament songs Bootsy had recorded, and Boogie played the rest.

"Boogie took a break around the time of the *One Nation Under a Groove* tour in late '78, and by the time he came back a couple of years later, the Baltimore crew was in there, which included the horn section, Dennis Chambers on drums, and me. Boogie switched over to rhythm guitar.

"I've always tried to make everybody else's stuff conform to my playing, so I never tried to play the P-Funk songs like they were played before. I twisted the rhythm arrangements in a jazzy way, and George found it refreshing. He just let me go for it without giving much direction, and when I went 'out' now and then I heard him tell other guys, 'Don't go out with Skeet. I *know* he can get back, but I don't know if you can.'

"My influences were Jamerson, Stanley Clarke, Jaco Pastorius, and Larry Graham, so I'm pretty funky for a jazz player and jazzy for a funk player. I thump and pop a lot when I play P-Funk stuff, and I do more fingerstyle playing on my current gig with Maceo Parker. I do a lot of left-hand muting to get a very staccato sound. Lige Curry calls it 'the Claw' because it looks like my whole hand is sliding up and down the neck without any finger movement. I double-stroke my right thumb up and down like a pick while I mute with the back of my palm for a percussive effect. It works almost like a hi-hat, where I've got a possible 16th note going almost all the time.

"I was in and out of the band over the years; my most recent stint ended in 1998. P-Funk has been leaning toward hip-hop for a while now, and I had an argument with some old funk fan from the '70s who didn't appreciate it. I said, 'Dude, you and those fans pretty much deserted P-Funk. It's not about nostalgia now; it's a whole new thing for a new audience. Do you want everything to be like it was?' Life dictates otherwise, so my hat's off to them."

LIGE CURRY: FLAME KEEPER

Tenure 1979–present
Style Varied, out of necessity
Can be heard on Funkadelic's "Funk Gets Stronger (Part 1)," "Shockwaves," "Icka Prick," from *The Electric Spanking of War Babies*; Parliament's "New Doo Review," from *Trombipulation*; P-Funk Allstars' "Viagravation" from 2005's *How Late Do U Have 2BB4UR Absent?*
George Clinton says "Even though Lige always knew the songs, it took him a while to get the pocket. Now he's excellent at hitting and holding it."

"I first encountered P-Funk at a 1974 post-show party jam in Cleveland with my cousin, guitarist Michael Hampton. We nailed 'Maggot Brain,' and they called him up right away, but I didn't hook up with them again until 1978 when I started doing business and crew work. When Skeet Curtis left in 1979, I earned the bass gig by auditioning. I knew the songs, but relaxing and hitting the laid-back feel was trickier than I expected. The only way to truly understand the nuances is to be shown by one of the guys who created the music.

"I've been lucky enough to learn from all the main bassists. At one point in the mid '90s, Billy, Skeet, and I shared the bass spot. Billy would play the early Funkadelic songs, Skeet would play the later-era Parliament stuff, and I'd play the rest. Billy taught me the Jamerson style, and to be as raw as you possibly can. Skeet taught me to be progressive and daring with note choices. I learned about effects from Bootsy, but Boogie was my true mentor.

"I approached him with a balance of enthusiasm and respect in order to get him to show me the nooks and crannies of the material. For example, Boogie uses right-hand attack positions that vary from way back by the bridge to way up by the neck in order to bob and weave like a boxer on stuff like 'Nappy Dugout,' or to get the staccato rhythmic effect on a song like 'Give Up the Funk (Tear the Roof off the Sucker).' He also plays open strings a lot, which can be magical but hard to incorporate. For example, I was playing the second note of the 'Cosmic Slop' line by hitting the 5th fret of the *E* string, but Boogie hit the open *A* string on the recording, which gives the line a different feel. When those roundwounds start ringing out and rattling against the frets—*that's* funk. I'm taking it to another level by playing a 6-string bass. It's my way of making the material my own, and all George cares about is the pocket.

"Only now, 26 years into this, do I truly have the feel together, and I'm passing that knowledge down to Ronald 'RonKat' Spearman, who is primarily a singer with P-Funk. I wanted to give someone from the next generation the same opportunity I got, because that's what the Mothership Connection is all about. Besides, I needed someone to give me a break at the end of these four-and-a-half-hour shows!

"I'm excited about the new record and the way the younger generation has rediscovered funk through hip-hop. It freaked me out to hear that Snoop Dogg now has a band called the Snoopadelics! We even did a show with Nelly at an NBA All-Star game party where he had a band. It's all coming back around, and P-Funk is going to be right there. I'm in this thing for life. Like George said to me recently, 'This shit ain't over yet!'"

★ DEEP CUTS: A P-FUNK BASS SAMPLER ★

Billy "Bass" Nelson on Funkadelic's "Hit It and Quit It" from 1971's *Maggot Brain*. Like a lot of early Funkadelic, the bass line from "Hit It and Quit It" has a raw and bluesy feel. Every chance he gets, Billy bends the *G*'s to hit the "blue note" in between the scale's minor and major 3rd.

"Boogie" Mosson on Funkadelic's "Nappy Dugout" from 1973's *Cosmic Slop*. Dig Boogie's improvised, syncopated flow in the first chorus. He cues the chorus with a neck-spanning slide, then loads the phrase with smaller chromatic slides.

Bootsy Collins on "Give Up the Funk (Tear the Roof off the Sucker)" from 1976's *Mothership Connection*. Starting with the verse at 0:20, this line never neglects the *one*. But more important, the tension set up by the syncopation within the bars—particularly the descending 16th-note funs anticipating beat *three*—emphasizes the downbeat to such a degree that booty-bumping on *two* and *four* is almost compulsory.

"Skeet" Curtis on Funkadelic's "Grooveallegiance" from 1978's *One Nation Under a Groove*. It's part jazz, part calypso, totally P-Funk, and completely Skeet—courtesy of his extended bass solo. Skeet shreds *B* Dorian over the *Bm7* chords and *F♯* Aeolian over the *F♯m* chords.

Lige Curry on Funkadelic's "Shockwaves" from 1981's *The Electric Spanking of War Babies*. The bass-driven reggae track spotlights Lige Curry, whose16th-note rhythms, ample rests, and melodic note choices give the line a happy lilt while reinforcing the reggae feel.

★ IT'S BOOTSY, BABY! BY BILL LEIGH ★

"Oh, yeah!" cried the familiar voice over the phone, in a mellifluous tone instantly recognizable to anyone who has ever been near a Bootsy Collins record. No cosmic drip-drops of Mu-Tron–infused Space Bass, though—just the friendly, hometown speech of the real William Collins, a Cincinnati native who helped define and then reinvent funk bass. From his teen years playing with James Brown to his pivotal role in Parliament/Funkadelic to the complete wackiness of Bootsy's Rubber Band, Bootsy—as he became known—has stood at funk's ground zero for most of his life.

Recently returning home from a tour of Europe, Bootsy is back on his rigorous recording schedule, cutting tracks at the Bootzilla Re-hab P-Form School, the studio attached to his Cincinnati home. Between sessions Bootsy graciously squeezed in time to talk about his history at the forefront of funk bass, but it was clear his time was limited—he had to get back to the studio.

Why keep up the constant activity? "You've got to keep it going while you got it going, right? Oh yeah!" he offers, asking and answering his own question. "I really like doing a lot of the studio thing now because I get a chance to be more creative and work with other people, too. That's really key with me. Back when I was with P-Funk was a good time for me, but I was always cutting something—Parliament, Funkadelic, Bootsy—and that took up all my time. I never really got a chance to work with anyone else. Since that wound down I've had a chance to stretch out a little. That's why I'm going nuts with it now."

For a versatile musician whose bread and butter has been far-out experimentation, Bootsy's newer works lean more toward hip-hop and modern R&B, though with a definite Bootsy bent, both in bass sounds and sense of humor. "The goal was to have a record that would help us play bigger places so I can pay the band. Trying to straighten up and do stuff at least halfway right was really hard work. I can always go back to doing crazy stuff; that's what I really love doing."

Long before the star glasses and star-shaped Space Bass, long before the wild outfits and effects-laden bass sound, William Collins was just a scrawny kid from Cincinnati, tagging along with his guitar-slinging brother Phelps—also called Catfish—nine years his elder. The two brothers put together a band with drummer Frankie Waddy and horn players Clayton Gunnels, Daryl Jamison, and Robert McCollough, and when they began to turn local heads, the group began doing sessions at nearby King Records. There they met King's star, James Brown, and got to know his band members. Eventually hired on as a band for James Brown Productions, the group did short tours supporting Hank Ballard and Marva Whitney. That put them in the right spot in March 1970, when most of Brown's disgruntled musicians rebelled just before a show in Columbus, Georgia. James sent for the youngsters on his private jet, and they soon became the JB's. For just over a year, Bootsy made music history by reinventing the Godfather's grooves with his over-the-top playing on such songs as "Get Up (I Feel Like Being a) Sex Machine," "Super Bad," and "Talkin' Loud and Sayin' Nothing."

You've been playing funk bass for a long time. Has your understanding of funk changed at all?

Funk to me is where I came from; it's the way I grew up. It's even deeper than the music. It's the way we communicated; actually the way we lived. It's like ten people in a small room and it's 110 degrees outside and there's no air conditioner. It's when the bill collector comes and you don't have any money to pay. It's when you've had as much as you can take and you can't take no more. What do you do? Funk it. That's when you grow into the funk.

What is the essence of funk bass?

It started off with the *one*. Then the *ands* and the *ifs* were added—all the in-between things. That's pretty much what I started doing. Nowadays it's been developed to a whole other level; people are doing different things with the *ands* and the *ifs*. It's their interpretation of what funk is for them. But as long as the *one* is there, your *ands* and *ifs* mean something. If the *one* is not there, it's kind of like daydreaming [*laughs*].

What is the most significant event from your early career that helped you develop into the person you became?

The first group I was in, the Pacemakers, or Pacesetters—we were kind of confused on which name to use—helped me start searching for who and what I wanted to be. That was when I started dressing crazy. I must have been 13 or 14 because I met up with James at the studio when I was around 15.

James Brown has a reputation for being quite a disciplinarian bandleader.

Oh, he was! But you know as a kid, I didn't really care about that. I respected him, but at the same time I had this kid inside me who felt like he was the baddest cat in the world. You know how cocky kids are, man! I had that all over me—and James knew it—so he treated me like his son. Everybody was calling him Mr. Brown, but I was calling him James. I figured I could get away with a lot of stuff and I pretty much did. I really thought I had it going on. I didn't even think about it until after I wasn't there. Then it was, Man, what were you doing?

We were with James Brown—we were on top of the world! But we started thinking of things we wanted to do once we weren't with James. And the urge was coming on quicker than we anticipated. We weren't sure what we wanted to do, but every day it was growing in us. Each show we did with James took us more to the point of thinking, Wait till we get a chance to really do our thing. We didn't have a plan; I only knew we weren't going to be with James Brown forever.

The song "What So Never the Dance" [on *Back in the Day: The Best of Bootsy*] is from the period between James Brown and P-Funk, when you went back to Cincinnati. Your bass is so out front. Were you the leader?

I guess. I couldn't hold that boy back, man; that boy was crazy!

How is it your big brother let you step in front?

I think he was having more fun with it being on me than on him. For some reason he's always wanted to be in the band and watch my back. I didn't know what the heck was going on—I just wanted to be out there. It was the girls, it was the wine, you know, getting high. But he was acting as the group's manager and booking the shows. He was the older brother and I was the fool kid.

There you were in 1971, stepping out front with the bass at a time when few players had done that. What made you different?

Jimi Hendrix is the one I was looking at. I was freaked out about what he was doing, and I thought, Wow—maybe I can do that with the bass. That's what did it. I was probably going to do something crazy anyway, but hearing Jimi put the icing on the cake.

Who were some of your early bass influences?

The major one was James Jamerson. Before I knew anything about bass we used to listen to all those Motown records when we'd go to house parties. He was so perfect in what he played—I always wanted to be like that. You didn't really know who bass players were then; they didn't put it on the 45 record. But when I found out who it was, I thought, Wow—that's the cat.

You knew you wouldn't be with James Brown forever. Is that how you felt about George Clinton and P-Funk as well?

Well, George and I had an understanding going in: If I did Parliament and Funkadelic with him, then he would help me do Bootsy's Rubber Band in return. I didn't have a plan when I was with James, but George helped me plan things. That made it totally different. James was more like a father; he really acted like a father. George was more like a brother. I could have fun with him in ways I couldn't with James.

Your musical role was probably pretty different, too.

George really wanted me involved. He gave me free clearance to do anything and everything I wanted, while James wanted to look like he did everything.

You weren't P-Funk's only bassist; Billy Bass Nelson, Cordell "Boogie" Mosson, and Skeet Curtis were also around. How did you decide who would cut a track?

If they came up with a song they cut it; if I came up with a song I cut it. That's pretty much the way it was, unless George stepped in and said, 'Bootsy, I want Billy's bass on this one.' I was probably on more of the commercial stuff. I did some stupid stuff too, but that's me on most of the Parliament hits, and the Funkadelic hits "(Not Just) Knee Deep" and "One Nation Under a Groove." Most people don't know I actually played drums on those, too, as well as on "Flashlight," "Stretchin' Out in a Rubber Band," and "Bootzilla." If you see my name on it as a writer, it's generally me on bass.

How did you get into using effects?

Again I have to credit Jimi. When I listened to his records I didn't know what he was using, but I knew he was using something. So I went out on a mission to find something to make the bass sound different and develop my own sound. I tried the wah-wah, but it wasn't really happening. I tried this box called the BassBalls that was all right. But until I found the Mu-Tron I never heard anything that totally made it wacko. When I played it for some girls in the studio, they said, 'Ooh, what's that wet, watery sound? That's sexy!' Oh, man—all of that rattle made me want to play every song with that sound! I would say I started using it around 1976.

Did you know any other bass players who were using pedals?

Larry Graham was the only other one I knew of that was even thinking about it. He was using a Maestro Bass Brassmaster, which gave it that sustain. But I had started wanting to use pedals when I was with James. I actually tried using a wah-wah with James, but he wasn't going for it! I knew I'd have to wait until I was away from him to really get off into it. And when I did I went crazy with it.

As the founding father of bass effects, how do you feel a bassist should use them?

Go through them one by one and check out what they do. How you hit the note—the fingers or thumb you use—tells the gadget what to do. If it seems like it doesn't work for a certain song, it might work if you play differently—if you change how you talk to the pedal. And certain pedals sound better on certain songs. You have to search it out and find the right ingredient.

Not only did you just use some pedals, you used a lot of pedals.

Aw, yeah—and I still do. I was hooked on the Mu-Tron—that and the Electro-Harmonix Big Muff. Of course I started adding a whole lot of other stuff: MXR digital delays, Electro-Harmonix Bass Micro Synthesizer, the Morley pedal with the fuzz and the wah built in—it goes on and on. I had a board built for all those pedals. Nowadays it's a much bigger pedalboard, and I've got the old pedals mixed with the new ones.

Are you constantly turning on and off effects while you're playing parts?

It depends on the song. Sometimes I'll play straight Mu-Tron or straight bass. Actually very seldom do I play straight bass, but I've been known to do that, too.

But when I kick on the effects, that's the gooey part—it's like, *Ooh, yeah*! I've got different things that come out of different sides of the speakers: Mu-Tron on the right speaker and a wet whammy pedal coming out in another octave on the left. That's how I have it panned for live shows and recording.

How do you record?

Usually I go direct, or if the song is supposed to sound live, I'll do more of a live thing and mix a little of the direct in with the live. I record four tracks at a time—one from each output.

Your newer material has some great bass hooks, but you seem to have backed off some on your playing to leave more room for the song.

That's exactly what we did to try to be more commercial. I learned a lot from the other producers and artists. Working with other people really helps me clock in on what's happening. The way we came up is just doing things the way you feel. Today the groove is so perfect and you can fix everything, so I'm learning how to do that.

Do you think that's less funky than playing with a live band?

Yeah, it is, but it's a new day. People are growing up a new way than when I came up. The closest thing you'd get to a sample in my day was the real James Brown or Parliament/Funkadelic. Today nothing has to be a mistake; you can make everything right. But our mistakes usually were the groove. The mistakes we made, rappers use for samples! [*Laughs.*]

In your song "Pinocchio Theory" you said, "If you fake the funk your nose will grow." Does today's way of making music fake the funk?

It depends upon the angle of the dangle. If you compare it to the stuff of today, it's the funky stuff. But if you compare it to the stuff we were used to—the real funk—definitely some noses would be growing. But it's two different worlds. I think what's happening today is best for today. However the process changes with computers, we are the DNA of what's to come, and the funk will always be encoded in that.

★ DEEPER CUTS: BOOTSY COLLINS ON PARLIAMENT'S "P-FUNK (WANTS TO GET FUNKED UP)" BY BILL LEIGH ★

Once upon a time called *right now*, the extraterrestrial brothers, broadcasting direct from the Mothership, take over your radio and do it to you in your earhole. That's the premise behind "P-Funk (Wants to Get Funked Up)," the opening track of Parliament's 1975 concept album *Mothership Connection*, a veritable master class in funk bass syncopation, courtesy of Bootsy Collins. (Don't stress about your radio;

they'll return control to you "as soon as you are groovy.")

The late '70s was the creative and commercial peak for P-Funk, and *Mothership Connection* is among the best of a dozen or so tremendous P-Funk recordings produced between 1975 and 1979. The album also represents two watershed moments in funk history: the addition of saxophonist Maceo Parker and trombonist Fred Wesley, long-time funk veterans from the James Brown regiment, to the P-Funk fold; and Bootsy Collins's emerging mastery of his signature effect—the Mu-Tron III envelope filter pedal.

Bootsy's sophisticated syncopation sense would have been enough to make him the stuff of funk-bass legend without the Mu-Tron. He had already revolutionized funk bass at age 19, when a year-long stint with James Brown yielded such bottom-bouncing classics as "Get Up (I Feel Like Being a) Sex Machine" and "Super Bad." But that Mu-Tron added extra *stank* to Bootsy's deliciously dancing style.

The key to copping Bootsy's P-Funk groove isn't an envelope filter, though. Most important is to internalize the seriously swung 16th-note feel. At the moderately slow tempo of "P-Funk (Wants to Get Funked Up)," those swinging 16ths provide a kind of internal propulsion, making every beat feel nearly as strong as the almighty *one*. Be sure to feel that underlying rhythm even as you play the quarter- and eighth-notes of the verse's staccato unison riff. The eerily quiet verses, where Bootsy keeps his tone clean and his notes clipped, are all potential energy. But Bootsy cuts loose in the louder choruses, whipping out juicy syncopated lines and the Mu-Tron's *bwap*, which kicks in more the harder he plays.

In the choruses, Bootsy almost never fails to play the *one*. He begins nearly every two-bar phrase with straight eighth-notes followed by syncopated 16ths, and a beat *three* rest, matching the straight-then-syncopated rhythm of the "Make my funk the P-Funk" chorus lyric. From there he cuts loose with booty-bumping barrages of slippery licks, bent-string slurs, phrase-ending accent slides, hammered riffs, and even a temporary shift to a straight-16th rhythm near the end.

13

PROFESSIONAL FUNK: THE SESSION PLAYERS AND SIDEMEN OF THE '70S AND '80S

★ JOSEPH "LUCKY" SCOTT WITH CURTIS MAYFIELD BY CHRIS JISI ★

Although he never quite achieved the high profile and chart status of fellow soul-men James Brown, Marvin Gaye, or Stevie Wonder, Curtis Mayfield stands as an R&B giant. The late Chicago-born singer/songwriter/guitarist first came to prominence as a member of the Impressions, reaching his creative pinnacle in the early '70s. With hits like "People Get Ready," "Superfly," and "Freddie's Dead," Mayfield was among the very first to write openly about the struggles and pride of African Americans, all while helping to tailor the Chicago soul sound: a blend of Latin-influenced rhythms, punctuating horns, and Mayfield's trademark open-string-tuned guitar. In short, it was emancipation through syncopation.

On the bottom, Curtis benefited from the loose, probing, persistent lines of the late Joseph "Lucky" Scott, a Chicago bassist whose other recording credits included Aretha Franklin and Natalie Cole, and whose own songs (such as the R&B standard "Never Let Me Go") have been covered by everyone from the Impressions and Bobby "Blue" Bland to Van Morrison and Luther Vandross. Scott's most famous sub-hook is the minor-3rd-leaning riff of "Freddie's Dead"—but a great bass line that captures the offbeat syncopation of Mayfield's pioneering psychedelic funk brew is "Pusherman," from the same *Superfly* soundtrack album. In the song's main A-section groove, which is doubled by guitar, Scott puts the emphasis on beat *two*, locking up with Mayfield's accented 13th chord. From there, he keeps it funky with upbeats through the end of the phrase. Dig Scott's fills during the vocals-free transition, and the vibrato slides up to high *C* in the bridge.

★ DEEPER CUTS: WILTON FELDER ON THE JACKSON 5'S "I WANT YOU BACK" BY CHRIS JISI ★

With his free-as-the-wind phrasing and Texas-size tenor-sax tone, Wilton Felder is a crossover-jazz pioneer. He and his fellow Crusaders added R&B, blues, and gospel to their jazz-rooted Gulf Coast sound to become the best-selling instrumental group of all time. What many people don't know is that Felder forged a dual career as a first-call Los Angeles session bassist, too. "In fact," laughs the Houston native, "in the studio world hardly anyone knew I even played sax." During his peak plucking period, from 1969 to '81, Felder appeared on hundreds of albums for artists including the Jackson 5, Marvin Gaye, the Four Tops, Joni Mitchell, Steely Dan, Billy Joel, B. B.

King, Jackson Browne, Tina Turner, and Ringo Starr.

Felder found his way to the bass shortly after the Crusaders found their way from Houston to Los Angeles in 1958. With original bassist Henry Wilson having departed, Joe Sample was providing the bottom on Hammond B-3 organ—until Felder decided to try out a '59 Jazz Bass that belonged to a club owner. "I seemed to have a natural affinity for it," he recalls.

Because of the Crusaders' preference for recording live in the studio, Felder played bass on only a few of the group's albums—although Sample credits him with forging the Crusaders' bass style. The "Fifth Crusader" was actually any one of a revolving series of such top-flight bassists as Buster Williams, Monk Montgomery, Max Bennett, Chuck Rainey, James Jamerson (Jr. as well as Sr.), Pops Popwell, and Alphonso Johnson. "I enjoyed all of them," enthuses Wilton, "especially Pops, who was our most-recorded bassist."

Felder's session career began in 1969 when bassist Ron Brown recommended him for a recording date at Motown. His Motown work led to calls from outside producers, and Felder's credits began to grow. Surprisingly, Wilton's most famous bass line can be found on his first hit-record appearance: His bouncy, twisting part on the Jackson 5's No. 1 pop and R&B hit, "I Want You Back." The song was composed by the Corporation, the 5's four-man production team that included Motown king Berry Gordy. Felder recalls, "The bass part, which essentially mirrors and counters the melody, was mostly written out; I added just a bit of myself to it. I used my '60s Telecaster Bass with flatwound strings and recorded direct."

As the track begins, Wilton grabs the bass line in unison with the piano. He admits, "As a sax player I related to the line's hip chromatic movement—but being self-taught, I found the fingerings a bit intimidating." Though many of the fills were written, Wilton added his input via 16th notes, ghost notes, and root-5th-octave flourishes occasionally inserted into the chorus's descending line. Corporation member Freddie Perrin came up with the killer arpeggiated bass figure in the song's vocal breakdown, which Wilton pulls off smoothly, accenting the 16th-note upbeats. As the final chorus rides out, Wilton continues adding rhythmic motion both subtle and dramatic. "The bass is all about how you get from one chord to another and from one downbeat to the next," says Felder. "A lot of the notes, false notes, and rhythms I play in between come from my sax experience as well as from James Jamerson's influence."

"I like it when the bassist and drummer play independent of each other but paint the groove together," says Felder, summing up his bass approach. "The key is to be aware of the multiple feels and subdivisions going on in the song. In other words, you have to know what you aren't hearing, and then play as if you're hearing it!"

★ REGGIE MCBRIDE: HAVING DONE SOMETHIN' BY JIMMY LESLIE ★

If the music business had a Best Supporting Musician award, Reggie McBride would have one helluva trophy case. Stevie Wonder, George Clinton, Elton John, and a long list of others have hired McBride and his bass to make their best songs sound better. McBride currently resides in Corona, California, but he grew up in Detroit during Motown's golden age. "James Jamerson lived down the street when I was a teenager," McBride recalls. Aretha Franklin asked him to go on the road, but Reggie's parents wouldn't allow their young son to miss school. The prestigious Berklee College of Music offered him a scholarship, but by that time, the streetwise McBride already had the tools he needed to succeed. Reggie is renowned for his mastery of the Motown sound and his naturally laid-back funk feel; you've heard it on classics such as Funkadelic's booty-shakin' "Good to Your Earhole," the Elton John gem "Little Jeannie," and Wonder's throwdown "You Haven't Done Nothin'." McBride's main gig since 1997 has been holding down the low end for country blues phenom Keb' Mo.'

What inspired you to play bass in the first place?

I grew up in Detroit during the '60s, and James Jamerson was the main man. My family went to the Motown Revue religiously every year, and Jamerson would be onstage with the Funk Brothers backing up all the singers, so I was aware of him by age five. I started playing Motown songs in a band when I was about eight. The drummer said that we needed a bass, but I didn't know what one was until he said, "It's the low notes that James Jamerson plays." I understood what he meant then, so I detuned my guitar until we could find a bass to borrow. My family moved out of the city for about five years, but when we moved back to town, the Jamersons lived four houses down.

I would never see James at home, but his son would come by our house, and we used to wrestle. I would see James out at clubs sometimes. I met him and had a long talk with him one night when he was playing with the Teddy Harris Big Band. We talked about what he was up to, his style, and I took a look at his charts. It was just a general conversation about how we both loved to play bass. That's the only time we ever spoke, but I saw him again when I was playing with Stevie Wonder. Jamerson came in and played on "They Won't Go When I Go," for Fulfillingness' First Finale.

How did you wind up playing with Stevie Wonder?

I played a lot of talent shows and clubs around Detroit. I was 14 when Aretha Franklin asked me to go on the road. My parents wouldn't allow me to miss school, but when I got an opportunity to tour with the Dramatics the following year, they let me go. We toured with James Brown, and both bands were on the same bus, so I got to know Fred Thomas and all those guys. In 1973 the phone rang again, and there was a voice claiming to be Stevie Wonder. I replied, "You're bullshitting me." He said, "No. I want you to come to New York and audition for my band." Ray Parker Jr. had recommended me, and I was excited because I knew all of Stevie's stuff like the back of my hand. He sent me a ticket, and I was led to a room at the 5th Avenue Hotel where his keyboards were set up. We played "Superstition," and then we got into about four bars of "Higher Ground" before Stevie jumped off the keyboards and wrestled me to the ground! At first I was confused, but I soon figured out that it meant I had the gig [*laughs*].

What instructions did he offer?

Not much. Stevie favored flat keys; he'd stay on the black keys with his left hand. "Superstition" and "Higher Ground" were in Eb, so I tuned down to Eb, which worked perfect with everything he did. I developed a sense for where he was going next. The whole gig was about listening to him, watching his left hand, and just nailing it.

What were the *Fulfillingness' First Finale* sessions like?

Stevie and I tracked together most of the time, but we overdubbed some things. For a new song, he would show me the root part, and he was usually specific about the bass line. If he wasn't specific, I'd add my ideas, but he taught me that locking down a simple bass line was key to a hit record.

"You Haven't Done Nothin'" was a huge hit. How did that go down?

Stevie had a Rhythm Ace—a primitive drum machine—playing the clave beat at the beginning, and he was playing a Clavinet. I started playing the bass line he suggested, but he said, "I want you to literally strike down on the string with your first finger like a hammer, but leave your wrist loose." I tried, but he wasn't satisfied, so he grabbed my bass and showed me exactly what he meant. I eventually got it, and I played the whole song by hitting the flatwound strings on my 1970 Fender Precision Bass right on the pickup, so it sounded something like a drumstick. The engineer yelled, "You can't do that—the speakers are popping out!" And Stevie said, "Shut up—I know what the hell I'm doing." [*Laughs.*] Eventually the engineer tamed the signal with a Pultec compressor/limiter, which stopped the speakers from popping and also magnified the effect so that you could really hear the hit. I overdubbed another bass part that walks down and does a quick slap-and-pop in the prechorus.

How much more work did you do with Stevie Wonder?

I did one European tour and a few television shows, and we recorded constantly. Some songs were in the can for future albums, and lots of things were for other people. I worked with Stevie on Minnie Riperton's *Perfect Angel* and *Stevie Wonder Presents Syreeta Wright*. I had more freedom to create parts on those sessions. I left after the tour to join Rare Earth.

How did you hook up with George Clinton?

George Clinton hired the Rare Earth rhythm section. We were credited as "Guest Funkadelic" on *Let's Take It to the Stage*, which is actually a studio record. We played on "Good to Your Earhole" and "Stuffs and Things." "Stuffs and Things" was really funky, so I played staccato, doubling Bernie Worrell's keyboard line.

What's the most surprising thing about your career as a bass player?

That I've been around this long! [*Laughs.*]

★ MR. EVERYTHING: WILLIE WEEKS DOES IT ALL BY RICHARD JOHNSTON ★

Willie Weeks—Donny Hathaway's *Live*—"Voices Inside (Everything Is Everything)"—Bass Solo. For a generation of bassists and R&B fans, those elements exist as a single thought. In the finale of Hathaway's classic 1972 album, Weeks—playing a flatwound-strung '62 P-Bass through an Ampeg SVT—takes a three-and-a-half-minute ride that is a seamless melding of groove, melody, and drama, making it one of the deepest bass solos on record. "Every bass player should own a copy of Donny Hathaway's *Live* album," says blues bass maven Tommy Shannon. "It's just about perfection."

Weeks deserves the renown the track has brought him, but in the past four decades his career has soared far beyond that moment of glory. In the studio he's worked with a spectrum of pop, rock, R&B, blues, and country icons—artists such as George Harrison, the Rolling Stones, Stevie Wonder, Aretha Franklin, Michael McDonald, Wynonna Judd, and Vince Gill—and onstage he has backed Harrison, Judd, the Doobie Brothers, Lyle Lovett, and Gregg Allman.

Born in Salemburg, North Carolina, Weeks grew up working in the fields and listening to country, pop, and R&B on the radio. He honed his bass skills in the early '60s in a variety of bands and locations, from Alvin Cash & the Crawlers in Buffalo, New York, to Les Watson & the Panthers in Dallas, Texas. In St. Paul, Minnesota, it was the Fabulous Amazers and prog-rockers Gypsy, whose self-titled '70 album with Weeks on bass has become a cult item. Willie found his '62 P-Bass at a California pawnshop before heading to Chicago, where he played with a pre–Chaka Khan lineup of the band Rufus before joining up with soul star Hathaway. That gig would change Weeks's life in ways beyond his famous solo.

"That band was such an incredible musical experience that I just couldn't get into any music I played after that," Weeks says. "Finally I said, 'I'm just through with it.' I went to Puerto Rico and hung out there for a year."

It wasn't the last time Weeks would take a hiatus and then re-emerge at a new level in his career. From Puerto Rico he traveled to New York and then London, where he joined drummer Andy Newmark in laying down tracks for future Rolling Stone Ron Wood. Weeks and Newmark went on to do sessions with Rod Stewart, the Rolling Stones, and George Harrison, playing on the former Beatle's *Dark Horse* and *Extra Texture* albums and backing him on tour.

In the late '70s and early '80s, Weeks enjoyed a busy stateside studio career and played the Doobie Brothers' '82 farewell tour. The death of his wife, however, left him at another crossroads, this time with a young daughter to raise. "I needed more of a family-oriented place. A buddy of mine said, 'Why don't you go to Nashville?' And I thought, Well, why not?"

In Nashville, Weeks worked his way onto the A-list of session players, logged steady roadwork with Wynonna Judd, and did a stint with Lyle Lovett. His sessions have leaned toward country but have also included blues, soul, and pop.

People around the world associate you with your break in "Voices Inside (Everything Is Everything)." What's it like to be known for one solo?

[*Laughs.*] It's incredible. Everywhere I go somebody knows my name. I don't get mobbed—but I am famous, and I like it. It's as incredible as that night Donny said, "On bass, ladies and gentlemen, the baddest bass player in the country—Willie Weeks, y'all!" I'm like, Oh, my God! What did he say? What am I going to do? I thought, I'd better build slow!

Was that solo edited for the album?

The only thing they did was make it shorter. There were other nights that the solo was sort of choppy—it didn't really tell a story. The solo on the record was very, very simple, but it had a story. It was a little song.

What do folks know they're going to get when they hire you for a session?

They know they're going to get a solid groove. It may be simple, but it will be melodic, it will be solid, and it will be a great sound.

How did you develop your groove?

It all started in church. Normally we didn't have any instruments except tambourine, and it would be *foot-stomp-clap*, *foot-stomp-clap* [two-eighth-note/quarter-note rhythm]. That was a strong groove—all of us people together, clapping and stomping. That was the basis for it. And Donny Hathaway, man—his music was like an *army* coming at you, a groove so deep it would hypnotize you. That didn't hurt as far as me developing.

Do you have a different mindset for live shows compared to doing sessions?

Basically it's the same: I want to play the music better than I played it the last time—I want to play this music *great*. I just think, I don't know whether I'll ever play this again, so I want to just kill it! [*Laughs.*] Every chance I get.

You've gotten discouraged with the music business a few times in your career. How did you overcome that?

I would try to hear some music that inspired me, like Motown and James Jamerson. And there have been times when I just picked up my instrument and tried to learn something different. If you find something that inspires you to learn, it lights the fire.

★ LOUIS JOHNSON: "THUNDER THUMBS" BY JIM ROBERTS ★

The passing of the torch from Larry Graham went to the slapper who burned with the purest flame: Louis Johnson. Louis, a.k.a. "Thunder Thumbs," is best known as a co-leader of the Brothers Johnson, whose gold-selling funk anthems included "Get the Funk Out Ma Face," "I'll Be Good to You," and "Strawberry Letter 23." At the same time, he also emerged as an L.A. studio ace under the guidance of the Brothers' producer/mentor Quincy Jones, appearing on dozens of sessions with a diverse array of artists including Paul McCartney, Stevie Wonder, John Mellencamp, Herbie Hancock, Chaka Khan, Sergio Mendes, George Benson, and Peggy Lee. His potent finger-and-thumb work is also present on every Michael Jackson album.

Born in Los Angeles on April 13, 1955, Johnson started slapping 14 years later, having never heard Larry Graham (or anyone else) use the technique. He explains: "My brother George and I both started out playing guitar, until my dad decided we would be better off from a band point of view if I moved to bass. Slapping was a matter of natural evolution for me. I plucked the strings with my thumb and tried to find the little clicks and pops I got when I strummed chords on the guitar. Gradually, as I struck the strings harder and harder with my thumb, I discovered all these percussive sounds that coincided with the note. For years I slapped and popped the standard way, with my thumb and index finger. When I got tired of that I made up other ways to do it, like pulling out the strings, or using just my thumb, or smacking the strings with the palm of my hand. I also developed a strumming technique where I hit all the strings with my fingers as if I were holding a pick but muted the strings so only one note sounded."

Louis and George hooked up with Billy Preston in 1972, and the bassist immediately began hearing people saying he played like Graham. "It was frustrating," he says. "I'd still never heard him; my two big influences were Ray Brown and James Jamerson." Not long after, Quincy Jones heard the brothers on a demo, setting the stage for the ascension of the Brothers Johnson.

Johnson continues to record everything from hip-hop to jazz in his home studio, and he's listening closely to what's happening in modern music. "The bottom line is that the evolution of the bass will continue to occur regardless of who gets the credit. I just feel very fortunate that the Lord chose to put it in my hands when he did, and that I was able to make a contribution."

★ DEEPER CUTS: LOUIS JOHNSON ON THE BROTHERS JOHNSON'S "STOMP!" BY CHRIS JISI ★

"Stomp!" was the Brothers Johnson's biggest hit, reaching No. 1 on the R&B and dance charts, and No. 3 on the pop charts. Infectious and multi-sectioned, the dance hit clocked in at 6:20 on the *Light Up the Night* LP, with over two minutes shaved off for radio. But both versions had a most pleasantly surprising centerpiece: a slap solo (although cut from 16 to 8 bars for radio).

The late-1979 session for "Stomp!" took place at A&M Studios in Los Angeles. Recalls Louis, "I started writing the song on bass first and then guitar at my home studio. Next, Quincy had Rod Temperton, George, and my wife, Valerie, help out with some melodies and lyrics; Jerry Hey did the horn and string arrangements." He adds, "We had it in about two takes, and I made no punches or fixes; the funk was there as soon as we hit it." Johnson used a natural Music Man StingRay strung with new D'Addario roundwounds, his bass recorded direct and through a miked and baffled Fender Bassman amp.

Anchored by four-on-the-floor kick drum, the track launches with an extended intro based on the chorus changes, with Johnson providing roots and rhythmic motion. Finally, with the full drum kit entering, Louis settles into a funky fingerstyle octave-swapping phrase that continues into the first verse. "I used fingers at first because Quincy taught me when you create a song you don't start out at level ten and leave yourself with nowhere to go," recalls Johnson. "You start simple, build to a highpoint, and then go back down slowly. I wanted to tell a musical story in 'Stomp!' and build up to the thumping." Johnson, true to his word, subtly builds via classic R&B pickup notes, telegraphing the prechorus downshift to *E* minor before it arrives. Disco octaves welcome the chorus, which brings more vocals, horns, and strings, and the drums continuing a quarter-note stomp, while Johnson pitches eighth-note-based syncopation on the bottom.

After a recap of the verse and chorus, thunder strikes—initiated by a vicious bass slide. Generally, Johnson starts each measure with a similar rhythmic figure, varying its ending on beats *three* and *four*. Listen for his left-hand-aided triplets and bar-ending walk-ups, usually with octaves or similar notes added on top. "It's all about the rhythmic counterpoint between the right and left hands," says Louis of his basic approach to slapping. "I'll tend to think about two or three traditional folk rhythms at once, maybe an African-type rhythm on the *one* and the downbeats, which is key in funk, then, say, a Native American rhythm over that, and maybe a Japanese rhythm on top. It's sort of like having a bass, mid, and treble going on in the rhythm."

Johnson reverts to greasy finger plucking for the keyboard solo, then back to the chorus. Finally, "to take it to one more place," Johnson introduces a two-bar outro lick built around a finger-plucked sub-hook that beckons the ear with the sliding upper-register lick at the end of the phrase. "I've always said, when I play, I become the bass," Louis declares, with his Bruce Lee–inspired intensity on the fingerboard. "I'm no longer Louis Johnson, I *am* the bass—so the bass is in trouble!"

★ DEEP CUTS: LOUIS JOHNSON ★

Michael McDonald's "I Keep Forgettin' (Every Time You're Near)." Johnson provides the funky backbone behind the chicken-pickin' guitars and funky keyboards.
Quincy Jones's "One Hundred Ways." In this 1980 James Ingram ballad, from Jones's album *The Dude*, Johnson keeps the groove moving with deliciously swinging pickup notes and subtly dancing fills.
Michael Jackson's "The Lady in My Life." This ballad may be the slowest song on the top-selling *Thriller* album, but it's also among the funkiest, courtesy of Louis's thumb thunder.
Earl Klugh's "Kiko." Louis applies his juicy funk chops to guitar-centered Latin jazz fusion.

★ WILBUR "BAD" BASCOMB BY CHRIS JISI ★

Coming off the success of 1975's *Blow by Blow*, guitar god Jeff Beck decided to funk things up for his next tour by calling "that bloke from America," drummer Bernard Purdie. Asked to recommend a bass player, Purdie tapped frequent rhythm-section mate Wilbur "Bad" Bascomb. The tour—opposite John McLaughlin's Mahavishnu Orchestra—and the subsequent recording of Beck's gold-selling instrumental album *Wired*, brought Bascomb and his melodic jazz/funk grooves instant notoriety during the player-conscious fusion era. But Bascomb was already emerging as a top New York City session bassist, a low-profile career he prefers to this day.

The son of noted Duke Ellington and Erskine Hawkins trumpet player Wilbur "Dud" Bascomb, Wilbur Jr. was born in 1950 in uptown Manhattan, where he acquired his nickname from the old Wallace Beery western *Bad Bascomb*. Having tried drums and trumpet before his teens, he switched from violin to string bass in his junior high school orchestra to accommodate a fellow student whose mother insisted he play violin. "It turned out my dad always loved bass," Wilbur says. "When I'd lug it home from school he would play it for fun." A first-call session trumpeter, Bascomb Sr. urged his son to take up electric after noticing a void in the early '60s studio scene. Though he loved upright—inspired by Ray Brown, Sam Jones, and George Duvivier—and was receiving classical lessons at New York's prestigious Music & Art High School, Wilbur heeded his father's advice and bought a '66 P-Bass. "I'd have Dad give me nightly reports on what he saw Chuck Rainey or Jerry Jemmott do in the studio that day," he recalls.

Bascomb quickly went from local nightclub gigs to the house band at Harlem's famed Apollo Theater, backing stars from Nancy Wilson to Stevie Wonder. A 1972 recommendation from Bob Cranshaw led to a doubling gig with pianist Billy Taylor that included a morning radio program, David Frost's TV show, and nightly sets at the Village Vanguard. The exposure soon got Bascomb session work from top TV, movie, jingle, and record producers. Purdie's Beck offer led to Wilbur's visit to Europe. "I loved playing with Jeff and contributing to his music," Bascomb says.

After his stint with Beck, Bascomb landed in liner notes on albums by James Brown, B. B. King, Luther Vandross, Michael Bolton, Cissy Houston, Chuck Berry, Grace Jones, George Benson, and others. His uncredited roles include the Persuasions' soul anthem "Thin Line Between Love and Hate" and the star-studded 1978 movie soundtrack *Sgt. Pepper's Lonely Hearts Club Band*.

Bascomb has recently stayed busy on Broadway, subbing in the '90s on *Bring In da Noise, Bring In da Funk* and *The Lion King*, and appearing on the 2009 Broadway Revival Cast recording of *Hair*. Ultimately, though, Wilbur remains his own man. "I've always pursued originality. I think it's the single greatest quality any musician can have."

★ SCOTT EDWARDS: NO. 1 WINNER BY CHRIS JISI ★

When it comes to the upper rungs on the ladder of unsung bassists, it would be difficult to place much higher than Scott Edwards. Between 1972 and 1982, Edwards appeared on 12 Billboard No. 1 Hits as a first-call L.A. session bassist. From R&B and rock to disco and pop to TV and film scores, Edwards' rhythmically righteous, melodically savvy lines were everywhere. He laughs, "I remember turning on the Grammys one night and realizing I had played on three of the winning songs."

Born and raised in Atlanta, Edwards started on trombone at age five and switched to bass guitar at 18, shedding along with James Jamerson–driven Motown radio hits. In 1970, Stevie Wonder came through town having yet to replace Michael Henderson, who had left to join Miles Davis. Edwards's brother and cousin were hired as part of the regional horn section, and they recommended him on bass. After the show Scott was offered the gig. Three years and two albums later, he followed guitarist Ray Parker Jr. out of Stevie's band and on to Los Angeles, where Parker recommended him to Motown arrangers. Additionally, Wilton Felder gave Edwards his session work whenever he hit the road with the Crusaders.

Edwards really hit his groove when the disco scene exploded, leading to seminal sides with reigning dance divas Gloria Gaynor and Donna Summer, and a key role in the *Saturday Night Fever* soundtrack. When the disco backlash swept out many of the producers and contractors he knew, Scott's worked slowed down and he graciously stepped aside. "It was time to pass the mantle to new players, like Nathan East." Today, Edwards lives in Long Beach, doing tracks in his home studio for industrials and enjoying his residual-fed retirement.

★ **DEEPER CUTS: BASIL FEARRINGTON ON ROBERTA FLACK AND DONNY HATHAWAY'S "BACK TOGETHER AGAIN"** BY JONATHAN HERRERA ★

He may not have been among the most elite of pop session bassists, but Philadelphian Basil Fearrington has exceptional musical instincts. The evidence? Roberta Flack and Donny Hathaway's 1980 hit, "Back Together Again." In the late '70s and early '80s, Fearrington was the first call for a successful Philadelphia production team fronted by former Miles Davis sidemen James Mtume and Reggie Lucas. Fearrington explains, "We had been working together in Roberta's live band, so the chemistry was there. Mtume and Lucas didn't have to give [the band] much direction. We were their sound." The duo penned several hits for Hathaway and Flack, notably "The Closer I Get to You" and "Back Together Again." "I got called because I had big ears and did what was asked—at least that was my initial objective. After everything locked up, my secondary objective was to embellish my part to give it distinctive flavor."

Fearrington tracked "Back Together Again" with a custom Carl Thompson 4-string that he came to via Anthony Jackson. "I was very close with Anthony. When he migrated away from Fender, so did I. The luthier he settled on was Carl, and I followed his lead." The track's dominant rhythmic figure came from Mtume's original keyboard idea. "I'd always start with Mtume's left hand, just to see if it was worth keeping. In this case, I ended up basing my part around that *boom . . . da-boom-da . . . boom* figure."

As for the overdubbed slap track, Fearrington notes, "At that time, slapping was not something I had developed. I remember being insulted the first time Mtume came up to me and said, 'Hey man, you ever check out Louis Johnson?' But I knew what he was saying; that was the sound of the day. Mtume preferred to do it as an overdub because it sounded like two basses. But if it had been up to me, I probably would have left out the slap stuff."

An early protégé and friend of bass icons Alphonso Johnson and Anthony Jackson, and a devout disciple of James Jamerson, Fearrington isn't afraid to cite their overwhelming influence. "A lot of times when I'm playing—even now, after what feels like a thousand years—I'm always thinking, What would those guys do in this position?" For example, Fearrington points to the sweet upper-register lick that first appears in beat *three* of the second bar. "That lick, especially the little trill at the end, comes straight from Alphonso. I heard him do it, thought it sounded slick, and worked it into the part. Initially we tried to work it in as a pattern that happened every 'X' number of bars, but it was really hard to play over and over again. My hand was starting to swell up and blood was coming out of my ears, you know? Eventually, I just did it when it felt right." Fearrington also credits his frequent practice of scales and patterns in 4ths up and down the neck with giving him the necessary skills to pull off the lick. "If I hadn't worked on that stuff, there's no way I could have done it."

Hathaway and Flack's elegantly playful verses and choruses crank along with a consistent groove until a profound rhythmic and harmonic shift signal the bridge, which has the ever-soulful Hathaway croons over sugary background vocals. Here, Fearrington introduces some of his tastiest work. Anthony Jackson–like octave bounces, Jamerson-style passages that drop down to the 3rd, and a surprisingly jazz-ified unison lick, capped with an ear-twisting bar of 5/4 before the main groove returns. The outro is where the overdubbed slap part emerges most prominently, with a succession of artfully syncopated pops.

Fearrington's heroes—Johnson, Jackson, and Jamerson—are all individualists with a singular style and sound, but Fearrington sees his role differently. "In every situation, I've allowed myself to do whatever the producer wanted. I mean, guys like Anthony would say, 'Look, this part stinks and I can make it better.' I never did that kind of thing. Anthony or Chuck Rainey can do their own thing because they're phenomenal, but I didn't want to get the reputation as 'the guy who can play his ass off, but . . . .' I didn't want there to be a 'but' about me."

★ DEEPER CUTS: DAVID HUNGATE ON BOZ SCAGGS'S "LOW DOWN" BY CHRIS JISI ★

In the mid '70s, Los Angeles was the epicenter of the record industry and an exciting place to be. As compelling new talent supplanted veterans on label rosters, the session-player ranks also received a youthful infusion. In 1975, former Steve Miller Band vocalist and yet-to-break-big solo artist Boz Scaggs was producing guitarist Les Dudek's self-titled debut when he encountered the rhythm team of drummer Jeff Porcaro, keyboardist David Paich, and bassist David Hungate on the session. The trio had been playing together since Paich and Porcaro were in high school. Impressed, Scaggs hired the twentysomethings to work on his upcoming album for Columbia. The result was *Silk Degrees*, which rose to the No. 2 pop position and yielded six radio singles, including the hits "Lido Shuffle" and "We're All Alone." Behind-the-scenes buzz about the platter led to a boatload of sessions for Porcaro, Paich, and Hungate, as well as offers from labels to start a band. Within a year, the three had formed Toto, which went on to sell millions of records and score numerous hits.

Silk Degrees' chart-topping single "Low Down" became an instant anthem, eventually winning the 1976 Grammy for R&B Song of the Year. The *Silk Degrees* sessions, which took place at L.A.'s Davelin Studios in mid-September 1975, were no different. Hungate remembers, "The sessions were in the evening and very informal; we'd do one or two tunes a night. There was no sense that we were making a hit record—it was more of a jam atmosphere. Plus, we were all a little buzzed!"

For "Low Down," Hungate, Porcaro, Paich, and guitarist Fred Tackett jammed for a while to come up with parts, with each eventually scribbling their own basic charts. They then recorded live to Scaggs's scratch vocal, nailing it in three takes. Hungate used his '62 Fender Precision strung with almost-new Rotosound roundwounds, his signal going direct and through his Versatone amp. Paich liked a little phrase-ending hammered fill that Hungate had played at one point in the jam—inspired by a similar move the Meters' George Porter Jr. makes on Dr. John's "Right Place, Wrong Time"—so he asked him to stay put and record a second bass track with those verse fills. While playing along, Hungate added upper-register fills to the other sections of the tune just for fun, and was later surprised to hear they were kept in the final version.

"When I went on tour with Boz after the album came out, I actually used thumb slaps to play the low *E* and *A* groove because it was the most efficient way to play both parts at once, live. For the track, though, I played the main groove with my index, middle, and ring fingers. The groove was something Jeff and I locked into during the jam; the 16th-note pickup was common in R&B at the time. I kept it straight and simple, alluding to a turnaround every so often that Jeff mirrored with his kick." He laughs, "We were young, so there's a fair amount of pushing and pulling, but it all adds to the charm of the track!"

For the first bridge, Hungate ups the syncopation of the main groove to change the feel. On the top, he adds cool sliding double-stops that outline the changes. "Those were influenced by fills the great studio guitarist David T. Walker would use, and also by Chuck Rainey's upper-register work on songs like Aretha Franklin's 'Until You Come Back to Me,' which is my all-time favorite record." Hungate and Porcaro bump up the intensity during the guitar solo. David says, "Jeff and I tended to start intense and build from there! He was our leader on sessions, the way Jamerson was at Motown; he was our truth meter, and if he liked what you played, he let you know."

★ ABRAHAM LABORIEL BY RICHARD JOHNSTON ★

One of bassdom's most creative soloists is also a veteran of more than 3,000 sessions in a myriad of styles. Already a studio guitarist at 17 in his native Mexico City, Laboriel began playing electric bass while at Berklee College of Music in Boston. After some studio work in Boston, he played on vibist Gary Burton's *The New Quartet*, and then went on the road backing Johnny Mathis with the Count Basie Orchestra. Through that gig, the young bassist met Henry Mancini, who encouraged him to come to Los Angeles. Abe's arm-long list of session credits now covers everyone from Herb Alpert to Joe Zawinul.

How do you maintain both virtuosic solo technique and the ability to fit into any musical situation?

When I first started to make records, I heard that most players who spend a lot of time in the studio quickly learn to become very economical—to get rid of the fat and play only the simple things that are essential to communicate the crucial feeling of that moment. If I overplay, it doesn't translate well onto tape, and some things that I feel are boring or uninspired really sound great on tape.

Among all your sessions, are there any favorites that stand out?

There's an Al Jarreau song called "Mornin'" that was one of the really high points, because we recorded that live. Al was singing with such *power*, the feeling was so strong and the song was so lovely, we literally could have played it all night. It was one of the rare things we got on an early take.

For a while early in your career you used just one bass. Does that in part account for the way you can get so many sounds out of your hands?

I think so. But also, my attention span was really short when I was first learning bass. Pretty soon I started adding rhythmic and harmonic interest, just to make it sound fuller. In my bass clinics, I tell people that all music goes *oom-pah-pah*: the bass is the *oom*, and everything else is the *pah-pah*. So when you practice bass by itself, all you practice is a series of *ooms*, and there's a lot of space between them. You could say that when I was younger, I was incorporating the *pah-pah* into my thing.

★ NATHAN WATTS: STEVIE WONDER'S LEFT-HAND MAN BY CHRIS JISI ★

Holding it down for a force of nature like Steveland Morris Wonder seems an unenviable task. In addition to being one of most prolific songwriting geniuses of the last century, and possessing perhaps the most imitated vocal style since Louis Armstrong, Wonder's keyboard-born left-hand lines have been as influential on thumpers as those of a short list of essential bass players. But none of that daunts Nathan Watts, having played more than 35 years with the man he casually refers to as Steve—a third of that time as his musical director. In fact, Nathan's muscular, rhythm-rife parts on such Wonder standards as "I Wish," "Sir Duke," "Master Blaster," and "Do I Do" have firmly established him as a cornerstone figure in R&B bass. This, in turn, has led to his appearance on hit singles such as Paul McCartney and Michael Jackson's "Say, Say, Say," the Pointer Sisters' "I'm So Excited" and "Slow Hand," Diana Ross's "Muscles," the Jacksons' "This Place Hotel" (originally titled "Heartbreak Hotel"), and Jermaine Jackson's "Let's Get Serious."

Born in Detroit on March 25, 1954, Nathan Lamar Watts was raised an only child on the city's gritty west side. Inspired by jazz great Lee Morgan, he took up trumpet in elementary school, forming a trio with friends and fellow future session stars Ollie Brown on drums and Ray Parker Jr. on clarinet. When he wasn't in school, Nathan would stroll over to Motown's Hitsville Studios to watch through the window as the Funk Brothers worked their magic. Another passion was the rock & roll of Jimi Hendrix, Deep Purple, Rare Earth, Mahogany Rush, and Steppenwolf, many of whom played at the nearby Grande Ballroom—"a rock club in the middle of the ghetto." When Parker Jr. switched to guitar, he and Brown encouraged Watts to pick up bass so they could remain a trio. Watts learned his first bass line, James Brown's "Cold Sweat," and began soaking up the influence of Motor City heavies like James Jamerson, Tony Newton, and Bob Babbitt. ("You had to know Babbitt's bass solo from [Dennis Coffey's] 'Scorpio' to work in Detroit.") By then, Parker had moved on to join Marvin Gaye's band, so Nathan joined a local group called the Final Decision. As a backup plan, he went to school to study accounting. That would all change on a sunny August day in 1974, when his mom yelled down the street to tell him he had a call from Stevie Wonder's office.

How did you come to join Stevie Wonder's band?

Steve's people told me he needed a bassist and someone had recommended me—I later found out it was Ray Parker Jr. Reggie McBride, who I knew from Detroit, was the previous bassist; he had replaced Michael Henderson, who left Steve for Miles Davis. Reggie was doing the road gigs, as well as some of Steve's

West Coast recordings, along with Scott Edwards. But he left to join Rare Earth, so the chair was open. I was told to learn as many of Steve's songs as I could, because they were going to fly me down to Memphis on the weekend for a gig. Here I was as green as an apple—I had never been on a plane. I got there and walked into the hotel room to find Steve sitting with Jesse Jackson. The show was a Push for Equality concert, in front of 250,000 people! There was no rehearsal; we went over a few tunes backstage and we were on. The first two tunes were "Superstition" and "My Cherie Amour," and I was fine. Then they called "Contusion," which I'd never heard, and I froze up! I went over and started watching Steve's left hand and somehow got through it. Afterwards, I was informed they were bringing me to L.A. to audition. At the audition there were two other bassists who were better, more advanced players than me. But I noticed when Steve played a line and asked us to play it back, I was getting it quicker; I'd always had big ears. A week later I got the greatest blessing of my life: They had selected me. From there, we went on a tour of Japan, returning in March '75, and then we began recording *Songs in the Key of Life*, in L.A. and New York.

What are some of your favorite bass tracks?

With Steve, it's "I Wish," "As," "Do I Do," and "I Ain't Gonna Stand for It"; I also like "Let's Get Serious," which Stevie wrote and produced for Jermaine Jackson, and "The Real Thing," which Steve wrote and we all recorded for Sergio Mendes's *Brasil '77* album. And Sergio's version of "The Waters of March," from *Brasil '88*, is cool. My all-time favorite Steve song, although I didn't play on it, is "Pastime Paradise" [from *Songs in the Key of Life*, later adapted for Coolio's 1995 rap smash "Gangsta Paradise"].

How do you and Stevie arrive at a bass part in the studio?

Well, Steve plays keyboard bass on at least 60 percent of his albums, but if he asks me to play on a track he'll usually have a demo or an idea, and he'll have me embellish it and come up with my own part. Then he'll say, "Yeah, that's what I want," or, "I don't like that, try something else." There are times when he has me cut a track first and then he goes with keyboard bass on the final version; that happened on "Isn't She Lovely," "Knocks Me off My Feet," and "Go Home." Whoever I'm recording with, I listen to the song, look at the chord structure, and do what I think fits. My whole concept is what I call melodic rhythm. I try to play something basic and solid, but if you listen closely, you'll hear a lot of subtle rhythmic movement—pickups and approaches. That all comes from my three main influences: Jamerson, Chuck Rainey, and Joseph "Lucky" Scott, who played with Curtis Mayfield.

Can you describe your basic technique?

I pluck with three right-hand fingers, and I have a heavy touch; I was using two fingers early on with Steve, but the day before we played at Human Kindness Day in Washington D.C., he accidentally closed a cab door on my middle finger, so I had to use the first and third fingers for the concert. Sly Stone was on the bill and Larry Graham came over to tell me I sounded great, so I've been using all three fingers ever since! My slapping is conventional: thumb across the strings down by the bottom of the neck, and pops with my index and second fingers. I also like to mute the strings with my palm and pluck with my first two fingers. With my left hand I do some muting, hammering, trilling, and a lot of slides.

Who influences Stevie's keyboard bass playing?

James Jamerson! Think about it—from the time Steve was 12 years old through his early '70s albums, who was he hearing? That's where his bass concept came from. He became one of the greatest, most original keyboard bassists—and Greg Phillinganes, who is also incredible, picked up a lot of Steve's keyboard bass style when he joined us, but it's all rooted in Jamerson.

How about having to play Stevie's keyboard bass lines on bass, live?

I'm used to it by now, since I've had to play everything over the years—"Boogie On Reggae Woman," "Too High." I just learned them all by ear; we've never had charts in the band. *Natural Wonder* is a good live double CD to hear what I do and how I cover Steve's keyboard bass lines. I actually played some keyboard bass on tour with Steve in the '70s. He wanted it live because a lot of his songs had keyboard bass, but at the time, there wasn't anything for electric bass that sounded like a synth bass, so I got an ARP 2600 and then a Yamaha DX7. Eventually, I went back to just electric bass, but I was probably the first R&B bassist to double on key-bass; now it's almost mandatory.

What about playing Jamerson parts?

You know I love all of those: "For Once in My Life," "Uptight," "My Cherie Amour," and "Signed, Sealed, Delivered," which I believe is Bob Babbitt. Knowing the bass line to "I Was Made to Love Her" on that first concert with Steve impressed him and helped me to get the gig. My favorite Jamerson part on a Steve song is "It's a Shame" [by the Spinners].

Stevie is known to be quite spontaneous live.

It's always a challenge; the sets can include anything. That's why I've enjoyed being here so long. While we were rehearsing for the Super Bowl pregame show, Steve tried a tune we hadn't done in over 20 years. He said, "Nate, remember this?" And it was an unreleased song! The rest of the band was like, *Huh?* Or he'll pull out an Ellington or Coltrane cover; he always keeps you guessing. There's no official list, but I figure I know 80 to 100 songs from his astounding catalog. At this point, we laugh because I know him so well; I know his musical patterns, so I know where he's going before he goes there.

★ DEEP CUTS: NATHAN WATTS WITH STEVIE WONDER ★

"Sir Duke." Nate's $E\flat$ tuning required him to bend up at the 20th fret of his '74 Fender Precision to get the high $E\flat$ in the middle of the pentatonic unison riff. "Stevie rehearsed the whole band, and then we cut it live," says Nathan. "Stevie let me come up with the two-feel bass line, and I cut loose a bit on the out-chorus."

"I Wish." "That was cut at 3 AM on a Jazz Bass I had bought. I had been recording all day, and I had just gotten home and into bed exhausted, when Stevie called and said, "I need you to come back—I've got this *bad* song." I came in and he had the eighth-note keyboard bass line, so I joined in, adding my Jamerson grace notes, which he liked. Then he said, "Nate, do this," and he sang some growly roars—so I started adding my slides. The engineer, Gary Olazabal, suggested I plug into an Alembic tube preamp, which he overdrove to get the growl. Other than that, the slides sound angry because it was 3 in the morning and I had to come all the way back to the studio!"

"As." "That was a magical session at the Hit Factory in New York City. I walked in with my P-Bass, and the first person I saw was Herbie Hancock! We all sat there— me, Stevie, Herbie, [drummer] Greg Brown, and [guitarist] Dean Parks—and just grooved. I've never felt anything like it. The song meant so much and the lyrics were so great that as we heard them, we kept taking it up another level. I actually made two rhythmic mistakes—right before the first chorus and right before the last chorus—and I asked Stevie if I could fix them, but he said no, he liked the way they felt."

"Do I Do." Nathan's ten-and-a-half-minute bass tour de force is an all-time bottom classic, packed with delightful fills, Jamerson-like syncopation, and a spontaneous slapped lick at 9:57.

★ THAT SWEET, FUNKY STUFF: OSCAR ALSTON WITH RICK JAMES BY CHRIS JISI ★

When funk legend Rick James died in his sleep at his Los Angeles home on the morning of August 6, 2004, at age 56, few felt the loss more intensely than Oscar Alston. Alston was James's bass player on record and onstage during his six-year reign at the top of the charts. Both James and Alston were born and raised in the same section of Buffalo, New York. The two didn't formally meet, though, until 1978, when Oscar and his local group became James's permanent Stone City Band.

Alston had taken up bass in a neighborhood band at age 15 to stay out of trouble. Inspired by James Jamerson and James Brown bassist Tim Drummond, he worked his way up to stints with Blue Magic and the Manhattans. One night, Rick James keyboardist Levi Ruffin saw Alston on *Don Kirshner's Rock Concert* with the Manhattans, directing the musicians. Impressed, Ruffin recommended him to his leader. Alston brought along three of his bandmates, and the unit worked for James on Teena Marie's debut disc, *Wild and Peaceful*. James had already released his Motown debut album and scored the hits "You and I" and "Mary Jane," but the Buffalo musicians who copied Rick's demo parts for the recordings didn't stick around, "because the money wasn't there," Oscar explains. "That opened the door for us."

Musically, it was a match made in hit heaven. Although rooted in Motown, James Brown, and George Clinton, Rick James acquired a heavy rock & roll side from time spent in Canada playing in the Mynah Birds with Neil Young. Alston and his crew brought the funk back front and center, laying the groovework for the hits to come. As for James's multi-instrumental skills, Oscar offers, "Rick was an amazing talent with a natural feel for all instruments. He played keyboard—which he wrote on—plus guitar, drums, congas, harmonica, and bass." Bass, of course, was what James became associated with, mainly because, liking the look of the instrument, he posed with it on the covers of *Fire It Up* and his biggest album, *Street Songs*, which shows him with his white Rickenbacker—a nod to his rock roots but an instrument he rarely played. Oscar continues, "In rehearsals, Rick would come around and play all of our instruments and suggest parts. His style on bass was aggressive and raw, because he didn't play enough to have a refined technique. He'd use a lot of up-and-down slides and just jump headfirst into a line. That was his main influence on my playing—the attitude, abandon, and presence he had on any instrument. It would pump you up and make you go, Wow, I wanna play along with that!"

Though generally not credited, the Stone City Band played a key role in writing as well as recording James's music. "Rick would bring in songs and ideas for parts, and we'd sort of jam our parts and finish the songs. A lot of his bass lines were conceived, but other times he'd play a one-note groove and rely on me to add my flavor and other notes to it. You could tell by his expression if he liked what you were doing." For 1981's *Street Songs* the band really stepped forward and "had their way with the music," as James had only four songs when recording started. Of the hits, Oscar recalls, "'Give It to Me Baby' was pretty much intact. The only thing I added to Rick's bass line was my inflections. On the other hand, 'Ghetto Life' was a studio jam by the band; Rick contributed only the lyrics. 'Fire and Desire' was a band song—we changed the tempo and chords. Part of it had to do with how Rick relayed the songs to us. Musically, he didn't have the training to express exactly what he wanted, so we would do something in response, and at times he would like it better than his original idea."

The disc's smash hit "Super Freak," which M. C. Hammer would later recycle in his 1990 hit "U Can't Touch This," was an interesting case. On his Web site James explained, "'Super Freak' came about after *Street Songs* was complete. I was listening to the tracks, just riffing on my bass, when I hit on this punky-funky-sounding line. It reminded me of how punkers look funny when they try to dance. I heard it as a goof and never dreamed it'd take off." Alston recalls, "Rick came in with the song and the famous riff, to which Erskine Williams contributed his stabbing keyboard part, but Rick told us he wanted to add a section that changed slightly, and he didn't know quite how. We tried for an hour and nothing was working. I had been playing jazz gigs back in Buffalo between tours, and I remembered how sometimes the bass would pedal while the chords changed, or my notes would change while the chords stayed the same. So I asked the guys to play their same parts, and instead of playing the riff *D–C–B–A–B–G–B–A*, I played *D–C–B–A–C–F–C–A* [first heard 0:43 into the track]—outlining *Am–F–Am* instead of *Am–G–Am*—and Rick said, 'That's it!' He was so happy he told us we were all going to be given co-writing credit. Of course, it never happened! The thing with Rick was, more than having to pay co-writers, he didn't want to have to say his music was written by anyone else."

> "That was his main influence on my playing—the attitude, abandon, and presence he had on any instrument."
>
> —OSCAR ALSTON,
> ON RICK JAMES

In the studio, James had his Rickenbacker and a Music Man StingRay, but it was Alston who always developed and recorded the bass lines, usually on his own Music Man StingRay, direct to the board. Live, James would strap on his Music Man for a few tunes, such as "Fire It Up," with his trademark slides. Oscar would remain on his Music Man, holding down the bottom, and James would riff and fill. In all, Alston played on six Rick James albums, four Teena Marie discs, the Temptations' *Reunion* album, and the James-produced self-titled debut disc by the Mary Jane Girls in 1983 (including their hit "Candy Man"). It was during the making of that platter that Alston, having had his fill of Rick's substance abuse problems and continuing money hassles, left the music business. He eventually resurfaced and moved to St. Louis in 1997, where he currently plays and writes contemporary Christian music via a home studio and a late '60s Fender Precision he bought as a teen.

Rick James's tale is better known and all too familiar. After releasing three post-Alston discs, in 1986 he had a major falling out with Motown over, among other things, sexually explicit lyric content. In '88 he released one album on

Reprise, *Wonderful*. Falling deeper into his drug abyss, he was charged with assault and wrongful imprisonment for incidents in 1991 and '92, for which he served jail time from 1993 to 1995. In 1997, he returned with *Urban Rapsody*, but while touring for the disc he suffered a stroke, and soon after, had to get a hip replacement. Afterward James stayed behind the scenes, writing his book (*The Confessions of Rick James: Memoirs of a Super Freak*), working on a movie bio, and creating his next solo album, *Deeper Still*, which was released posthumously.

Alston reconnected with Rick a few months before he died. While in Atlanta visiting friends, he discovered that James was coming to town to be a special guest at a Mary Jane Girls concert. He paid a surprise visit backstage before the show and was glad he did. "I was with my friend's 20-year-old daughter, and Rick was alone in a room, and when he saw me his face lit up. He gave me a hug and said to the young lady, 'Do you see this man here? He's responsible for all of the success I've had.' And then he toasted me. I had to leave the room, it was so emotional. Later, we all had dinner with the Mary Jane Girls and Teena Marie, and Rick said everything the band and I wanted to hear 20 years before. Then he said he and the Stone City Band needed to do one last tour, so we could get properly paid and credited for all the work we'd done over the years. He even had a few dates booked in the fall." He continues, "I got all the guys together and we agreed to do it. We hammered out more details on the Sunday before Rick passed, and I was going to call him on Friday, August 6, to tell him to go ahead and send us the plane tickets. That morning my sister called with the tragic news."

"They don't make them like Rick James anymore," sums up Alston. "He was so genuine. He was smart, well read, and funny, and people would just gravitate to his personality. Artistically, he was a creative genius. His contribution to funk and contemporary music was a whole lot of attitude and a whole lot of heart."

★ DEEPER CUTS: "READY" FREDDIE WASHINGTON ON PATRICE RUSHEN'S "FORGET ME NOTS" BY CHRIS JISI ★

At the dawn of the '80s, the first wave of Larry Graham–inspired would-be thumb-slingers receded, leaving a number of true slap standards glistening on bassdom's beachfront. Patrice Rushen's "Forget Me Nots" is one such classic. The song was conceived and played by veteran first-call L.A. session bassist "Ready" Freddie Washington. Washington, who grew up in Graham's native Oakland, California, started on upright bass in the eighth grade and switched to electric bass soon after. His mentor was another great Bay Area bassist, Paul Jackson, whom Freddie eventually replaced in Herbie Hancock's Headhunters in 1977. Rushen heard Freddie while performing with the band in San Francisco and brought him to Los Angeles in 1978, where he embarked on a hugely successful session career. His résumé eventually included work with Michael Jackson, Kenny Loggins, Al Jarreau, and George Duke; such hit tracks as Dionne Warwick's "That's What Friends Are For" and Anita Baker's "Sweet Love"; and the bass chair for TV's legendary *Motown 25th Anniversary Special*. "I always knew what I wanted to do: play on records," Washington says. "I scrutinized thousands of album tracks growing up, always thinking, How could I fit in and bring something to this song?"

Freddie brought both his playing and composing skills to Rushen's first six solo outings, but it was "Forget Me Nots" that fueled her 1982 breakout album, *Straight from the Heart*. The song exploded again in 1997 when Will Smith sampled the chorus for his Grammy-winning soundtrack rap, "Men in Black." Washington recalls the writing process: "I was sitting on my bed at home, jamming on my bass, when this line came to me. I just went where my fingers took me, and it wrote itself into an entire song. I made a demo at a friend's house, playing to a little rhythm box he had. I took it to lyricist Terry McFadden, who came up with the poetic flower concept. From there I brought it to Patrice, and she and I hashed out the verse melody, chords, and arrangement."

On the session Freddie played his rosewood-board '72 Precision with new round-wound strings. He laid down his bass line first, along with his friend's beatbox pattern "because it had become an integral part of the song." Next to record was Gap Band/LTD drummer Melvin Webb, chosen by Washington for "a certain lope and swing he added to dance grooves." Rushen followed with her keyboards and vocals, Roy Galloway added background vocals, and Gerald Albright contributed an alto sax solo.

The track begins instrumentally on the main four-bar bass hook, a bouncing slap line that sits in contrast to sparse melody and rhythm parts. "I purposely kept the drum part simple," Freddie notes, "because the bass drives the track and adds all the little subdivisions and 'feel' elements. When it came to the fills, my focus was rhythmic more than melodic. I thought of myself as the drummer, building up to Melvin's cymbal crashes on beat *one*."

The third chorus is marked by a catchy 16th-note alteration that leads into an interesting breakdown bridge. "I wanted to go somewhere totally different with the song," explains Freddie, "so I switched to finger-plucked notes that I muted with my left-hand 3rd and 4th fingers. It's pure Paul Jackson; that's me just coming right out of Paul's bag." After Albright's solo, the song rides out over the chorus, with Washington peppering the bass hook with funky fills. "The bass line is the whole song. If I had switched to a different line in one of the choruses or on the rideout, I

★ **L.A. SESSION GREAT NATHAN EAST** BY CHRIS JISI ★

As a first-call session bassist, Nathan East boasts over 1,000 albums and numerous jingles and soundtracks to his credit. On the road, he's held it down for rock royalty, pop divas, and jazz geniuses. He began his career at 16, touring and recording with Barry White's Love Unlimited Orchestra. After college, he went on to record with the likes of Quincy Jones, Whitney Houston, Lionel Richie, Madonna, and Babyface, while frequently touring with Eric Clapton, Phil Collins, and Al Jarreau.

As a teenager, Nathan's main training tools were the record player and the radio. "I was playing along with James Brown, Motown, the Beatles, Sly Stone, Cream, Hendrix, and horn bands like Chicago, Blood, Sweat & Tears, and Tower of Power. I focused on prominent bass parts, which meant I was being driven crazy by James Jamerson, Chuck Rainey, Verdine White, and especially Rocco Prestia, whose lines I couldn't even play! On top of that, I was checking out the fusion and jazz side—Stanley Clarke, Ray Brown, Ron Carter, and Scott LaFaro."

You became established in the L.A. studios at a time when the bass scene was in flux.

That's right. There was a bit of a void around 1980; Chuck Rainey, Joe Osborn, Carol Kaye, and Anthony Jackson had left town, and players like Max Bennett, Wilton Felder, and Eddie Watkins had pretty much stopped taking dates. Lee Sklar and Louis Johnson were busy. My peers—Abe Laboriel, Jimmy Johnson, Neil Stubenhaus, and Freddie Washington—were all in L.A. a little before me, and they were on their way to becoming established. It was the perfect time for bassists who could read and play. I was fortunate to get a lot of recommendations from people like Abe, Patrice Rushen, and especially Jeff Porcaro. I got tight with all the drummers, and they've remained good friends of mine.

What were your key early projects in L.A.?

There was always a big project going on—Dionne Warwick or Johnny Mathis sessions with 60-piece orchestras. I played on Whitney Houston's and Madonna's first records, and they were complete unknowns then. Lionel Richie was the first major artist to make a big commitment to me and use me on everything he did. "Endless Love" was my first gold record; he also wrote "Lady" for Kenny Rogers, and I played on that.

Over the years, some top bass players have been critical of studio bassists for "sacrificing their artistry" and producing "sterile" music.

I think there's plenty to be said for someone who can create with a lot of heart for a wide spectrum of recording artists under the circumstances and pressures of the studio. The bassists who say those things are invariably bandleaders who seem to have forgotten that the nature of the instrument is supportive. I have a solo side, but I pride myself on being an excellent support system—being The Man next to The Man. A studio bassist is simply an artist of a different kind—just listen to James Jamerson.

You replaced Jamerson's part on "Lady" near the end of his career. Do you think part of his downfall resulted from his reluctance to alter his approach and sound, based on his earlier success in Detroit?

That may have been one aspect of it—but I think it had more to do with his performances not being up to his usual high standards, because of the personal problems he was experiencing. I remember being called to replace one of his parts and refusing, only to find out later that I had replaced him on "Lady."

★ DOUG WIMBISH & THE SUGAR HILL HOUSE BAND BY CHRIS JISI ★

When Grandmaster Melle Mel rapped the immortal phrase "The bass is in your face," he was referring to the imposing lines of Doug Wimbish. In 1979, Wimbish—along with guitarist Skip McDonald and drummer Keith LeBlanc—formed the house rhythm section for the pioneering rap/hip-hop label Sugar Hill. Over the next five years, the trio unleashed a torrent of menacing, machine-mocking grooves behind such artists as Melle Mel, the Sugar Hill Gang, Grandmaster Flash & the Furious Five, Spoonie Gee, and the Sequence.

Working around the clock at Sugar Hill's two studios in Englewood, New Jersey, Wimbish, McDonald, and LeBlanc—who traveled from their home base near Hartford, Connecticut—played on and arranged (and often wrote, produced, and engineered) more than 30 different artists from 1979 through '85. Augmented by a range of musicians, the Sugar Hill house band functioned in the same way as Motown's legendary Funk Brothers. "Like Motown's musicians," explains Wimbish, "we were there at the dawn of a new musical form, so there were no rules or traditions to follow. As a result, we had the freedom to experiment and be completely creative using our backgrounds in R&B, jazz, and rock."

Given McDonald's sparse, percussive guitar punctuations and LeBlanc's preference for the lower half of his kit, Wimbish himself assumed a James Jamerson-like role. On track after track, his forward-mixed bass can be heard covering the entire frequency range while filling the open spaces between lyrics with a wicked assortment of slaps, pops, taps, harmonics, dive-bombing low notes, and overdriven squeals—all locked so deeply into the groove it was often unclear what instrument or machine was producing the sounds.

The single that started an era, the Sugar Hill Gang's "Rapper's Delight," features a rap over a cover of the rhythm tracks from Chic's "Good Times." These were recorded by a group called Positive Force, but Wimbish and company, as the quickly formed house band taking its place, recorded nearly everything else on Sugar Hill, including such mega-hits as "The Message" by Grandmaster Flash & the Furious Five, "8th Wonder" and "Apache" by the Sugar Hill Gang, and "Funk You Up" by the female rap group Sequence.

While earlier cuts retain the organic flavor of the horn-heavy '70s R&B, with a touch of techno and a rap on top, later Sugar Hill tracks feature the trio's amazing interplay with the drum machines, sequencers, and samplers that began dominating the genre. The ever-increasing use of mechanization ended up driving the trio from Sugar Hill by 1985.

Two classic tracks that showcase Wimbish's work in both an organic and more mechanized setting were recorded and released in 1983: "White Lines," the anti-drug anthem by Grandmaster Flash & Melle Mel, and "New York, New York" by Grandmaster Flash & the Furious Five.

"White Lines" begins with a mechanized flavor, employing a hi-hat-triggered sample of Wimbish's bass. When Doug's most famous Sugar Hill bass line jumps in, it prompts a shout of "Bass!" from Melle Mel. Wimbish played the familiar two-note, four-bar phrase with his right-hand fingers, fretting the *A* on the 5th fret of the *E* string and the *C* on the 3rd fret of the *A* string. Of the throbbing, hypnotic line, he says, "The general idea for the groove came from a group called Liquid, Liquid. As for the bass, I tried to be simplistic, through the use of just two notes—but at the same time I wanted to create the illusion of two bass parts overlapping."

The phrase is played countless times over the course of the track's seven minutes and 39 seconds—standard procedure in the days of the 12-inch single. "It definitely built up your endurance—but it was never tedious, because we often recorded live with the rappers right in the studio. That kept up the energy and enabled us to respond to their lyrics with everything from subtle phrase changes to over-the-top fills." In the classic James Brown tradition, relief from eight-minute ostinatos usually came in the form of a bridge section.

Though the feel of "New York, New York" is more mechanized than "White Lines," Wimbish was given greater creative freedom. "The music was written by Reggie Griffin, who laid down a bass part with his Fender Mustang," he explains. "I was then given the part to make my own, which I did by reinterpreting the phrasing and adding the fills."

Following Sugar Hill, Wimbish, McDonald, and LeBlanc remained on the cutting edge by forming the band Tackhead with London dance-music producer Adrian Sherwood. Wimbish went on to become a first-call session bassist in the U.S. and Europe, with a recording résumé that includes Mick Jagger, Madonna, Seal, Living Colour, Jeff Beck, George Clinton, Carly Simon, Peter Wolf, Depeche Mode, Billy Idol, Freddie Jackson, and Squeeze.

Summing up his Sugar Hill days, Doug says, "Like any house band, we were underpaid in general and under-credited as writers—but I'm not bitter at all. I'm proud to have been around at the dawn of rap and hip-hop, and to have contributed to a music that's still going strong."

14.
FUNKY BANDS

★ GET DOWN, GET DOWN: ROBERT "KOOL" WITH KOOL & THE GANG BY MIKAEL JANSSON AND BILL LEIGH ★

For more than four decades, Robert "Kool" Bell's funky bass has driven Kool & the Gang. The New Jersey band's hitmaking career started in the early '70s with tunes such as "Hollywood Swinging" and "Jungle Boogie," which feature strings of jazzy, razor-sharp horn riffs over fat funk vamps.

Kool's first attempt at playing bass was live onstage at Greenwich Village's Café Wha? in the mid '60s with one of the first incarnations of the Gang. "We didn't have a bass player at the time. We played this Herbie Mann tune, 'Coming Home Baby'—which I had fooled around with on guitar—so I borrowed a bass and

played the bass line on one string, the *E*," Bell laughs. "Later on I started to get serious about it, so I began to study by ear." Bell was heavily into jazz, so early influences were upright players Ron Carter, Paul Chambers, and Reggie Workman. But as the band got more involved in funk and R&B, he listened to Motown's James Jamerson.

The Kool & the Gang library of funky bass grooves is huge. Kool has come up with most of them himself—"but if another band member has written a song, he may have his own idea for a bass line, though I usually add some of myself to it." Does he have a favorite? "Well, a lot of musicians seem to like 'Funky Stuff.' I'm quite fond of the first part of 'Jungle Boogie,' with just the bass and the horns. Of the '80s songs, I'd say 'Ladies' Night.'"

During the '80s, the group hired outside producer Eumir Deodato, recruited singer James "JT" Taylor, and focused more on vocals for another string of hits: "Ladies' Night," "Celebration," "Joanna," and "Cherish." At the decade's end, times were leaner for funk acts, and the band suffered financial problems. Thanks to a fair share of hard roadwork and authorized hip-hop sampling, Kool & the Gang have made a comeback and stayed fairly busy.

★ DEEP CUTS: ROBERT "KOOL" BELL WITH KOOL & THE GANG ★

"Funky Stuff." The lower notes by themselves make a simple, on-the-*one* bass part that leaves ample room for the rest of the rhythm track. The upper notes are almost like another instrument voice, and their syncopation pushes the snare hit on beat *two*.

"Hollywood Swinging." Bell's four-bar bass line is a self-contained call-and-response: The descending figures in the second and fourth bars answer the simple quarter-note questions, and in so doing, also respond to the vocals. The spacious groove also leaves room for a guitar response at the end of the first and third bars, which he joins in the second and fourth bars.

"Jungle Boogie." The masterfully constructed bass and horn line ascends and descends the *G* minor pentatonic scale, with well-placed chromatic passing tones and heavy syncopation.

"Too Hot." Bell's bass line rhythm hits right before beat *two*'s snare drum, giving the smooth and melancholy track a boogie-inducing groove.

"Ladies' Night." Similarly, in this roller-disco staple Bell's bass part anticipates beat *four* in the first bar and beat *three* in the second bar.

★ DEEPER CUTS: RUSTEE ALLEN ON SLY & THE FAMILY STONE'S "IF YOU WANT ME TO STAY" BY CHRIS JISI ★

In the sunny summer of 1973, Sly & the Family Stone was still on top with its unifying blend of funk, soul, gospel, blues, and psychedelic rock and anthems like "Dance to the Music," "I Want to Take You Higher," "Everyday People," and "Family Affair." It seemed like an era was ending, though, with Sylvester "Sly Stone" Stewart's erratic behavior having already driven drummer Greg Errico and slap pioneer Larry Graham from the band in late 1971. But Sly had one more gem left in him: the ambitiously named *Fresh*, which hit the streets in early July. The raw, more stripped-down outing was boosted by the bass waves of Graham's hand-picked replacement, Rustee Allen. Sly himself laid down some of the album's bass tracks, but it was Rustee whose lilting line drove the disc's hit single, "If You Want Me to Stay."

Born in Monroe, Louisiana, and raised in Oakland, California, Allen started on guitar at 12 and, in a local band, was assigned to play the bass parts on the bottom four strings. Penciling in a moustache to obscure his being underage, he was soon playing in bars with blues guitarist Johnny Talbot. A stint with the Edwin Hawkins Singers led him to meet Sly's brother Freddie, who hired him for Stone vocalist Little Sister's band. On Freddie and Larry Graham's recommendation, he became a member of the Family Stone in late 1971, recording three albums before leaving and eventually joining Robin Trower's band. He has played with Bobby Womack since 1994.

It was on an afternoon late in 1972 that Allen arrived at the Record Plant in Sausalito, California, to overdub a bass part on the song. He plugged his fairly new sunburst Jazz Bass, freshly strung with Rotosound roundwounds, into the board, and listened to the track, which had Sly's own scratch bass part. Sly stood next to Allen in the control room and coached him through the part. After a few run-throughs, Rustee nailed the first take, making one or two punched fixes.

"If You Want Me to Stay" rides a repeated four-bar progression borrowed from singer Bobby Hebb's much-covered 1966 hit, "Sunny." The three-minute track begins with Allen's pickup and three bars of bass and drums, which reflect his heavy James Jamerson influence. Rustee recalls, "Sly's scratch bass had the bouncing eighth-note pattern, and he told me his concept for the part upfront. When we recorded, he just turned his back to me and grooved with my interpretation, giving a shout when he really liked what he heard. Rather than being controlling, he encouraged the tune's spirit and vibe. He wanted me to be myself and put my nuances in the part."

Several key elements of the part have already taken shape by the time the verse vocals enter. The first is the alternating short-long eighth-note feel, which Rustee attained using thumb plucks. "That's Larry and Sly's trademark bass approach, like on 'Everyday People.' Although I've always been primarily a fingerstyle player, I was able to adapt. It's sort of a light slap in which you hold your thumb perpendicular to the strings and using just the side of your thumb, you strike the string, sometimes using a little bit of your nail. You control the notes' duration with your left hand." He continues, "I learned that from Sly, who is a *great* bass player; he actually took it even further than Larry by incorporating up- and downstrokes—the way Victor Wooten does so incredibly now."

The feel of the part is eighth-notes, but, as Allen advises, "There's so much going on underneath, like the light swing in the 16th-note pickups. It's most important to relax and lay back in the pocket; if you play right on the beat or push it, it's all over!" Allen's important contribution to the part is the use of accented finger pops on the V7 chord turnaround. Note also his preference for the bluesy $A\flat$ against the $F7$ chord in those bars. Rustee's chromatic 16th-note fills reveal his jazzy, Jamerson roots. Bobby Vega, who replaced Allen in Sly Stone's band, enthuses, "Rustee Allen is funky with a capital *Ohh!*"

★ ALAN GORRIE WITH AVERAGE WHITE BAND BY KEVIN OWENS ★

Thirty years after the Average White Band's seminal instrumental funk tune "Pick Up the Pieces" topped the pop and R&B charts, bassist/vocalist Alan Gorrie finds himself in the same place he's been for the majority of those years: on the road, delivering AWB's resonant blend of soul-funk to a devoted international fan base. Says Gorrie, "We were lucky to land a song like "Pick Up the Pieces" and then be able to keep a career going for another 30 years on top of it. That kind of longevity is rare outside of the jazz world."

What kind of a tone do you go for?

I love the "bump" that my Fender produces because it goes so perfectly with the kick drum. That's been my quest all along—to be one half of the *sock* sound that you get when the drum and bass hit together. Rather than stand out as a separate instrument, I like to blend in with the kick drum.

Your bass lines are uncomplicated, but they really propel the songs. How do you develop those grooves?

I often start a basic groove with a busy, multi-note guitar line. Then I try to create a bass line to punctuate that groove. The bass part should take up only a fraction of the space that the guitar is taking, and it should begin to spell out some wider chord possibilities by moving the root note to different places.

Can you point to any songs that use that type of approach?

Motown bass lines are the best examples. James Jamerson sometimes never played the root at all. He would play a 5th or a 3rd, and it would color the chord beautifully. His playing on Stevie Wonder's "I Was Made to Love Her" epitomizes what I call "the Fundamental": the ability of the bass to expand the size and shape of the chord by going off on musical tangents without playing the obvious root note.

★ MARSHALL JONES OF THE OHIO PLAYERS BY KEVIN OWENS ★

"In a 1968 *Downbeat* interview, James Brown said, 'That bass player in the Ohio Players doesn't have any frets, so he must know what he's doing.' He was talking about *me*," says Marshall Jones, original Ohio Players bassist and self-credited inventor of the fretless electric bass. "In 1965, I yanked the frets out of my Fender Jazz Bass, sanded over the grooves, and applied some epoxy. It wasn't a bad job. But then I realized that I didn't know what I was doing, so I started to study position playing—like on a slide trombone. Eventually I started getting proficient."

While there may be some differing opinions on the roots of fretless bass, the Godfather of Soul was right on the mark about the Dayton, Ohio, native knowing his way around his instrument. Jones's silky, sultry, and downright sexy fretted bass grooves anchored such seminal Players tracks as "Love Rollercoaster," "Fire," "Skin Tight," and "Jive Turkey," tunes that helped to define the Ohio funk and R&B sound of the '60s and '70s alongside hits by Lakeside, the Dazz Band, Sun, Slave, and Zapp. Though Marshall left the Ohio Players in 1984, he continues to work as a bassist in and around Dayton, recording commercial jingles and gigging with his band, the Marshall Jones Blues News.

When developing lines, Marshall likes to keep things simple. "I start off with the tonic, because you always have to keep that in your ear, and I think more in terms of tone centers than of scales. I take those four strings and try to play something interesting without getting in the way of the other instruments," he says. "Too many players today get caught up trying to play too many notes. I like to keep you in the groove until you feel me, and then I play a little something to keep it interesting. When I'm recording for jingles, producers tell me, 'Man, just give us the meat. We've got guitar players to add the potatoes and biscuits.'"

Rhythmically, Marshall favors "a quarter-note bebop feel that bounces and swings," but he's more concerned with feel than with adhering to strict time. "When I used to play small clubs, I'd watch the women's hips as they moved. Whichever way those hips went, I'd change my feel to match. Of course I'm cognizant of the *one*, but whatever I do after that is based completely on feel."

A proud citizen of "the Big O," as he calls his home state of Ohio, Jones points to Dayton's geographical location when asked how the city became such a hotbed of funk activity. "Well, Dayton is right at the crossroads of Chicago, New York, Philadelphia, Atlanta, St. Louis, and Indianapolis. We get a little blues, Southern R&B, rock & roll, the Chicago sound—all that stuff is mixed up here. I like to say that God put his heel down right here and created the Miami Valley, and that the Dayton funk is the sweat off of God's feet."

★ DEEP CUT: THE OHIO PLAYERS' "LOVE ROLLERCOASTER" ★

Marshall puts tremendous bounce into the song's main groove, then he really funks it up on the break. "I imagined circus elephants playing bassoon, so I tried to make it sound like that. I've always dreamt of being a bassoonist; the song would have come out even greater if I had been able to play one."

★ DEEPER CUTS: RAY RANSOM ON BRICK'S "DAZZ" BY BILL LEIGH ★

"Music makes your body move—*well all right!*" That's the lyric in the verse hook of "Dazz" by Atlanta band Brick, a song that remains a playlist staple on "jammin' oldies" and "classic soul" radio decades after it topped the charts in 1976. There's hardly a better line to express the impact of the song's thick, syncopated groove, with its juicy keyboard stabs, taut guitar rhythms, and sturdy, memorable bass line. The word "Dazz" describes the group's funky "disco-jazz" fusion, which singer/bassist Ray Ransom says was the goal when he and Reggie Hargis founded the group a few years after both earned music degrees at Morris Brown College. "I had formed a jazz combo and Reggie had been playing dance music, so when we got together we thought that combination would be our niche."

There are two versions of "Dazz": the original three-and-a-half-minute single and the 5:38 extended version, which showcases Ransom's bass playing midway through the added flute solo. In the studio, "Dazz" started out with a click track, Hargis's guitar, and Ransom's Fender Precision plugged straight into the board.

Hargis sang the main bass line to Ransom, who in turn wrote the melody and bridge section. Drums, keys, and vocals were added later. "When you're working on something, you never know what you've got," muses Ransom. "But the first time I heard 'Dazz' played on the radio, I knew we had a hit because you could *feel* it. So three months later we went back to add the breakdown for the extended-play version. For the breakdown, we made a loop of the drums and the keys, and Jimmy Brown—a genius multi-instrumentalist who had only been playing flute for two weeks—created his solo. Then I addressed the flute solo with the bass: I went in, I started to feel it, and I came up with the bass line. I just played it once, straight up, no rehearsal."

Ransom's simple, on-the-*one* bass line sits hard on every downbeat and syncopates in between, with a mix of shortened and full-length notes that gives the line shape and life, especially in the second half of each two-bar phrase. In his pulsing bridge lines, he breaks up the even rhythm with held, hammered octave notes that contrast with the carefully clipped beats.

In the long version, the bass sits out for an instrumental verse, reentering midway through the flute solo with Ransom's thumb-slapping lick against Hargis's backbeat guitar. As Ransom recalls: "The pocket was there; the drums and keyboard vamp were just looping. I was just trying to ride the groove and help it build, using the flute solo for cues. Jimmy got to a certain point in his licks where his solo seemed to need a transition, and eventually, the bass sort of takes over." Indeed, by the time Ray gets into ascending fingerstyle lick, everyone else is helping build *his* intensity. Note how he funkifies the two-bar phrase by stopping short of the *one* in every other bar, instead letting the drums and Clavinet hammer the downbeat. He also gives the phrase's last note a subtle bluesy bend. "I bend strings a lot. It's kind of a melodic attitude I have: It's lead-like, only it's just bass." The entire bass solo has that quality: It's definitely a solo, but it stays down low and holds the pocket together like a bass line.

Ransom, Hargis, and Brown still perform with Brick about twice a month, especially at summer and fall outdoor festivals. As for "Dazz," Ransom reports hearing one of the two versions on the radio at least once a week. What does he think when hears it? "*Mmm!* Still happenin'! It still has the impact of the first time I heard it."

★ **JANICE-MARIE JOHNSON WITH A TASTE OF HONEY** BY E. E. BRADMAN ★

Watching Janice-Marie Johnson perform may make you tired. In between working both ends of the stage—singing, dancing, and playing bass—she simultaneously manages an onstage costume change while talking to the audience and playing acoustic guitar, one foot on a volume pedal. You can bet that at some point in the show she'll launch into the chorused bass intro and disco funk riff of A Taste of Honey's "Boogie Oogie Oogie," the No. 1 R&B and pop hit that earned her a 1978 Grammy.

A singer since age ten, Johnson picked up bass while she was a business major in 1971. Although she took private lessons, she credits bassist/keyboardist Perry Kibble with teaching her theory basics. "He would run over scales, reading charts and intervals. He would say, 'Learn your neck—don't be askin' me.'" She also listened to plenty of Willie Weeks, got pointers from Rufus's Bobby Watson, and hung out with Charles Meeks, Chuck Mangione's bassist. "Two weeks after I started learning from Perry, I was working nightclubs, playing stuff like 'Let's Stay Together' and the Isley Brothers' 'It's Your Thing.' I wasn't making any money, but I was gigging. I was making all kinds of mistakes, but the musicians would encourage me—'Keep on going, try it again!'"

On one of these gigs Johnson, faced with an audience of apathetic military personnel, improvised the words to "Boogie Oogie Oogie." The groove came later, co-written with Kibble, and the bass intro was a chance recording of Johnson warming up. The buzz around the band—led by two women who sang, danced, and played their instruments well—earned them a meeting with Capitol producer Larkin Arnold, who was still skeptical of Johnson's instrumental skills. "We weren't the greatest musicians, but I was doing my thang. I was holding my own, and we were already playing all our songs live." *A Taste of Honey*, released in 1978, eventually sold more than a million copies; two subsequent albums also produced the successful singles "Rescue Me," "Sukiyaki," and "I'll Try Something New."

★ DEEP CUTS: JANICE-MARIE JOHNSON ON A TASTE OF HONEY'S "BOOGIE OOGIE OOGIE" ★

The chorused intro—recorded by chance while Janice-Marie was warming up in the studio—has Johnson moving upward along the *G*, letting the notes ring as she bounces off her '75 Fender Jazz Bass's open *D*'s. For most of the song, Johnson keeps things moving with the signature octave groove, which she played fingerstyle—no thumps and pops, please, at least not until the end of the bass break.

★ MARK ADAMS WITH SLAVE BY THE *BASS PLAYER* STAFF ★

Of all the funk bands Dayton, Ohio, produced in the late '70s, Slave was among the most prominent, bass-wise. The group was fronted by drummer-turned-lead-vocalist Steve Arrington, but it was Mark Adams who grounded the groove with his bold and funky bass work. The group scored hits with the 1977 R&B No. 1 single "Slide," 1980's "Just a Touch of Love," and 1981's "Watching You."

How do you describe the groove in Slave?

From where I stand, the groove begins with bass and drums. In Slave, either Steve Arrington or I would start a groove and it would inspire the rest of the band. That was the only way we knew how to do what we did; we seldom planned a groove. It was spontaneous. What I do is listen for the space between the hi-hat, snare, and kick—the overall ambience and the subliminal sounds.

Your bass playing is really out front.

I've been fortunate in Slave that the band has always given me space to be a melody instrument and to lead the groove. I talk through my bass and step forward like a lead singer riffing; I'm constantly in freestyle mode. Steve calls it "anointing bass." I also look at my bass like a drum kit, using my thumb for the kick and my pops for the snare-like Larry Graham does. That's what I did on "Just a Touch of Love." I don't know how Slave grooves like it does. It's hard to put into words, but it will always be in us.

★ DEEPER CUTS: NATE PHILLIPS ON PLEASURE'S "GLIDE" BY BRIAN FOX ★

At a time when funk had a firm foothold in the Midwest, Pleasure was happy to blaze its own jazzy dance trail in the Northwest. "We were sort of isolated up there," says Portland, Oregon, native Nate Phillips, "so we just did our own thing." The group's fusion-influenced dance music reached its peak with 1979's "Glide." The tune sports some of the finest bass work of the era, as Nate drives the track with his formidable slap-and-pop technique. It's the kind of dense, booty-shaking line every would-be funkateer wishes *they* had written.

Nate spawned the lick that became "Glide" on a visit to his mother's house in Portland. "I had my Fender Jazz Bass with me—I always took it wherever I went. I was messing around playing 10ths, because I had noticed guys like Chuck Rainey doing that a lot. After about 20 minutes of working it out, I taped it and left it alone until our next rehearsal. When I played the line, everybody just fell in perfectly—I didn't have to say anything. I have to give it up to them and their energy and enthusiasm. I'm deeply flattered and humbled by the comments young bass players make about the song—it blows me away. But I didn't do it alone."

Nate kicks off the intro groove with a string of slap-and-pop disco octaves, positioning his hand so his thumb is roughly parallel to the strings and popping with his index finger. Things start to heat up around the third bar, where Nate follows up his hip-dipping hammer-on with a slide into a sturdy syncopated figure. On various repeats of this intro line, Nate fills out his line with muted ghost notes. "I throw those little ghost notes in there to keep the line moving," he says. Nate sits out the fourth bar of the phrase, leaving room for Marlon "the Magician" McClain's snaky guitar licks. Finally the intro gives way to the good part: a tight little four-bar verse phrase that has just about every trick in a funk bassist's tool kit—double-stops, slides, hammer-ons, double-thumbing, triplets—you name it. Nate gets a jump on the verse groove by anticipating the *one*, where he first plucks the verse lick's double-stopped 10ths with his thumb and index finger. At the end of the vocal phrase, Nate's bass line becomes hyper-kinetic as he uses a double-stop slide to connect two impossibly funky licks.

"Everybody asks how I got that tone," says Nate. "I used my '70 Fender Jazz, which has a maple fingerboard with block inlays. I remember putting a fresh set of Rotosound roundwounds on right before doing that take. Our engineer Phil Kaffel said, 'Your bass sounds so good, let's just go straight into the 24-track.' They had to fight to get the bass that high in the mix. I thought it was too much; I love hearing other bass players real loud, but not myself."

Pleasure disbanded back in 1981, but Nate has continued to play actively, producing and playing in the Dazz Band through the '90s. In 2000 and 2001 he played alongside members of the SOS Band, Con Funk Shun, the Gap Band, and the Bar-Kays as part of the United We Funk All-Stars project. Nate continues to find inspiration in exciting jazz and fusion players who can "go crazy," but he feels deeply connected to his R&B roots. "When I hear Motown records I just have to smile, because that's the *stuff.* That's me. Forget soloing; there ain't no messing around, it's holding it down!"

⋆ CHIC'S BERNARD EDWARDS
BY CHRIS JISI, MARCO PASSARELLI, AND BILL LEIGH ⋆

His liquid lines advanced the art of R&B bass playing while almost singlehandedly rewriting the book on disco low end. Yet the late Bernard Edwards's work remains better known via the name of the group he founded with guitarist Nile Rodgers: Chic. Such late '70s smashes as "Good Times," "Le Freak," "Dance, Dance, Dance," "Everybody Dance," and "I Want Your Love," as well as such Chic-produced hits as Sister Sledge's "We Are Family" and Diana Ross's "I'm Coming Out," heavily influenced the ensuing new wave, rap, and dance-pop movements, and continue to have a profound impact.

Edwards, who liked to stay mainly on the first five frets of the *E* and *A* strings for a "fat, chunky sound," once told an interviewer that his subtly sophisticated sub-hooks were mostly a reaction to Rodgers's guitar parts. Nile clarifies, "I would play chords, and he would define my inversions with different notes and passing tones until he came up with his part." Rodgers laughs, "What he didn't mention is he wouldn't start playing until I came up with something he liked. If he played along, I knew the song was going to be cool because Bernard was ten times hipper than everyone else."

After moving to New York at age ten, the North Carolina-born Edwards tried tenor sax and guitar before purchasing a Fender Precision—and a stack of R&B records featuring session heavies James Jamerson, Chuck Rainey, Jerry Jemmott, and Wilbur "Bad" Bascomb—in order to secure an open spot in a local band. A short time later he hooked up with Rodgers while gigging in the neighborhood clubs that dotted New York City in the early '70s. Faced with reproducing hit records in trios and quartets, Bernard and Nile became adept at covering two or three different parts at once. Those skills, along with the solid, four-on-the-floor drumming of Tony Thompson, became the keys to the Chic style.

Rodgers says Chic worked hard to create a unique sound. "We analyzed the Brothers Johnson and Rufus with Chaka Khan, and we decided we needed to have a sound that people knew was Chic when they heard it. We spent a great deal of time working on that." For inspiration, Bernard would also turn to Motown's James Jamerson, Atlantic session great Jerry Jemmott, and Larry Graham, Sly & the Family Stone's slap-and-pop pioneer. "He thought Larry Graham was unreal," says Nile. "He just couldn't believe that technique." But Rodgers also remembers other musicians checking out Edwards's unusual playing style. "When we were on the tour with the Brothers Johnson, I used to see them standing at the side of the stage staring and going, 'How the hell is he doing that?'"

Rodgers explains: "Bernard was a guitar player before he played the bass, but the last thing that he wanted to be was a bass player who used a pick. So he played with his forefinger and thumb, like he was holding a pick. He'd strike the string with the bottom and top of his finger. The strength of the low end comes from his thumb on top and the other three fingers curled up underneath, so he had the fattest pick you could ever imagine!"

"Bernard's fingers would often bleed," says Nile. "If we played a two- or three-hour show, the blood would be dripping down the bass! But he was used to it; that's how he played."

"Everybody Dance" opens with Bernard's bombastic four-bar bass theme, which clips along at a brisk, disco-licious 16th-note pace. During the song's breakdown and outro, Edwards took this riff and went *off.* "'Everybody Dance' was infectious," says Duran Duran's John Taylor, an Edwards disciple. "But 'Good Times' was the sealer. It changed the way records were made. From that point on, all great modern pop demanded a great bass line." The punchy quarter-notes followed by tight syncopation inspired Queen's John Deacon, who wrote "Another One Bites the Dust." Moreover, "Good Times" is one of the few songs that can be said to help launch a whole genre of music, when Sugar Hill Records' house band copped the groove for the Sugar Hill Gang's "Rapper's Delight," the seminal rap song whose lyrics yielded the term "hip-hop."

After Chic split up in the early '80s, Edwards went on to produce Rod Stewart, Robert Palmer, and Power Station, with Rodgers doing the same for David Bowie, Madonna, and Duran Duran, among others. In 1992 the duo reunited for the album *Chic-ism*, and a new edition of Chic began playing sold-out shows across Japan in 1995. It was at the end of one of those tours in the spring of '96 that Edwards, weakened by a cancer few knew about, succumbed to pneumonia at age 43. Rodgers has bittersweet memories of Edwards's final days. "At the last show of the tour, Bernard passed out onstage during a verse of 'Let's Dance,' and when the bass stopped it happened in such a hip place that I thought, Wow, I wonder why we didn't do the record like that? He recovered and came in exactly six bars later, and I turned around and gave him the thumbs-up, not knowing he had passed out! That's how he was; everything he did was musical." Rodgers discovered Edwards's body in his hotel room the next day. "Obviously it was a painful shock," he allows. "But spiritually, we were so tight at the time of his death I quickly realized he went out the way he wanted: playing his music with his best friend."

★ DEEPER CUTS: RUFUS'S BOBBY WATSON ON MICHAEL JACKSON'S "ROCK WITH YOU" BY BILL LEIGH ★

"Wow—cool playing. That was me?" That's how Bobby Watson reacted to his bass line on Michael Jackson's 1978 hit "Rock With You," having not heard in years. Modesty aside, the longtime Rufus bassist acknowledges that "a lot of people like that song and that bass line for some reason," a fact confirmed by occasional queries from fans around the world, asking him about the line. But Watson remembers the rhythm-section session as "basically a jam," with "Rock With You" recorded in an afternoon along with two other Rod Temperton-penned tunes. Ultimately, it would end up as Watson's sole contribution to Jackson's breakout solo album, *Off the Wall*, which—like many Quincy Jones crossover R&B productions at the time—had Louis Johnson's thunder thumb and keyboardist Greg Phillinganes's left hand dominating the low end. Bobby's drum-locked, fill-peppered line is part of what makes "Rock with You" stand apart both from the album's other tracks and from most of the era's disco-funk singles. His groovy, melodic approach helps create the track's smooth, mellow swing, which was perfect for the hip-swaying dance that dominated discotheques and roller rinks whenever the song played. "It's funny," reminisces Bobby. "You go into the studio and hang out for an afternoon, order Chinese food, and just have fun playing, and you never know that stuff is going to be magic."

Watson had already earned two gold records with Billy Preston, playing on the hit singles "Nothing from Nothing" and "Outa-Space," when he replaced Dennis Belfield in Rufus upon the Chicago-based band's move to Los Angeles. His first big single with Rufus was "Once You Get Started," from the 1974 album *Rufusized*. Quincy Jones's *Off the Wall* sessions were starting up just as he and Temperton were helping Rufus finish *Masterjam.* "Quincy liked the way we sounded as a rhythm section," remembers Bobby. "So he said, 'Come on over.' If a band plays together through soundchecks and rehearsals for years, they're going to have a tight sound that's different from a set of studio guys." Along with Watson, the session included Rufus drummer John "J. R." Robinson and keyboardist David "Hawk" Wolinski, with Michael Jackson guitarist David Williams taking the place of Rufus's Tony Maiden. "We got simple chord charts and were told, 'Play what you feel.' Rod Temperton was there kind of directing and setting the tempo. 'Rock with You' was probably no more than two takes with no overdubs, but it was the last tune of the day, so we were warmed up by then. We were swinging."

Bobby tuned his P-Bass down a half-step so he'd be able to use open strings on the *E♭* grooves, but he notes that he would have naturally gravitated toward "sweet"-sounding notes in the middle of the neck rather than playing them in open position or around the 2nd fret. "I'm not one of those studied guys like Ron Brown or James Jamerson," he explains. "Those guys play down there where the string is taut and you get a different tone. But those guys read, too. I don't, so I just play it right where the notes sound best."

The song kicks off with a one-bar drum fill before launching into the main groove, a restrained yet funky drum-locked feel. "I don't really play that kind of *bump . . . ba-dump* kind of beat," says Bobby, whose signature style is more loose and liquid. "But the way I think about bass, the first thing I do is I make sure I'm locked with the drums and try to set up the groove. Once the groove is locked, I start looking for riffs and stuff to try to make it interesting, because it's got to be interesting. You can't be boring." It's not long before Watson begins adding rhythmic variations, but generally he stays tight with the straightforward first-verse drum part by working note lengths and adding ghost note pickups. The sparse groove leaves room for more rhythmic play and phrase-ending fills. Things start getting really deep in the second verse as Bobby starts getting tastefully busy. Dig, for example, his upper-register flourishes between vocal phrases, and how he lets it breathe a bit by playing quarter-notes in the next obvious spot for a fill. Bobby never quite plays the chorus phrase the same, instead letting it develop through constant variations.

The bridge is the only time Rod Temperton's jazzy changes solidly resolve to the tonic chord, *B♭* minor; Bobby punctuates the moment with an accented descending scalar line and a long-held tritone shimmy-slide in the middle of the bridge. "That little melody might have been something new that just came to me that day. But the shimmy thing? I do that all the time."

"When I listen to my bass line now I can hear where I took some risks. More than half of the riffs I played are just things I threw out there, hoping they would stick. For example, I did a lick to lead into the second half of the flute solo that was definitely a risk, but it seems to work well."

The end of the solo marks a modulation up a half-step to *B* minor, with the chorus riff now dominated by low *E*'s rather than the open *E♭* string. "When the song modulated, I didn't play in the middle of the bass anymore," notes Bobby. "I stayed in the 1st-fret position through to the end. There was a song in *F* on *Masterjam* called 'Do You Love What You Feel' that I had been rehearsing for hours and hours, so I got real comfortable playing in 1st position." This outro section is full of luminescent bass moments.

"Louis Johnson redid all the tunes I did," says Bobby, who explained that it was Quincy and engineer Bruce Swedien's practice at the time to link together consoles, record 80 to 100 tracks, and then consider optional parts to see which "snapshot" best suited the song. "Luckily for me they went back to my part on 'Rock with You.' Bruce told me later that Louis played a tighter bass line, but it lost the magic. He said, 'Man, we pulled up that 'Rock with You' track, and we *had* to keep your bass. You were pumpin' it! We took out your bass and the whole song died. Your bass *made* that tune.' That made me feel really good."

★ CAMEO'S AARON MILLS BY ALAN GOLDSHER ★

"Aaron Mills is one bad mutha to have in the studio," says Andre Benjamin, a.k.a. Dre, of hip-hop iconoclasts OutKast. Dre ought to know—after all, Mills's fat lines are all over OutKast's Grammy-winning rap milestone, *Stankonia*. A Chicago-based electric and upright bassist who has been performing, recording, thumping, and slapping with classic funksters Cameo on and off since 1979, Aaron provided the backbone for *Stankonia*'s two biggest hits, "Ms. Jackson" and "So Fresh, So Clean." And in an unusual move for the programmed, looped world of hip-hop, Mills laid down his pulsating lines all the way through each track. Then again, when you dig his foundation-laying with Cameo, his ability to hold it down—and down and down—it shouldn't be a surprise.

How did you get started in music?

My parents were both musicians. My daddy, Elvin Mills, played saxophone with Lionel Hampton, and my mother, Ruth Mills, played in the church. I started playing bass when I was about 11 years old in Asheville, North Carolina. I actually played guitar first, but my family band needed a bass player—and my brother wanted to play guitar. I was just a kid, but I could read music, so when guys like Sam & Dave or Percy Sledge would come through town, I got to back them up. I started playing professionally when I was about 19. I went to college at North Carolina Central, where I met and recorded with [trumpeter] Donald Byrd & the Blackbyrds. Then Donald produced my group the New Central Connection Unlimited in 1974, and we toured with the Blackbyrds.

At what point did you get together with Cameo?

After the New Central Connection Unlimited broke up. One Sunday, I had just gotten home from church, and the phone was ringing. I ran to get it, and it was [Cameo frontman] Larry Blackmon. By Tuesday, I was in New York at a Cameo rehearsal. It was a piece of cake, because I was used to playing jazz. I intended to make some money and bail out; I wanted to be on the West Coast. After I'd been with them for a couple of months, we went into the studio and did *Secret Omen*. When the damn thing went gold, I decided to hang around. We had four or five gold records in a row, and then a platinum album with *Word Up*.

By the early 1990s things were getting rocky for Old School funk bands.

Rap was taking over, and all the A&R people at record companies were signing young talent. Bands were falling off, and it was especially tough on a lot of black acts like us, Con Funk Shun, the Gap Band, and the Ohio Players. It hurt to lose our record deal, but we have a lot of fans, and we still tour a lot.

On many classic Cameo tunes like "Word Up" and "Candy" you pop and slap like there's no tomorrow. How did you perfect your thumb technique?

It's *all* in the wrist. You've got to have a downstroke and an upstroke with your thumb; I used to walk around slapping my thumb against my chest or my leg so I could get that rhythm in my wrist. Sit around with a metronome and practice slowly, and then speed up. It takes time—but who wants to hear someone who can play fast but not slow?

How did you hook up with OutKast?

My good friend Sean "Shyboy" Davis—the engineer for Atlanta's Dungeon Family, the group OutKast is part of—woke me up at 3:30 one morning to work on *Stankonia*, and by 4, we were in the studio. They put up "Ms. Jackson" and we played it down twice. I came back a couple days later, and we did "So Fresh, So Clean," and I also played *that* right down the track—no loops.

What kind of mindset do you need to play hip-hop?

It's a challenge to play repetitively—to do the same thing consistently over and over again. I like that challenge. I can play this simple, same bass line in time, without missing a beat, for five minutes. I could make the energy level keep growing—that doesn't mean the time is going to speed up. There's nothing like a human feel.

Some younger musicians are amazed when I come in and they're expecting me to loop it, and when I say that playing it live is a piece of cake, they're almost shocked. I'll say, "Let me play it for you, and I can expand on it if you want me to. But if you want the same thing all the way through, I can give it to you like that."

★ ROBERT WILSON OF THE GAP BAND BY KEVIN OWENS ★

When Robert Wilson took the call from keyboardist Billy Preston inviting him on a short tour, the then-19-year-old bassist hesitated—not because he didn't want the gig, but because he had to clear it with his mother first. "She told me I couldn't leave because I had other responsibilities that weekend," says Wilson. "But I had to set her straight. The next day I was onstage at the Spectrum in Philadelphia, sharing the bill with Larry Graham, the Whispers, and Blue Magic."

It was the mid '70s, and word was spreading quickly about Robert, whom Preston contacted through Tulsa, Oklahoma, session great Leon Russell. Robert, his older brothers Charlie and Ronnie, and the rest of the Greenwood, Archer & Pine Streets Band—they would soon shorten the name to the more marquee-friendly "GAP" Band—had been discovered by Russell at a Tulsa nightspot. "Leon heard us one night and snatched up the whole band," explains Wilson. "He basically removed his band and installed us."

The Gap Band really took off when the Wilson brothers moved to Los Angeles, pared down to a three-piece core, and hooked up with producer Lonnie Simmons. 1979's "Shake" was the first of several high-energy, synth- and bass-heavy party anthems, followed by "Burn Rubber (Why You Wanna Hurt Me Bad)" and "You Dropped a Bomb on Me."

At the root of the group's influential style lies Robert's vivacious bass work, which anchors the band's groove and provides the foundation for his brother Charlie's synth-bass parts. "I go for a sound that's warm but still has enough guts to cut through," explains Robert. "I put my parts down and Charlie comes behind me. Whatever the lick, he doubles it. He'll cut some breaks here and there, but his parts basically follow mine." Restraint is a key ingredient in Robert's groove recipe. "I don't like players whose main goal is to show that they're technical wizards. Bass is all about creating a mood."

When crafting his parts, Robert—who developed his bass chops in church bands—often appeals to a higher source. "I connect with the spirit and let it take over," he says. "If you think too much about your next lick, you won't be able to find its spirit. I try to take my mind out of it."

Sometimes, however, his inspiration has more earthly origins. "I always wanted to play lead guitar," says Robert, "so I'll play the lead licks that I hear in my head. As long as you leave the bottom on the *one*, you can be more aggressive on beats *two* and *four*. You just have to know how to get back to the *one*. That way you can keep your licks in perspective."

15.
PRINCE

★ **THE ARTIST: A BASS INTERVIEW** BY KARL CORYAT ★

In 1999, during a period in which he had renounced his name and was only known by an unpronounceable symbol, the multitalented yet reclusive Prince granted an interview about his bass playing. He didn't make it easy.

"I like to start by feeling out a person through conversation," The Artist said as I began to scrawl whatever I could in my notebook. I was sitting alone with The Artist in a studio control room at Paisley Park, his recording/performance complex just outside the Twin Cities. For our interview, he had disallowed tape recording and at the last minute, he dismissed the stenographer I brought along. "These walls are completely soundproof. I prefer it this way. When we talk in here, it's your word against mine." Hoping the real interview had yet to begin, I managed a few general questions about the nature of funk, causing The Artist to wax spiritual in his rich but slightly nasal timbre. Finally he burst forth with a delighted cackle and then paused to think. "See that? Would words on a page capture my laugh, or the irony in what I just said? I'd much rather you write about the vibe of our conversation, rather than trying to get my exact words so people can analyze them to death. Why do you need to know exactly what I'm saying? How would that make for a better article?"

Hoo-boy. Beginning to sweat, I tried to explain I had planned a Q&A in which I'd ask very specific, technical questions that would interest only other musicians—in a context where bassists would want to absorb every word. "Then ask me something," he replied. "Ask me any question on that list of yours, and we'll see what happens."

Skipping my planned opening query, I quick-searched the page for the most technical question I could find. "Okay. Do you have a tone recipe for great funk bass?"

Without a pause: "Larry Graham. Larry Graham is my teacher." The Artist continued, veering quickly away from funk tone to God, to all of us being connected by the spirit—but just as suddenly he clapped his hands sharply, jumped up from his seat, and bellowed a joyful noise. "Why do you need a stenographer to type out 'Larry Graham'? That's my answer to your question—it is all you need to know. Just write down 'Larry Graham' in your notebook!"

Things went much smoother once I had been paisley-whipped into shape. Yet it seemed no matter what I asked, the conversation turned to either God, Larry Graham, or both—The Artist freely admitting he modeled his bass style after

Graham's. Prince first briefly met the slap pioneer at a Warner Bros. company pic-nic in 1978, by which time Larry had moved on from Sly & the Family Stone and was a star in his own right fronting Graham Central Station. The two met again a few years later, this time at a Nashville jam. "Larry's wife came up to him and pulled an effects box and cord out of her purse," The Artist remembers warmly. "Now *that's* love." But Graham and the man he calls "Little Brother" didn't devel-op a real relationship until the '90s—"relationship" perhaps being an inadequate description. "Here's a guy who has a brother hug for you every day," says The Artist. "And once Larry taught me The Truth, everything changed. My agoraphobia went away. I used to have night-mares about going to the mall, with everyone looking at me strange. No more." The couple forged an ocean-deep spiritual connection—The Artist is a Seventh Day Adventist, Graham a Jehovah's Witness. "I mean, Larry still goes around knocking on doors telling people The Truth. You don't see *me* doing that!"

> "Why do people feel they have to take credit for everything they do? Ego—that's the only reason."

The Artist invited his "older brother" to Minneapolis, set him up with a house of his own, and welcomed him into the Paisley Park family, "signing" him to a handshake-based deal with NPG Records. Before long Graham was playing with The Artist's band New Power Generation and feasting Graham Central Station on Paisley's incredible rehearsal and studio facilities. And ever since, after years of always picking up the bass for at least a few numbers per set, The Artist has hardly touched the instrument onstage. "I can't even physically reach for it anymore," he laughed. Why? "I don't know. I hope it's out of respect for Larry, and not because I feel inadequate compared to him."

The Artist had plenty to say about the dangers of ego in a musical context. "My first bass player was André Cymone," he recalled, "and André's ego always got in the way of his playing. He always played on top of the beat, and I'm convinced that was just because he wanted to be heard. André and I would fight every night, because I was always trying to get him to sound like Larry Graham. Larry's happy just going [*mimics thumping open-string quarter-notes*]—he's not interested in showing off. When you're showing off it means you aren't listening." The Artist shifted gears to describe a present-day rehearsal and grows excited again. "Space!"

he bellowed. "Space is what it's all about. I'm always telling people in rehearsal you've got to shut up once in a while. Solo spotlights are fun and everything, but if you make music *people* want to hear, they'll keep that tape. You can listen to one groove all night, but if everyone's playing all over the place all night and not hearing each other—not respecting the *music*—ain't nobody gonna want to listen."

The Artist first picked up bass years after he began playing guitar in 1975—which, in turn, was years after he started playing the family piano. "Bass was a necessity," he confessed. "I needed it to make my first album." Already a solid drummer, he translated his rhythmic chops to the bass, and everything fell into place fairly quickly. "That's the thing about playing both bass and drums—the parts just lock together. Lenny Kravitz is the same way. If you solo his drum part on 'Are You Gonna Go My Way,' it sounds like, hey—he ain't that good. But put everything on top and it comes together. He just gets high on the funk."

So how can a bassist achieve that kind of lock with a live drummer? "I'll tell you how Larry Graham does it: through his relationship with God. Bootsy plays a little behind the beat—the way Mavis Staples sings—but Larry makes the drummer get with *him*. If he wants to, he can stand up there and go [*mimics 16th-note slap line*] all night long and never break a sweat." Like the whirling dervishes of Sufi tradition? Exactly. But isn't it possible to create music as deep as Graham's without drawing inspiration from a higher power? "No, it isn't. All things come from God and return to God. I wouldn't say it necessarily needs to come from a higher place—but it does need to come from another place."

The Artist's all-time biggest hit, "When Doves Cry" from *Purple Rain*, is most distinctive because of its lack of a bass line. The song had one but it was pulled at the last minute. "They were almost done editing the movie," he explained, referring to his big-screen debut in *Purple Rain*. "'When Doves Cry' was the last song to be mixed, and it just wasn't sounding right." Prince was sitting with his head on the console listening to a rough mix when one of his singers, Jill Jones, walked in and asked what was wrong. "It was just sounding too conventional, like every other song with drums and bass and keyboards. So I said, 'If I could have it my way it would sound like this,' and I pulled the bass out of the mix. She said, 'Why *don't* you have it your way?'" From the beginning Prince had an inkling the tune would be better bass-free, even though he hated to see the part go. "Sometimes your brain kind of splits in two—your ego tells you one thing, and the rest of you says something else. You have to go with what you *know* is right."

So bass can work against a song then? "Not necessarily. 'When Doves Cry' *does* have bass in it—the bass is in the kick drum. It's the same with 'Kiss': The bass is in the tone of the reverb on the kick. Bass is a lot more than that instrument over there. Bass to me means B-A-S-E. B-A-S-S is a fish."

Prince's first four albums were basically one-man efforts, with a few guest spots (though he kept all bass duties to himself). One of the most prolific artists in rock history, he also wrote, produced, and recorded for others—most notably fellow Minneapolis band the Time. In fact, he performed nearly all the instrumental parts on the Time's first two records, choosing to take only a production credit under the pseudonym Jamie Starr. "I was just getting tired of seeing my name," he explained. "Why do people feel they have to take credit for everything they do? Ego—that's the only reason."

Starting with 1982's *1999*, Prince began crediting a band, the Revolution, on his recordings. Though he still played many of the parts, over the next few albums the Revolution played an increasingly important role. "I wanted community more than anything else. These days if I have Rhonda [Smith] play on something, she'll bring in her Jaco influence, which is something I wouldn't add if I played it myself. I did listen to Jaco—I love his Joni Mitchell stuff—but I never wanted to play like him." The Artist still raves about the original Revolution bassist, Brown Mark (who took over for André Cymone), calling him the tightest bass player next to Graham himself.

With most of my questions answered (or at least chewed up and spit out), I posed another: Of all the bass lines you've created and played over the years, which stands out the most? As if he's answered the query in every interview, he instantly volleys back, "777-9311," from the Time's *What Time Is It?* Why? "Because nobody can play that line like I can. It's like 'Hair,' or 'Lopsy Lu'—nobody can play those parts better than Larry and Stanley." I mentioned I was glad to hear him dig up "Let's Work" for the previous night's show. "Hmmm . . . that might be a tie with '777.'" The Artist gets up and heads over to the bass sitting in the corner but then waves a hand at it. "Oh, 5-string—a mutant animal." I started to scribble down the quote. "Don't print that! People will say I don't like the 5-string because I can't play it. We do have to keep an open mind to things. We need to be open to evolution."

The Artist picks up a phone receiver and—without dialing—summons Hans-Martin Buff, his engineer, who fetches Graham's white Moon bass. "Now imagine *me* teaching Larry Graham how to play this," he scoffs as he plugs into the board and lays into the "Let's Work" line. With no rhythm track, his feel isn't *quite* as slinky as on record, but all the elements are there—subtle ghost notes, vibrato, funky push-and-pull.

Suddenly he stopped and handed me the bass. "Let's see what you can do." As I grabbed the neck he snatched my notebook and crossed his legs. "Now I'm gonna ask *you* some questions." Stalling, I inquired about the XLR jack on the upper horn. "For his mike," he said, as if I needed to ask. I tentatively tried out a generic finger-funk groove in *A*. (I was *not* going to slap in front of the "Let's Work" guy.) "That's *the* sound, isn't it?," asked The Artist. The tone is indeed perfect, but aside from the very low action and super-zingy strings, there's nothing terribly magical about the instrument's feel. And of course it sounded like me coming out of the monitors, not Graham. "Do you ever practice?" I ask, handing back the bass. "Do you get rusty when you don't play for a while?" "No," he sighs, almost bored. "Playing is like breathing now."

We get up and start to move to the door. "I was a little worried there at the beginning," he says. "But it wasn't that bad, was it?" And I'm out of there—but not before one last awkward moment as I shake his hand, unsure how to address him. "It was very interesting. Thank you. Um, yeah—thanks."

★ DEEP CUTS: PRINCE ★

"Partyup." Though this track from 1980's *Dirty Mind* has a technically simple bass line, Prince's loose feel and careful articulation are key to his early style. Early in each bar, the eighth notes are staccato, but then they get tenuto in beats *three* and *four*. Vibrato on held notes is a Prince signature—he uses vibrato somewhere in most of his lines.

"Let's Work." The feel of this slapped line from 1982's *Controversy* is slinky and greasy; playing it straight destroys the vibe. The slid-into note at the end of the first bar is a little elastic—listen to how Prince sometimes hits it almost right on beat *four* rather than a 16th earlier.

The Time's "777-9311." This track from 1982's *What Time Is It?* is a real rhythmic challenge for the ears, let alone the fingers. Though it's in 4/4, the extreme syncopation means you have to internalize the rhythm; like the song's crazy drum-machine pattern, it's just too fast and syncopated to count.

"Automatic." Prince slips in a slick bass solo as this extended album track from *1999* comes to a close.

PART III:
MODERN FUNK BASS

If it could be said that the relatively young electric bass guitar has now reached some sort of maturity, then its moment of emerging from adolescence would undoubtedly have begun with Anthony Jackson. Jackson spent the early part of his career not only developing and refining the musical craft of bass playing per his own exacting standards, but also exploring the possibilities of the instrument itself, working with builders to develop the precursors to the extended range basses that have now become part of the musical landscape.

In the '80s, changing musical styles and the rise of synthesizers, drum machines, and mechanized production had the fortunes of many funk bands and studio funkateers in retreat. There were, however, some major funky developments: First, a young bassist named Marcus Miller created what became *the* sought-after funk-bass sound of modern music. Then, while sampling, sequencing, and synth bass took hold in R&B and hip-hop, a new generation of musicians who had grown up with the sounds of organic funk and soul began to incorporate Old School grooves and funk-bass techniques in other genres of music. First it emerged in an unlikely place: the punk, thrash, and the ska-soaked fringes of rock & roll. Then funky bass began to flourish in churches, driving a new modernized style gospel music.

In the '90s, players like Victor Wooten began to further explore the role of bass as an instrument of full musical expression, developing innovative techniques that helped legitimize bass as a solo instrument. Hip-hop and neo-soul producers began to use more real instruments, incorporating computer-based production with human feels. With artists like D'Angelo, bassist/producer Raphael Saadiq, and session chameleon Pino Palladino, the hip-hop aesthetic began to influence their approach to instrumental grooves.

16.
ANTHONY JACKSON: THE REINVENTOR

★ THE ANTHONY JACKSON INTERVIEW BY CHRIS JISI ★

Driven purely by an unshakable love for, and dedication to, music, Anthony Jackson has consistently broken down musical barriers. His mastery of various pick and fingerstyle techniques and startling ability to restructure instantly the melodic, harmonic, and rhythmic direction of a piece of music mark him as an innovator of the highest order. Jackson has also conducted exhaustive research into the instrument's design and sonic reproduction, and his idea for a "contrabass guitar" predated the current boom in extended-range basses by nearly 20 years. Most important, as an artist, his refusal to compromise his integrity for popular trends has enabled him to retain his individuality in all musical situations.

Anthony Jackson was born on June 23, 1952, in New York City, approximately one year after the introduction of the Fender bass. By age 12, his voracious listening habits, combined with a few years of "poking" at the piano, evolved into a desire to play the guitar. He started out on a standard 6-string but soon began to play bass guitar as well. By the time he was 16, he had moved to bass full-time, drawing from a diverse collection of musical mentors, chief among them James Jamerson, Jack Casady of the Jefferson Airplane, and French modernist composer Olivier Messiaen.

Jackson began to perform locally in 1966 and played on his first recording session in 1970. Two years later, he joined Billy Paul's band, receiving his first gold record for the hit "Me and Mrs. Jones." As a result, he started working regularly with the Philadelphia production team of Gamble & Huff. In 1973, he earned a writer's credit as well as an immediate reputation for his unforgettable bass line on the O'Jays' hit "For the Love of Money." Shortly after, an informal demo session in New York for arranger Leon Pendarvis led to a session with pianist/singer Roberta Flack, and word of Jackson's sophisticated style spread quickly through the Big Apple's studio scene.

A 13-month stint with Buddy Rich's sextet at the drummer's East Side club gave Jackson additional exposure. He then toured with both Flack and violinist Michael Urbaniak before the demands of session work kept him in town. Always one to disdain categorization, he nevertheless became known as a "studio musician," despite his seminal work with fusion artists such as Chick Corea, Al Di Meola, and John Scofield.

Beginning in the late '70s, Jackson reached new technical and creative levels, resulting in some of the finest contemporary bass playing ever recorded, with such diverse artists as Chaka Khan (*Naughty, What Cha' Gonna Do for Me*), Steely Dan (*Gaucho*), Al Di Meola (*Electric Rendezvous*), Paul Simon (*Greatest Hits, Etc.*), Eyewitness (*Modern Times*), and Michel Camillo (*In Trio*).

In 1975, Jackson "terrorized" luthier Carl Thompson into building his first contrabass guitar—a 6-string bass tuned (low to high) *B, E, A, D, G, C* —an idea he conceived while in his teens. Working with successive guitar makers to improve design and playability, he finally began playing the instrument exclusively in 1982.

Although his uncompromising commitment to the contrabass guitar, his refusal to "mindlessly" slap and pop, and the increasing mechanization of music have led to unpredictable career turns, Jackson has remained immutably on course. He fulfilled a lifelong goal by paying homage to his mentor James Jamerson, contributing three transcriptions and a thoughtful analysis to Allan Slutsky's now-classic volume *Standing in the Shadows of Motown: The Life and Music of Legendary Bassist James Jamerson*. Working with Fodera guitars, he continued his development of the contrabass guitar, and fit his instrument around projects with a host of top-shelf guitarists, vocalists, drummers, and composers.

Guitarist Steve Khan observes: "People are impressed by Anthony's technique, his sound, his incredible time and feel, and his innovative work in developing the 6-string contrabass guitar. But on our recordings, the quality that shines through is his unique sense of spontaneous reharmonization. He's willing to step into places where other bassists would not dare to go."

Along with Stanley Clarke, Alphonso Johnson, and Jaco Pastorius, you are one of the original voices of the "bass revolution" of the early '70s. What was the atmosphere that existed then?

There was more of a sense of adventure. Miles Davis's *Bitches Brew* was relatively new and had gotten a lot of people buzzing about new ideas and new avenues to try with rhythm sections. Even before that album came out, my best friend in high school, [guitarist/producer] Reggie Lucas, myself, and many of our friends were experimenting with the concept of putting jazz ideas on top of funk rhythms. We'd all grown up on the Beatles, James Brown, and John Coltrane, and there were endless clubs and loft spaces to play and experiment in. In 1972, I joined Billy Paul's band, Stanley was playing with Chick Corea, Alphonso had left Billy Paul's band and was with Woody Herman en route to Weather Report, and Jaco was down in Florida—a sensation, but not yet having attained international recognition.

Some of your peers in the fusion world were critical of fellow players who became studio musicians. How did you enter the session scene, and how did you feel about the criticism?

I didn't set out to be a "studio," "stage," or any other "type" of musician. Understand that I was a child when I started playing, and my only motivation, reflecting a child's innocent idealism, was to find the greatest music to play and the greatest musicians to play it with. My first major recording experiences were very intense, beginning with Gamble and Huff in Philadelphia in 1972, and later as a freelancer in New York in 1974. One of the first people I came across in New York was L. Leon Pendarvis Jr., a very great composer and arranger who managed to get me on a Roberta Flack recording project he was producing. That led me to one of his other sessions, which is where I first met the great Steve Gadd. Steve Gadd decisively influenced the way I hear music and is really the only drummer I've worked with who has. He is one of the important talents of the 20th century.

You also recorded three albums and did a 13-month stint with Buddy Rich's sextet at his East Side club around that time.

That was an equally rewarding, though totally different, situation. My first experience with Buddy was with the big band in 1973. I came in cold without a rehearsal and got sent home in shame after one show because I didn't read well enough. I boned up and about a year later I managed to get an audition with his sextet and was hired. I would say that Buddy is the only bona fide genius I've worked with.

How did you feel about Buddy's funk and rock conceptions?

Consider that when the various big bands began their flirtation with commercial music in the late '60s, the bass chair, formerly confined to the upright, became a doubler's chair. These people, often upright players of very high quality, generally possessed no redeeming qualities as bass guitarists other than good sight-reading skills. Their interpretations tended to be stiff, clichéd, and generally offensive, reflecting their disdain for the instrument that they usually played only out of economic necessity. On the other hand, genuine, committed bass guitarists capable of bringing good performance qualities to these bands could seldom read well—myself, at that time, included. Understand that big-band arrangers were generally a pretty pathetic lot as well, including some of the biggest names still active today. Their conception of the so-called "New Music" can be judged by the typical style indications at the top of their charts, such as "Funky Boogaloo," "Get-Down Feel," or "Real Funky Here." These bigoted, stylistically limited—however well-trained—writers, working with bigoted and incompetent "Fender bassists," combined to make our instrument a laughingstock. This attitude, though slowly dying out, persists to the present.

By all accounts, it was one thing to play your part while he guided the band, but quite another to initiate something and have him react or follow. Were you able to do that?

Astonishingly, yes. I never got over my fear of him, because he was such an intimidating figure, but onstage I was soon able to communicate with him and persuade him to "dialogue" with me. By sheer coincidence, my emerging Jamerson-based funk conception fit very well with Buddy's busy, polyrhythmically based conception, which was only a modern variation on the way he'd always played.

When did you discover James Jamerson, and what kind of impact did he have on you?

I heard him with the Four Tops on "Baby, I Need Your Lovin'," on which he played upright. Much of Jamerson's earliest Motown output is on the upright, but his character was nevertheless distinctive enough to catch my ear. The beginning of a lifetime of being knocked to the floor and stomped on came in the summer of 1966 when "Road Runner" by Junior Walker & the All Stars was released. The song opens with a classic fill by [drummer] Benny Benjamin followed by eight bars of Jamerson at his best. At that point, I knew I had my mentor, although I didn't know his name.

Was there something specific about his playing?

I could point to his tone or his rhythmic feel or his use of passing tones to redefine harmonic structures, but it was more the mentor relationship. He simply turned the key in the lock, in a very big way. A while later, in 1972, I discovered a 1968 Diana Ross and the Supremes album called *Love Child*, containing several major Jamerson performances and a consummate one—"How Long Has That Evening Train Been Gone?"—and was in a position to spend virtually every waking hour for several months playing along with and studying them. It was probably then that one of the foundations of my style took root.

Having Jack Casady as your other main influence seems like such a striking contrast, much like the vast difference between your pick performances and the way you play when using your fingers.

I was fortunate in having two very individualistic and diverse bass guitar talents as mentors. Casady, whom I'd first heard on the Jefferson Airplane's *Surrealistic Pillow* album in late 1966, had a big, rich, metallic sound with a full bottom and a curious, guitaristic way of playing that I was immediately drawn to. When I saw him perform live, I was struck by his dignity and serious mien. Both he and Jamerson were preoccupied with performance, not hype.

When did the idea for a 6-string contrabass occur to you?

As I progressed, I began consistently observing normal tuning discipline, but I continued feeling constrained when practicing to a particular record whose bass part would drop below low *E*. The numerous recordings of organist Jimmy Smith were important to me because practicing with them helped give me a firm foundation in swing, but there was one piece, now forgotten, that had an altogether different effect: I heard a significant note, one I simply had to play, that was below my range. I realized by this point that tuning down, while it allowed the note to be played, caused a loss of sonority.

For one reason or another, I decided I'd had enough of this very unfortunate need to compromise, and an idea that had been hovering just outside of awareness popped forward. That idea was a special instrument with an extra string on the bottom. This was probably 1970. At the time, I did not possess the slightest idea about how to carry this idea further, so I bandied it about for several months. Sometime during this period, the idea of simply putting an extra string on the bottom along with an extra string on the top began to sound logical. By the time I began traveling extensively, in 1972, the 6-string extended-range bass guitar had become, for me, an inevitability. By 1974, I was ready to search for a builder and begin the unending odyssey with the "big six."

Many of your concepts seemed to come together on the O'Jays' "For the Love of Money" in 1973: the tone of roundwound strings, the rhythmic and sonic possibilities of playing with a pick, and the use of time-delay effects. How did everything fall into place?

To me, the ideal bass guitar sound has always seemed to be the sound of a standard guitar dropped an octave or more in pitch. My acceptance of this principle predates my first experiences as a bass guitarist and can possibly be traced to experiments involving records played at half-speed. Sometime back in the very beginning, I can recall commenting to a school friend on the shimmering, exquisite beauty of a now-forgotten performer's bronze-stringed flat-top guitar heard on a record played at 16 RPM. At the time, I simply could not accept not being able to achieve this sound, even if my intention was not to use it all the time. A few people—Jack Casady, John Entwistle, and the Dead's Phil Lesh—achieved a sound that at least seemed to be on the right track.

I decided to try roundwound strings in 1972, when they were still a novelty and people were saying, "Don't be a fool. They're noisy, they'll eat your frets, and they make the bass sound too much like a guitar." They were a revelation. Combined with the flatpick, which I had been using since the beginning as well as fingerstyle, my instrument assumed an identity completely removed from my Jamerson self, accentuating Casady's influence.

Around the same time, the Maestro company released a phase shifter. I knew the theory behind the device, and I heard it demonstrated by a guitarist one day at Manny's Music in New York City. Henry Aldrich, the owner, insisted that the box simply would not work for me: "It's for guitar, not for bass." I bought it anyway, and when I plugged it in at home, the world changed. I was completely flabbergasted. Here was a sound I had never heard—it was beautiful and just plain *right*. After a few weeks, I took the unit apart and located the intensity adjustment. I did some careful tweaking and was able to subtly enhance the effect.

That particular unit and my recently purchased Fender Precision were used on "For the Love of Money." That was, as far as I know, the first time a recording was made with a phased bass guitar. Kudos to [producers] Gamble and Huff for taking a chance on the sound—I loved it desperately, but it was still alien to the marketplace, as was the right-hand technique I was using with it. It would have been understandable had they elected to follow a more conservative approach, as was their norm. The success of the record clearly vindicated my decision to incorporate the pure guitar-consciousness brought forth by the roundwound string-and-pick endeavors. I continued experimenting until I met Al Di Meola in 1975, when he saw the possibilities and thereafter provided a powerful developmental stimulus.

On Chaka Khan's *Naughty* and *What Cha' Gonna Do for Me*, you were able to express highly creative ideas while not only supporting the songs but kicking the hell out of the grooves. Is that the most freedom you've ever been given as a sideman?

Certainly those recordings are among the best examples of blatant commerciality infused with high art that I've been involved with. The basic tracks went down quickly and easily. They probably could have been left untouched, ready for overdubs and sweetening, were it not for my inability to find anything good to say about my own performances. They were competent, but I was absolutely not thrilled, and this was unacceptable. This situation has generally prevailed throughout my career, and in most cases I have had no recourse but to stuff a sock in my mouth and go quietly home. Those who know me, of course, know that often the sock came out and I let everyone know that if they had any sense they would let me redo my parts until I felt they were right. For the most part, this got me nowhere, though I did make many close enemies.

I will probably never know what could have been going through the minds of Chaka and her producer, Arif Mardin, in allowing me to redo every single note of every single track I played on. To make a fascinating but long story short, *Naughty*, which was recorded in New York in 1979, went on without concern for the bass tracks. I was given absolute artistic license, with one exception, and an unheard-of amount of time—three months—to recompose the bass parts, whereupon I notified Arif of my readiness to record. I was then given all the studio time that I required. I never found out how much my indulgence cost Chaka, but the end result is as pure an example as exists, in my own case, of the ends justifying the means.

The performances represent, with only scattered exceptions, the peak of my creative abilities at the time and in that genre. They are, hopefully, only elemental today, but I recall listening to the final mixes just before release and realizing that I was able, for the first time, to hear evidence of a defined, mature, and effective style coming through my playing. This was a revelation, a coming-of-age, and, I hoped, proof that my stubbornness in playing what I heard despite intense pressure to "conform or else" was paying off. The succeeding album, *What Cha' Gonna Do for Me*, recorded in Montreux in 1980, was made along similar "highbrow" lines, but with the first signs of an end of an era in sight—the budget was down and the time restricted—although the end result remains impressive.

Unfortunately, reality closed in around us after that album, and the crucial prerequisites to recordmaking of this quality are difficult to come by today. Producers are no longer inclined to grant sidemen, however esteemed, unlimited control of anything, and certainly time is more tightly rationed than anything else. The right combination of players is now highly unlikely, inasmuch as a full rhythm section is seldom seen. Machine augmentation is the rule. Most important of all, few artists of major stature have ever possessed the patience, supportiveness, musicality, and virtuosity of Chaka Khan. I've worked with countless singers, from divas to bicycle pumps, and none has been able to gather and harness such powerful creative forces as Chaka.

★ DEEP CUTS: ANTHONY JACKSON ★

Like most bassists, gospel session player Joel Smith first appreciated Anthony Jackson upon hearing the O'Jays' 1973 smash "For the Love of Money." He went on to study AJ's prodigious '70s and '80s studio output, and he remains firmly rooted in Jackson's sophisticated groove aesthetic. "Whatever he does, he's ferocious with it. At the same time he really knows his place, and you can hear his discipline." Here are five of Joel's favorite Jackson tracks.

Tania Maria's "Encanto Meu."

Chaka Khan's "Any Old Sunday." "The whole album is great. It's just an R&B setting, but he was playing some stuff!"

Quincy Jones's "Tell Me a Bedtime Story." "He has a certain approach that's hard to put into words. It's just a feel I understand."

Dave Grusin's "Montage." "I like the way Anthony is countering Steve Gadd's hi-hat and snare groove. I listen to how people make their space, because there are so many ways of going about it. That's what makes it intriguing."

Earl Klugh's "Keep Your Eye on the Sparrow." "It's a very simple line, and Anthony's using the phaser—one of the ways I can tell it's him."

Of the three consecutive Warner Bros. albums with Chaka Khan—*Chaka* (1979), *Naughty* (1980), and *What Cha' Gonna Do for Me?* (1981)—*Naughty* stands as Jackson's favorite, and a testament to an era of craftsmanship and indulgence long gone from the record business, and the track "Move Me No Mountain" best demonstrates Jackson's full range of skills: deep-in-the-pocket, precisely executed grooves; angular, bar-crossing fills; Jamerson-esque chromaticism; and a take-no-prisoners fearlessness and tenacity. Nathan East, who switched to 5-string after hearing Anthony's contrabass in the early '80s, says, "Anthony's performance on 'Move Me No Mountain' should be studied by all bassists as an example of a perfect bass part. For me, it was one of the greatest contributions to a song from the bass I had ever heard, and it represents a standard of creativity that should be the barometer for all of us who consider ourselves to be studio bassists."

MARCUS MILLER
(© PETER VAN BREUKELEN/REDFERNS)

17.
MARCUS MILLER: THE NEW STANDARD

★ MARCUS MILLER: THE QUINTESSENTIAL
MODERN BASSIST BY CHRIS JISI ★

When Marcus Miller was a 21-year-old studio-bass phenom, he told an interviewer: "I know there are a lot of people who would love to be studio bassists, and I'm very fortunate. But for it to happen so fast lets me know there must be some place further to go." Prophetic words. Since then, Miller has gone from being a much-sought-after bassist to a much-sought-after producer, arranger, and multi-instrumentalist in the pop, R&B, funk, and jazz fields. Best known for his chart-topping collaborations with saxophonist David Sanborn, vocalist Luther Vandross, and legendary bandleader Miles Davis, Miller's additional credits range from the Queen of Soul (Aretha Franklin) to the Chairman of the Board (Frank Sinatra). In between, Marcus has managed to sustain careers as a solo artist and film composer. All the while, a generation of bassists has tried to emulate his sound and musicality. The Marcus Miller sound is *the* sound of modern funk bass.

Marcus Miller was born on June 14, 1959, in Brooklyn and raised in Rochdale Village, in the Jamaica section of Queens, New York. His initial enchantment with music began in church, where his father, an organist, performed everything from classical music to gospel. Marcus acquired a taste for jazz as well, after hearing Wynton Kelly, a second cousin, play the piano. Inspired by what he heard, Marcus began singing, and then, at age ten, he took up the clarinet. Soon after, the pop sounds of such artists as Kool & the Gang, Stevie Wonder, the Jackson 5, and Isaac Hayes started to draw his attention. With little chance of getting into a local band as a clarinetist, he tried saxophone and organ before latching onto the bass at age 13. With help from his parents, he bought a semi-hollowbody Univox bass before moving on to his first Fender Jazz Bass.

While it was his aptitude on clarinet that gained him entry into New York City's prestigious High School of Music & Art and then Queens College, it was Miller's attitude on bass that landed him his first pro gigs with such local talent as Harlem River Drive and keyboardist Lonnie Liston Smith. Still a teenager, he made his first recording with flutist Bobbi Humphrey and went on the road with a fellow "Jamaica boy," drummer Lenny White. When Marcus returned, drummer Buddy Williams, his section-mate in Humphrey's band, got him an audition for the *Saturday Night Live* band. There he met Sanborn, who integrated the bassist into his *Voyeur* album and subsequent tours. Miller soon began to get calls for jingle and record dates, and he also joined Roberta Flack's band, where he met a backup singer named Luther Vandross. By the time Miles Davis called in 1981, the music world seemed to be unanimously acknowledging that it was, indeed, Miller Time.

As a slapper, you've developed a reputation for having a clear sound and for using mostly your thumb with only the occasional pop.

I strike the strings right in front of the chrome neck-pickup cover, not at the bottom of the neck where you get all the overtones. A lot of times I don't pluck at all. That developed during my jingle days, because I found that using my thumb was the best way to hear the bass coming out of a tiny TV speaker. Plus, if you use two alternating fingers, as I do when I play fingerstyle, there's always a strong note followed by a weak one; with the thumb, every note is strong. That became really important when I started doubling sequenced keyboard-bass parts. Then I began challenging myself to see if I could develop the speed to play entire charts using only my thumb. I still add plucks whenever they're necessary, as they were on "Teentown." But I think a lot of players tend to overuse them. The plucks are just accents, after-thoughts—the funk is in the thumb.

> "Ultimately, you should be able to lay down the baddest groove and blow the hottest solo."

Let's talk about your left-hand technique, especially with regard to intonation on the fretless.

Playing a 4-string requires a lot of hand-position changes; fortunately, studying bebop helped me to get up and down the neck. I'm basically a one-finger-per-fret guy. As far as the fretless goes, it's important to stick with one instrument and find where the pressure points on your fingers are in relation to the notes on the neck. Beyond that, you just have to keep putting in time, really using your ears. I'll check myself with open strings, but it's always a battle—especially when you play with other instruments that use tempered tunings, like keyboards.

How did you develop your muting technique?

That started when I was 21 and playing in [percussionist] Ralph MacDonald's rhythm section with [drummer] Steve Gadd, [keyboardist] Richard Tee, and [guitarist] Eric Gale, doing jingles and backing people like [saxmen] Grover Washington Jr. and Sadao Watanabe. Eric doubled on electric bass before me, and one day Ralph put on a track they'd done and said, "C'mere kid. Here's what a bass should sound like." I imitated it and he was thrilled. The way I do it is by muting the strings with my right palm near the bridge and plucking with my thumb. Sometimes I'll use a pick if I want more speed. You can also get a decent upright sound with muting.

How would you sum up your relationship with Miles?

Miles was like a musical father to me. In 1980, I was booked to play on a session for him, but he never showed up. A year later, during a country date, I got a note saying, "Call Miles." He answered the phone and asked me to meet him at CBS Studios in an hour. I went in and introduced myself and played with everybody for a while without much being said. When we were finished, he asked me to join his band. Early on, he occasionally gave me a hard time, but he was always very supportive and proud of my session career. He used to tell his girlfriend, "This is Marcus Miller. He drives a BMW." Eventually, as we grew together musically, he placed entire projects in my hands, which was incredibly scary yet extremely encouraging. In retrospect, I would say that my bass style solidified on *The Man with the Horn*, and my composing took giant strides beginning with *Tutu*.

The melody on "Panther," from *The Sun Don't Lie*, reminds me of Stanley Clarke.

I tried playing it with my thumb, and when I switched to my fingers for a bit more articulation and speed, the sound paled in comparison. I knew the only way to combine both approaches was to move my fingers closer to the neck and pluck very hard to get that popping sound. I wasn't trying to sound like Stanley, but he was certainly an important influence. At the time, to hear a young black musician come out of nowhere with such amazing technique and that aggressive bass-in-your-face sound was an inspiration.

What other bassists had an impact on you?

Robert "Kool" Bell, James Jamerson, Rocco Prestia, and all the Jacksons—Jermaine, Paul, and Anthony. I got into slapping through Larry Graham during his Graham Central Station period. In my neighborhood, if you couldn't play like Larry, you might as well put the bass down. We used to have slap competitions on a little cafeteria stage in high school to attract girls. When fusion hit and piqued my interest, I was fortunate to have a friend, [drummer] Kenny Washington, who sat me down and played me the history of jazz, which put things in perspective. That got me into upright players like Paul Chambers, Sam Jones, Ron Carter, and Eddie Gomez. Then Jaco came out and blew my mind. He had it all covered; I left his first album on my turntable for two years and learned every solo note for note. But without a true knowledge of harmony, I had no idea what the notes meant. Jaco's playing and writing were like a wake-up call; it led me to study bebop, which really got my harmony together.

How about Miles Davis's bass players?

For me, *the* bass player with Miles was Paul Chambers, especially at a tempo like the one on this tune. People think of him mainly as a groovemaster, but check out his bowed solo on "Moment's Notice" [on John Coltrane's *Blue Train*]. Coltrane handed him the changes and they recorded it! He's *the* cat as far as I'm concerned. He doesn't get his due.

Who are some of your favorite bassists today?

I don't get to hear that many players, but the guy I really like is Pino Palladino. Doug Wimbish is wicked. John Patitucci is bad, and so is Victor Wooten. And Anthony Jackson, of course.

How did your tone evolve?

I was pretty young when I started in the studio, and I assumed all engineers were experts at recording bass. So when they'd plug me into a direct box and ask for full volume, I'd turn the knobs on my Jazz Bass all the way up, and that became a key to my sound. Eventually, I started pulling the front pickup back a bit for certain situations. The more I recorded and began developing a style, the more I became aware of the sound I was looking for. When I met Roger Sadowsky in 1979, he took an interest in my playing and asked a lot of questions. Through his knowledge of wood and electronics, that sound became a reality. People describe it as being very bright, but what they don't realize is that they're also hearing clarity and punch over the full tone range.

How did you get your start as a composer?

I used to watch my cousin, Denzil Miller, write for a local band we were in, Harlem River Drive, and I just assumed you weren't a complete musician unless you wrote your own material. Later, when I met Sanborn in the *SNL* Band, I gave him a demo of some fusion tunes I'd written and he asked to record them. Shortly afterward, I began writing vocal demos with Luther Vandross; he's so talented I was able to gain a lot of insight. What I always try to do when I write for another artist is see his face in my mind. If I can envision him moving to the music, then I know it's appropriate. It was difficult trying to use that method for my songs on this album, though, since it's hard to get an objective view of yourself.

When you talk to young players, do you stress the importance of playing grooves?

No. Telling young players they have to play grooves is like telling painters they have to use blue. You have to encourage beginners to do whatever turns them on, because that's what they're going to do best. When they get a bit older, you can tell them the realities of the music business—that there are more opportunities to work if they learn to function as a bass player. The important thing is to listen to as much music as possible. The young ear is naturally drawn to the high frequencies played by solo bassists, but if you listen to a lot of groove players, you'll get caught up in that as well. Ultimately, you should be able to lay down the baddest groove *and* blow the hottest solo.

★ DEEP CUTS: MARCUS MILLER ★

"Run for Cover." Marcus Miller's composition "Run for Cover" first appeared on David Sanborn's 1980 album *Voyeur*, and it was recut on the live-in-the-studio 1984 Sanborn disc *Straight to the Heart*. As for his eight-bar slap solo, Marcus laughs: "A lot of people get hung up on this, but if you take out all that fast stuff and play what's left, what you have is Larry Graham." Two funky "Marcus-isms" to look for: his frequent use of the flatted 5th as a "blue note" approximation, often attained by bending up from the 4th; and his use of upper-register, slurred, descending runs.

"Boogie On Reggae Woman." Marcus's cover of this Stevie Wonder classic appears on his 2005 solo album *Silver Rain*. On the descending 7-chord opening—it was a warmup that he ended up liking—he thumb-slaps the roots and flamenco-plucks the 7ths and the 3rds, before using hammer-ons and pull-offs to cop Stevie Wonder's original synth bass line. "I wanted to claim that bass line for bass guitar! Stevie Wonder's part is brilliant; he's got his whole heart and soul in it, and it was really hard to make it sound natural on the electric. I listened to the original to remember all the lines, because he never plays the same thing twice—no doubt from his Jamerson influence."

Luther Vandross's "Bad Boy/Having a Party." Crooner Vandross's second album opens with tons of attitude, courtesy of Marcus Miller's thumb.

18.
FUNK MEETS ROCK

★ FLEA: FUNK CHOPS WITH PUNK ATTITUDE BY KARL CORYAT AND
SCOTT MALANDRONE, FROM 1992 AND 1995 INTERVIEWS ★

Flea's personal musical interests are centered around jazz, but it's the energy and
ethos of punk mixed with the style and techniques of funk that have driven him
and his band, the multimillion-selling Red Hot Chili Peppers. Despite three times
being voted Best Funk Bassist in the early '90s—granted, it was at the pinnacle of
funk-rock's ascendance—Flea would describe himself less as a funk bassist and
more as a player with an individual style, firmly grounded in punk. "My playing
has always been very physical," he noted in 1992. "A constant *whackeda-whacke-
da-whack*. I don't do it to impress people; I just play what's fun. Understand that
my roots are in punk, which was all about playing hard, fast, and loud. As the
Chili Peppers got more and more funky, it was a natural evolution: the energy of
punk translated into the music we felt like writing." Flea has also plied his funky
chops on such hit songs as Alanis Morissette's "You Oughta Know" and Young
M.C.'s "Bust a Move."

How did you first start slapping?

In high school, I saw some guy slapping on a bass, and I thought, "Wow,
that's cool." So I started doing it. When I got into punk, the way I slapped wasn't
really funky; it was more like WHUM—BACKA—BACKA—BACKA! as hard
as I could, just *abusing* the bass. I was really into the punk ethic: Play every note
like it's your last! You could be dead tomorrow! Play for today! You do it because
you mean it: You're pissed, because things are twisted. And that's beautiful—the
punk thing is so honest and sincere. Even though the music and the genre were
finished a long time ago, the intensity is still important to me. And a pretty song
can be just as intense as a hard, thrashing song.

**There are a bunch of different styles mixed together in the bass line of
"Aeroplane," from 1995's *One Hot Minute*. How did you come up with the
slap part in the verses?**

I was sitting in my garage with a bass Louis Johnson gave me—a Treker Louis
Johnson Signature 4-string—and I started playing that '70s funk line. The bass
had light strings on it and had that *whacka-whackita* sound. It's kind of a "been
done" groove, but it's nice and Anthony liked it. Actually, "Aeroplane" was the
only song [on *One Hot Minute*] I was worried about—I thought it sounded like
another stupid white boy trying to be funky! [*Laughs.*] I put it out anyway, but it's
the one thing I'd go back and fix. It was one of the few things I had to overdub.

The part kept feeling stiff to me, as if it wasn't my day; I wasn't flowing with the drums. I wanted to redo it, but Rick [Rubin] said, "It's cool."

What's your opinion of the role of the bass?

It's difficult to generalize, but I like hearing the bass when it's really locking in with the drums. I like it simple. I like it when it makes you want to make love— that warm, good feeling. Very seldom do I enjoy bass playing that takes center stage; even on a funk song where the bass is the focus, such as Funkadelic's "(Not Just) Knee Deep," it's just a funky groove—it's not "Look at me." Plenty of bass players have fancy chops, but they don't make you feel any emotions. You don't feel anger, fear, or love. That's what I call "all flash and no smash," a phrase I got from Lonnie Marshall of the band Weapon of Choice. Lonnie's one of the funkiest bass players alive today—I've *totally* copped stuff off him.

★ LES CLAYPOOL: EMBRACING THE MIX BY KARL CORYAT ★

Les Claypool is one of very few rock musicians to make a name for himself with bass in hand, but what makes him so unique is what he does with that bass: a tripped-out goulash of wild rock and freaked-out funk techniques, whether with the groundbreaking quirk-rock of Primus or his various other projects, including Oysterhead, Les Claypool's Frog Brigade, and Colonel Claypool's Bucket of Bernie Brains. Les isn't shy about calling out Rush frontman Geddy Lee as one of his all-time bass heroes, but his bass approach owes just as much to the pioneers of funk.

How did you discover funk?

One day, a friend of mine said, "Geddy Lee is good, but he's nothing compared to Stanley Clarke and Larry Graham." I told him he was crazy, even though I didn't know who those guys were. Then I saw Stanley's *I Want to Play for Ya* in a record store. I bought it, and it blew my mind. I also saw Louis Johnson on [the TV show] *Don Kirshner's Rock Concert*, saw him go *bang-bippety-bip-bang*, and thought, "Man, that's the coolest thing!" By my junior year, I was getting way into all the funk players. Guys would give me shit and call me "Disco Les" because I was playing all this funk stuff.

Around my senior year, I bought an Ibanez Musician EQ bass. I had always wanted a Rickenbacker before, but then I decided the Rickenbacker was no longer the cool bass to have. I hung around Leo's [music store] in Oakland all the time; they had tons of new and used stuff. One day, I saw a Carl Thompson piccolo bass sitting there. I had stared at the photo in *I Want to Play for Ya* where Stanley had all his basses lined up, and a couple of them were Carl Thompsons. I always thought, "Man, that sure is an ugly bass." I picked up the one in the store, though, and I couldn't believe it—it was so easy to play. It's still my main 4-string. In the '80s, it wasn't cool to have a fancy-woodwork custom bass; it was cooler to have a pink one or something the color of toothpaste. So people were constantly giving me shit for having a bass that looked like some weird piece of furniture.

Where did you pick up the strumming technique?

From Stanley Clarke, because of songs like "School Days." The first time I saw Stanley shoot the ol' chords—he'd start at the top and go *pow!* [*mimes strumming and sliding a chord down the fingerboard*]—I thought that was way cool, and I decided to do it. It hurt like hell when I first started.

Did Stanley also inspire you to start slapping?

Yeah, him and Louis Johnson. Louis's right arm would go way out away from the bass. Stanley, though, used minimal hand movement, and I was always into the minimal hand-movement thing. A friend of mine told me your thumb should just *graze* the string and rest against the next one, as opposed to whapping the string and bouncing off it. My thumb got pretty fast, since I was more into thumbing than plucking.

One thing that helped me a ton, probably more than anything in my career, was playing with a group called the Tommy Crank Band. I had been playing fusion, and when I played with them the first time I was like *bloobilla-bloobilla-bloobilla!* They said, "Cool," and I got the gig. I had to learn all these blues and R&B tunes; we played everything from James Brown to John Cougar. A lot of the time I overplayed, and everyone else in the band was always clamping down on me to mellow out. By playing these tunes four hours a night, three to five nights a week, my groove got really good, and I learned to improvise and pull off songs we hadn't even rehearsed.

★ ROBERT TRUJILLO: INFECTIOUSLY FUNKY
BY KARL CORYAT AND BILL LEIGH ★

Robert Trujillo grew up listening to his mother's Motown music and his father's roots rock: That explains why he became a natural at funk-rock bass. These days, as a member of Metallica, Robert Trujillo has largely put his huge thumping thumbs on the shelf. But when he joined perennial hardcore outfit Suicidal Tendencies in 1989 and helped form funk-rock offshoot Infectious Grooves, Trujillo had one of the hardest hitting thumbs in the business.

From a 1994 interview:

Do you have different approaches playing with Infectious and Suicidal?

With Infectious I have to concentrate a little harder live, because the bass and drums really carry the band. With Suicidal, everything's centered around the rhythm guitars and the drums; it requires a little more simplified—but equally intense—style, with a lot of slapping but not much popping. When I slap with Suicidal, I do it just to get a percussive effect; that way I'm complementing the rhythm and it sounds heavy, but it doesn't step on the guitar. I just let the bass add color.

How did you get started playing bass?

My dad played flamenco guitar, and when I was about eight years old I start-ed messing around with his guitar, playing it with just two right-hand fingers. Later I had a cousin who turned me onto Parliament/Funkadelic, the Ohio Players, and James Brown. That got me moving toward bass. When I was 18 I got my first real bass—a Kramer with an aluminum neck. By then I had started exper-imenting with slap. I wasn't very good at it, though; I would practice and practice, and then I'd listen to Larry Graham and get frustrated. That stuff was like Japanese to me—so I decided not to learn bass lines note-for-note. I realized music like that was based on feel, so I decided it was more important for me to develop my own feel. I knew a lot of people took things from records, but I decided I wanted to take *ideas* and use them my own way.

From a 2008 interview:

You've got these monster slap chops that you used for years with Suicidal and Infectious, but between Ozzy and Metallica, you haven't really had the chance to use them. Do you miss it?

I do. With Metallica I play pretty hard, and some of my fingering technique is almost borderline slap, but just with the fingers. There's a lot of fretboard attack and digging in, much the same way as if I were hammering down with the thumb. People tend to think Metallica fans or metal fans are very strict about what they like, so, you know, I'd better not bust out the thumb. "Seinfeld in the house," that kind of thing. But sometimes I incorporate some slap stuff in a little bass jam I do before "Orion," and the fans actually dig it.

I wasn't slapping at all for a while, but in the last year I've been reuniting with my thumb and my slap technique, and it feels good. I use it when I'm messing around at home, recording grooves and ideas. The slapping I tend to go for nowadays is on the *B* and *E* strings, with a lot of percussive stuff going on. I like to keep it funky but heavy, with the attitude of a metal player hammering down the heavy. I love Larry Graham; I mean I'm an absolute fan. As funky as he is, to me he's really a heavy play-er. He's pure metal. If he wanted to, Larry Graham could play in Metallica.

★ FISHBONE'S NORWOOD FISHER: THOROUGHLY UNHINGED
BY CHUCK CRISAFULLI, FROM A 1996 INTERVIEW ★

They call it nutmeg: the wild, adrenalized mix of punk, funk, thrash, and ska L.A.'s Fishbone has been pumping out for years. From their eponymous 1985 debut EP—the one that got revelers of all sorts grooving along with "Party at Ground Zero"—the band has demonstrated a unique ability to meld monster chops, imaginative arrangements, heavy lyrics, and a cartoonish sense of humor into one fine, genre-jumping musical rush.

Fishbone began as a family affair, with Norwood kicking out jams alongside his brother and bandmate, drummer Philip Fisher, a.k.a. Fish. It started shortly after a young Norwood had a revelation in which he realized his duty in life was to pick up a bass guitar. "A cousin took us to see Larry Graham—our very first concert," he remembers. "I was about six years old, and we sat in the next-to-last row at the Shrine Auditorium. The lights were shining down on the stage, and this beam was coming off Larry's bass. It hit me in the eyes, and I felt like I was chosen to do what he was doing."

> "Those P-Funk records made a big impression on me."

Another bit of serendipity gave Norwood his next step in bass education. When a cousin's aunt banned the playing of Funkadelic's *America Eats Its Young* in her house, he brought his records to Norwood's house, where Mother Fisher had a much more liberal in-house musical policy. "Those P-Funk records made a big impression on me," Norwood smiles. "I could just feel the music changing me."

"The same cousin who brought over the Funkadelic records also had Iron Butterfly, Chicago, Led Zeppelin, Sly Stone—we were listening to everything, and nobody ever told me there was anything wrong with that. Come to think of it, though, I do remember being in the car with the cousin who took me to see Larry Graham, and when some Sly Stone came on the radio she said, 'Turn this rock shit off.' I said, 'It's Sly—he's as black as us.' She didn't want to hear it, and I thought to myself, This is exactly what I need to listen to—stuff that gets people upset. It's beautiful, because now I know there are young black women who would say the same thing when their kids listen to Fishbone."

Norwood's parts are formidable, lightning-fingered constructions that manage to energize the band's grooves without ever sounding overly busy or willfully complicated. His bass lines tease around a groove, never landing in obvious places but also never pulling away from the beat. Fisher doesn't demean the band's wicked grooves, but he admits his parts aren't always entirely premeditated. "I play some ridiculous shit!" he grins. "I love this music, but sometimes I'm just laughing my ass off when we're recording. I listen back to some of those odd notes, and the only explanation I have is I didn't know what I was doing. I let myself get crazy without thinking too hard about it. I'm also usually the first one to say I should do my part over—but sometimes if you listen to the odd notes for a while, they don't sound like mistakes. Give 'em a chance, and they get kind of funky."

19

VICTOR WOOTEN: THE NEW PIONEER

★ **VICTOR WOOTEN: THE NEW PIONEER** BY JIM ROBERTS AND BILL LEIGH ★

Few modern players can combine technical innovation and musicality as well as Victor Wooten. He emerged on the mainstream musical stage as the bassist of Béla Fleck & the Flecktones, wowing audiences with his quick double-thumbing, mastery of tapping and harmonics, an incredible internal groove sense, and a flair for showmanship. He's gone on to wow the bass world with his solo albums, his work as a bandleader, his collaborations, and his commitment to education.

Wooten's 1995 solo debut, *A Show of Hands*, was a revelation of the expansive possibilities of electric bass. Armed only with one of his Fodera basses and having sworn off overdubs, Victor crafted a dissertation on solo bass that marked the culmination of years of advanced study and development of electric bass technique, using the language of jazz, classical, and R&B. And it was funky.

How did he develop into such an adventurous and innovative player? "My brothers and parents were the foundation," he says. "They prepared me for just about anything by teaching me to keep my mind open and to learn to adapt. Musically, that means not being rigid and not having to play in a certain way." The youngest of five musical brothers, Victor began his bass career as a toddler when his oldest brother, Regi, began teaching him to play on the bottom strings of a guitar. By age five Victor was joining his brothers on the nightclub circuit. By the time he was in middle school, a few years after the family settled in Newport News, Virginia, he was a veteran musician. His best schooling in the art of freestyling? The daily summertime jams at the Wooten home.

Victor also credits his home musical schooling for his extended array of techniques. "Everything I do on the bass Regi does on the guitar—tapping, thumb stuff, everything. Some things we developed together, and some things I've shown him, but he's really the basis of everything I do." One of the bands the Wootens covered early in their careers was Sly & the Family Stone, but Victor had a hard time getting a handle on Larry Graham's sound. "I wasn't getting the right tone and feel until my brother, Regi, showed me how to use my thumb. Then he showed me how to use my thumb in a down-and-up fashion, the way he played guitar. He said if I wanted to sound like Larry Graham, this was the way to do it. I'm not sure whether Larry used that technique or not, but it helped me to get that really funky, jumpy sound I was looking for—the sound that makes you move."

When he was about ten years old, Wooten first heard Stanley Clarke. "Someone played us some *Return to Forever*, and after that I started learning every

Stanley Clarke song I could get my hands on. I had been taking solos onstage since I was eight, but it wasn't until I got into Stanley that I started learning lines note-for-note." His second revelation came several years later, when he was exposed to Jaco Pastorius. "A drummer friend of mine invited me over one day, and he put on Jaco's 'Portrait of Tracy.' I heard this piano playing, and he told me it was a bass. It *floored* me. So I borrowed the record, and I learned the tune that night—I just found where the harmonic notes were on the neck, and I've never been the same since."

> "I know I'm doing stuff that a lot of people aren't doing right now, but because I know what I *can't* do, it keeps things in perspective."

The Wootens played together until the late '80s, along the way recording an eponymous album for Arista. Shortly after the band broke up, Victor hooked up with fusion banjoist Béla Fleck, whose music suited Wooten's style perfectly. With his bewildering arsenal of right- and left-hand techniques, Victor's solo during a Béla Fleck & the Flecktones show is mind-boggling, to say the least—but he asserts that wasn't the goal. "The techniques I use didn't really evolve out of my need to be different," he says. "They evolved because I needed to play what I was hearing. I'd listen to drum solos by Billy Cobham and Tony Williams, and I'd try to learn those rhythms. I couldn't play them with conventional techniques, so I had to come up with different ways to do it." But how does it feel to be able to blow almost anyone away with his chops? "I don't see it that way," said Victor in a 1992 interview. "I know I'm doing stuff that a lot of people aren't doing right now, but because I know what I *can't* do, it keeps things in perspective. I know there are guys out there who can blow *me* away, so to take that attitude wouldn't be the right approach."

Of course these days, a generation of players have copped Victor's approach to bass, both in terms of technique and how he thinks about music, which he has presented both at his Bass/Nature camps and his 2008 novel, *The Music Lesson*. Keenly conscious of his visibility in the bass world, Victor is always eager to share the spotlight, give back what he has gained from others, and continue to grow as a musician. "My main goal is always to make people forget I'm a bass player," he says. "If I do things well enough, I can make you focus on the music."

★ DEEP CUTS: VICTOR WOOTEN ★

"The Sinister Minister." While Victor's playing on the original track, from 1990's *Béla Fleck and the Flecktones*, the version on 1996's *Live Art* provides a glimpse at one his legendary bass showcase moments during a Flecktones concert.

"Me & My Bass Guitar." One of many funky tracks on Victor's solo debut, 1998's *A Show of Hands*, on which Victor displays his ability to create a multi-layered funk track with just his bass alone.

"Amazing Grace." Victor improvises the traditional tune on the Flecktones' *Live Art*, simultaneously playing the melody in harmonics and a fretted bass line. His various readings of the song include ostinato grooves and canny bass-note choices for jazzy reharmonization.

"Bass Tribute." On his 2005 solo album *Soul Circus*, Victor gathers a bevy of friends for a track that pays musical respect to a pantheon of bass heroes.

20.
FUNKY GOSPEL

★ JOEL SMITH: GOSPEL'S SESSION MAN BY E. E. BRADMAN ★

It's easy to miss the small building with gray double doors, somewhere near the middle of the 2200 block of East 14th Street, in Oakland, California. Inside, the gold and platinum records on the studio walls are more obvious, as are the immediate warmth and firm handshake of the smiling man who walks us into the main room. Nothing about Joel Smith's bearing indicates the ego to match his recording and live credits—on bass and drums—with Al Jarreau, the Jerry Garcia Band, Tony! Toni! Toné, and the brightest names in contemporary worship, including the Rev. James Moore, T. D. Jakes, Beverly Crawford, and Kim Burrell.

The Oakland native has developed his reputation with a savvy mix of low-

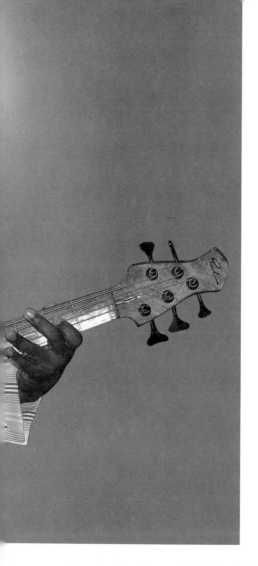

end focus and fluid technique, delivered with a throaty Jazz Bass tone heavy in low-mids. One producer called Joel the most incredible bassist or drummer he'd ever heard. Bassist/bandleader Fred Hammond, who grew up on Joel's playing, calls him a genius, and Joel himself acknowledges that sessions have been derailed by drummers too awestruck to play with him. Despite the praise, Smith remains down to earth—but he's fiercely loyal to the bottom line. "Everyone has their thing, and each is valid. A lot of guys like to play up high, for example, and that's great. I have nothing against it. But real, solid foundation—that's what bass is made for."

Joel was born on December 6, 1959, into one of the most distinguished gospel families. His mother, Feddie Hawkins, is a member of the Oakland-based Hawkins Singers, headed by her brothers Walter and Edwin Hawkins, who enjoyed huge success with the 1969 hit single "Oh Happy Day." Joel began playing drums at age six and took up bass at 12. He was hooked. "Right away, I had so much fun with bass because it was so related to what drums are to me—the foundation. That's the way I looked at the bass, 'cause that's what it is."

A year later Joel made his recording debut with his uncles, taking inspiration from both sides of the rhythm section. "I watched Gaylord Birch and Eddie Bayers on drums, and I listened to a lot of Chuck Rainey, Verdine White, and Anthony Jackson. They all had their signature styles, and they also knew how to lay a foundation. I was intrigued because they all had different approaches."

Mainly self-taught, Joel was lucky enough to receive one-on-one tutoring from Sly & the Family Stone bassist Rustee Allen; other top-notch players gave him encouragement, too. "When I was 13, my uncle Edwin asked me to play drums on a session for him, and I thought he was kidding, since I only played in church," says Smith. "He also said he had a surprise for me." The next day Joel stood speechless as Chuck Rainey began setting up his equipment. Joel's uncle came up to him. "Remember the surprise I told you about? This is it."

Those sessions—which resulted in the Grammy-winning *Wonderful* and an earful of praise from Rainey—helped Joel decide to get serious about bass and the importance of connecting the two instruments' roles. "As a young boy, being around cats like that made me grow up quick musically. I was always around older cats who showed me what could happen within the structure of a song, and all the different approaches. That was a blessing."

Smith's versatility is one of the keys to his success. "Joel's one of the best-kept secrets, but producers and artists—the people who keep you working—definitely know him," says Jerry Mannery, executive producer for the Rev. James Moore, with whom Joel recorded four albums. "We brought him in once to play bass and something happened to the drummer. We got another bass player, Joel got on drums, and he didn't miss a beat."

Mannery, director of Malaco Records' gospel division, says Smith had a great relationship with the late Rev. Moore. "Moore knew many musicians all over the country; he used the best of the best. Joel would usually wind up being musical director, tightening up the musicians and bringing them together. One thing that sets him apart is his humility; there are a lot less accomplished people out there tooting their own horns."

A distinct part of Smith's sound is the late '80s, neck-through F Bass 5-string he's owned for six years; the maple fingerboard and ash body are just right. "This bass is a gift. It fits me so well. It's so quiet and never brittle—some people think it's keyboard bass when they hear it," Joel laughs. "I didn't expect that tight sound from a neck-through. I can get a lot of different tones, including a Marcus tone, but everybody does that. I like a little more bottom. Joel emphasizes that he gets more low end from his instrument and less from his SWR amp. "I use my fingers to get a full tone. I like a lot of bottom, but the way I play, I want everything to be distinct—punchy but clean. When I'm making my moves, you know it."

★ MAURICE FITZGERALD: YOUNG LION BY E. E. BRADMAN ★

You can hardly fault Maurice Fitzgerald for sounding confident. Barely a decade after first picking up bass, he has amassed a résumé that includes some of gospel's best-known artists. He has toured extensively with Fred Hammond & Radical for Christ, the funky worship sensation that easily sells out Madison Square Garden. And his schedule just keeps getting busier.

What keeps the Chicago native gigging? His well-honed ability to recognize gospel changes anywhere, anytime, in any key. "In the churches where I grew up, there was no such thing as charts. You had to remember everything. It's all about ears: You hear it once and you get it. In the studio, that's what I've developed a reputation for—knocking a session out, no overdubs."

"Gospel musicians have to have great ears," says Fitzgerald. "There are patterns everybody uses. It's like a language—if the piano player plays a certain progression, you know what's next. You've got to have a good ear for what the piano player's doing, or you'll get lost in the sauce."

Fitzgerald started on drums in church, and by age 13 he was a regular visitor to rehearsals of the legendary Rev. Milton Brunson, whose band featured bassist/producer Steve Huff. After he switched to bass as a high school sophomore, Maurice woodshedded on gospel, Jaco, and Jamerson classics. He also worked hard to absorb the sound and feel of contemporary players like Marcus Miller and John Patitucci, a fact reflected in his advanced technique and bright, modern tone. Fitzgerald augmented his listening sessions with chart-reading lessons, scales, finger exercises—and the occasional undercover club date. "Sometimes my mom didn't even know where I was. I'd say I was going to a friend's house, and I'd go to a club," he laughs. "Learning different styles made me a more rounded bass player. I'm not saying every bassist should play clubs, but they should do whatever they can to broaden their horizons, be around good musicians, and challenge themselves."

At 19, Fitzgerald auditioned and landed the gig with popular North Carolina-based Rev. John P. Kee & the New Community Choir, a platform that gave him new visibility and musical exposure. "John was always surrounded by incredible musicians, and we would challenge and learn from each other. I spent hours working out, playing through changes, trying to push songs as far as we could go within the arrangement." In the end, however, Fitzgerald's five-year, three-album stint with Kee taught him more than theory. "It was my first big gospel gig, so I thought I was going to make a lot of money. But it was more of a learning experience than anything. John trusted me to be original, and I tried not to let him down. He pushed me to come up with parts I hadn't heard or played before."

Fitzgerald went on to bring his chops and youthful energy to Donnie McClurkin, Marvin Sapp, the Rev. Jackie McCullough, Kim Burrell, Bishop T. D. Jakes, and many others, including his high-profile post with Fred Hammond & Radical for Christ. Although he was honored by Fred Hammond's invitation, Fitzgerald says preparing for the audition was a harrowing experience. "Fred called me when bassist Terrance Palmer stepped down to focus on producing. I was excited, but I was really nervous knowing Terrance and Fred were both great bass players. But I was confident I could pull it off." Two weeks of studying a videotape of one of the band's shows paid off. "I went in, they counted off a song, and then went to the next one. Before I knew it, we had run through the whole set—and learned some new songs. After that, Fred was like, 'Here's the tour schedule.'"

Does Hammond suggest parts? "At times he does, but he pretty much just lets me do what I do. Sometimes in rehearsal he says, "Rice, why don't you try this?' For the most part, he never gives me bad advice. Fred knows bass, so when he asks me try something, I do it."

"Our styles are very similar," says Hammond. "Maurice knows how to play the pocket and move around in the pocket. He does things I would do, and he makes me feel comfortable when I'm singing. We think alike."

Fitzgerald notes that today's worship music poses particular spiritual and musical challenges. "Gospel has changed significantly in the last ten years; it's more hip-hop and jazz-oriented. Some people have been criticized for bringing other flavors to gospel, but you have to balance it out by doing hip-hop for young folks and traditional gospel for older people who don't want to change. You can stay true to the original style of gospel and give everybody a little of both."

★ DEEP CUT: MAURICE FITZGERALD ★

Rev. John P. Kee's "Thursday Love." "I tried to do something different, moving around the song like a guitar player would. A lot of people have commented on that."

★ TERRANCE PALMER TAKES GOSPEL TO A HIGHER PLACE BY CHRIS JISI ★

For those who haven't witnessed the exhilarating contemporary-gospel glow of Israel & New Breed, imagine Earth, Wind & Fire and P-Funk meeting for a Motown Revue on Cloud Nine. Leader Israel Houghton and his lineup of vocalists, keyboardists, guitarists, percussionists, and horns raise the roof on a nightly basis, secure in the knowledge that the mighty hands of Terrance Palmer have a firm grip on the foundation.

The Michigan-based Palmer has become as much a gospel bass hero as his peers Andrew Gouche, Joel Smith, Fred Hammond, and Maurice Fitzgerald—able to move from 5-string thud to scissor-sharp slap to heavenly fretless. But as any praise and worship plucker will tell you, glorifying the groove is Job One. "I try to get beneath everything and move it along," says Terrance. "There's a certain drive you have to provide at all times, but with so many people playing and singing you really have to pick your spots and keep it simple and tight. You don't want it to sound like everyone is competing with each other; that's the difference between a good gospel band and a not-so-good one." He continues, "I always keep eye contact with the drummer, and I listen to everyone onstage. It's all about communication. There's a place you get to when everyone hits the pocket; at that point it's all flowing, and it seems like whatever you play just fits right in."

Raised on the sounds of Stevie Wonder, Earth, Wind & Fire, and Motor City gospel greats like the Winans and the Clarks, Terrance showed a gift for music by age three. His mother, a pianist, had him try sax, trumpet, tuba, piano, and drums, which he settled on until his last year of high school, when the school's resident bassist graduated. Palmer had been attracted to the sound of the bass—he even removed the top two strings from his acoustic guitar—so when he was asked to try filling the vacant bass chair, he agreed. "Something clicked immediately when I picked up the electric bass and started playing it, like this is where I was meant to be," he recalls. Within two years he was backing no less than Dionne Warwick and Aretha Franklin at benefits, while landing in the band of legendary gospel composer/keyboardist Thomas Whitfield (replacing Mary J. Blige bassist and musical director Lanar Brantley).

Inspired by the low-end likes of Anthony Jackson ("I wore out a Grover Washington Jr. concert video"), Stanley Clarke, Marcus Miller, Richard Bona, and fellow Detroit thumper Al Turner, Palmer shaped his style on his own, but it was Whitfield who taught him his most valuable lessons. "I thought no one could touch me early on; I had chops and I was overplaying. But Reverend Whitfield straightened me out—he taught me discipline and gave me an appreciation of music. For an entire year he told me to play only the parts on his albums. When it finally sunk in, he said, 'Okay—now you can start expressing yourself.'" Having given himself to the groove, another key to Terrance's development was a founding role and six-year stint in Fred Hammond & Radical for Christ. "Fred is such a great bassist himself, with a drive and sound no one can duplicate. Listening to him I learned how to be aggressive yet in the pocket, and how to create song-suited bass lines. He also taught me all about studio production." Tiring of traveling and wanting to focus on the writing and production side, Palmer left Hammond in 1999 (he was replaced by Maurice Fitzgerald), built a home studio, and began writing commercials.

In 2001, musical director Aaron Lindsey called on Palmer for Israel & New Breed's Sony debut, *New Season*. Says Terrance, "Everyone in the band is into many different kinds of music, which is fortunate considering we cover R&B, pop, funk, jazz, blues, Latin, alternative rock, and hip-hop. You have to be on the ball because the shows are never the same, and Israel will change direction in a heartbeat." So how does he come up with his bass lines? "Israel and Aaron are very vocal about the direction they want, and they count on us to expand on their ideas. So I usually think of a particular artist or bassist—'What would Anthony play here?,' or, 'This has a John Mayer vibe.' Once I get the concept, I have the freedom to put myself into the part. Also, New Breed's music is all guitar- or keyboard-written, so there are a lot of chord inversions, with me playing the 3rd or the 5th. And we're big on unison sections; we like to show that we play together. But there's no bass book and very few charts," he says, pointing to his head. "It's all up here."

Palmer describes his technique as pretty basic: two-finger plucking, thumb-and-index slapping and popping, and palm-muting with thumb and index plucks. He gets a solo space in the New Breed show, for which he generally finds himself trying to play a Willie Weeks-like groove solo over a one- or two-chord vamp. "I love leaning on our drummer, Michael 'Big Mike' Clemons, who used to be in Usher's band. He hits hard, and he's so easy to lock with." The same can't be said of programmed drums on studio dates. "With sequenced drums, I have to work hard because you're creating the feel for both instruments. The machine is locked into one thing, and if I try to go somewhere, it's not going to follow. That's why I'm happy live drums are prevalent in gospel." Also widespread in gospel's new movement is "praise and worship." "Praise and worship goes beyond a musical style; it's a lifestyle, like hip-hop. It's inviting God to be a part of you and letting the music come through you to inspire others."

★ FRED HAMMOND: GOSPEL'S MULTI-TALENTED MINISTER OF BASS BY E. E. BRADMAN ★

"I knew the older Winans already had a bass player, so I didn't get my hopes up," remembers Fred Hammond. "And then the younger Winans asked me over for rehearsal. The family was competitive—all in fun, of course—and there was excitement in the air. It was a summer day, people were outside the house, and the rhythm section was tight! We were rehearsing and arranging when all of a sudden [elder Winan] Marvin takes over the piano. I'm on it; I had all their songs down, and we click right away. I'm in his back pocket! The house erupts. Mom and Pop Winans are tickled to death 'cause they know what's getting ready to happen. Marvin calls an emergency meeting in the basement. Finally, the Winans asked me to join. I said, 'Let me pray on it.' But I was ready."

From those auspicious beginnings, Hammond has become one of gospel's most sought-after bandleaders. Of the current generation of artists whose music owes equal debt to traditional gospel and Old School funk and soul, few enjoy the critical and popular success of Detroit-based Hammond, who has worked with the cream of contemporary praise music as a bassist, bandleader, producer, and vocalist.

Born in 1960, Hammond began formal music training in high school, picking up bass at 13 and vocals in the 11th grade. Almost immediately he immersed himself in Detroit's late '70s/early '80s gospel scene, which included the Winans family, Rance Allen, and many others. Events such as the Clark Sisters' bimonthly "midnight musicals," which began at 11 pm and lasted well into the morning, made a permanent impact on Hammond. "Anyone who aspired to be in the gospel scene was there. Two thousand people filled the place, and there were lines around the block. You could go at four in the morning and it would still be bumpin'!"

After a two-year stint with the Winans, Hammond struck out on his own with Commissioned, whose nine albums fused contemporary gospel with new jack swing, early hip-hop, and funk; he left the group in 1995. He released his first solo album, *I Am Persuaded*, in 1991; he founded Face to Face Productions in '92, and *Deliverance* followed the next year. Already an in-demand singer, producer, and bassist, Hammond has gained renown for his drum programming, vocal arrangements, keyboards, engineering, and mixing for a long list of contemporary and traditional gospel projects. His Radical for Christ project has released numerous albums since '95; he describes the sound as "a mix of contemporary gospel—Andrae Crouch, James Cleveland, and Walter Hawkins—with Stevie Wonder, LTD, and Earth, Wind & Fire."

Hammond's bass aesthetic reflects both secular and spiritual influences. He grew up listening to gospel session stars Joel Smith and Andrew Gouche, and he's been strongly influenced by Marcus Miller, Abraham Laboriel, and Anthony Jackson. "I was more into solid bass playing, so I gravitated to those three cats. I'm not flashy—put me in a solo and I'm done," he laughs. "But I know how to make your song phat, and I can move around in your track without sounding like an elephant." He also lists Stanley Clarke and Jaco among his favorites. "I would go to Stanley's concerts to see him make his basses sing. You can hear it on my albums, like 'The Lord Is Good' [from '96's *The Spirit of David*]. That's a slowed-down Stanley lick," he laughs. "On 'Give Me a Clean Heart,' from last year's *Purpose by Design*, that's a Jaco vibe. I play Weather Report's 'A Remark You Made' [*Heavy Weather*] on my boat all the time, and people still ask about it. It's so current today."

Hammond says a particular '80s Laboriel performance at L.A.'s Baked Potato was a revelation. "I was two feet from Abe and I watched his every move, and that's when I learned dynamics. He gave each note its full due. And then the touch—sometimes he was jumping up and down and hollering, and then he was barely touching the string, and working a volume pedal! That's when I really learned how to play bass."

Fred Hammond's snappy, bottom-heavy bass sound draws from many influences, but Marcus Miller towers above the rest. "Whatever Marcus had or was talking about, I had to get it," he says, referring to his blond 1970 Jazz Bass, Fender Marcus Miller Signature Jazz, and DR Hi-Beam strings. "I never really achieved it, but reaching for that 'Marcus sound' has helped me find my own."

Although Hammond plays on his studio albums, it's been Terrance Palmer or Maurice Fitzgerald laying it down live while Hammond fronts a nine-piece choir. "I pick guys who can play with my band—three keyboards, a horn section, drummer, guitar, and percussionist. These guys have to lay the foundation, and Maurice and Terrance do that." Of the two, Maurice "makes me feel comfortable when I'm singing; we think alike. Terrance approaches it a little differently—he's more linear. They're both very solid and extremely dependable. If something dropped out and they kept going, you wouldn't miss it."

Between his 60-plus gigs a year, hectic production and studio schedules, and commercials for Plymouth, Domino's Pizza, and K-Mart, Hammond works hard to maintain his priorities. "It's a challenge to keep the spirit strong. Some gospel artists think they need to sound like Jay-Z or Puffy to be accepted, but I disagree. We call ourselves Radical For Christ because our music is aggressive. We're like that guy who goes to Green Bay, paints his face, and takes off his shirt in 30-degree weather. He's crazy; he's radical. We're that enthusiastic about God and the things He's done."

★ ANDREW GOUCHE'S PILGRIMAGE TO PLUCKING PROPHET BY CHRIS JISI ★

When James Jamerson began creating his bible of bass guitar playing, it could be heard on the radio—chapter and verse, each week. With Jaco poised to turn jazz bass on its ear, it was but a five-year journey from Florida to the world. But for gospel bassdom's breakout innovator, Andrew Gouche, mainstream recognition has been a 30-year passage. He first gained cult status with bassists via his probing, present parts on recordings for gospel music's A-list, as well as his hugely popular residency at the Prayze Connection club in Los Angeles. But Gouche became a true underground underlord through the many web clips of his bass bravura, plus his crossover to become Chaka Khan's musical director. *Andrew Gouche*, his instrumental solo debut, is the perfect pulpit for Gouche's singular, spirited, singing 6-string. Like a resonant Reverend guiding his flock, Andrew spins lead lines and counter-melodies, triggers spontaneous grooves and unison riffs, and casts a joyous hue over his mixed set of inspirational covers and originals.

Born on May 27, 1959, and raised in the Crenshaw district of South Central Los Angeles, Andrew Gouche's initial exposure to music was the sound of his mother's piano playing and singing at his grandfather's church. Told at age eight that he had to join his siblings in picking an instrument, Andrew selected trumpet. He stayed with the horn until he was 14 and saw Larry Graham on *Soul Train*. He recalls, "I persuaded my mom to buy me a Teisco bass and Silvertone amp from Sears. My friends used to make fun of me because I would sit in front of the TV, pour a whole box of Cap'n Crunch cereal and a half-gallon of milk into a pot, and just eat and practice bass all day." While the grooves of Graham, Jamerson, Verdine White, and Stevie Wonder caught his ear, Gouche's main influence was Gap Band bassist Robert Wilson, whom he first heard on records by gospel vocalist D. J. Rogers. "His approach was different from everyone else. I remember he tuned his *E* string down to *B* on 'Yearning for Your Love'—he's definitely unsung."

Furthering his progress, Gouche happened to be singing in the choir at the church of the legendary Reverend James Cleveland, who revolutionized gospel music by incorporating R&B and jazz elements, thus setting the stage for modern-day gospel/secular music hybrids. Andrew relates, "Rev. Cleveland would let me sit on the side with my bass and amp and try to fig-ure out the songs. Eventually, I learned all about music and chords from the great keyboardists in his Gospel Music Workshops." Gouche began touring the world with Cleveland and meeting other praise & worship heavies, such as Andrae Crouch, who heard Andrew in Israel and had him in to record a few weeks later. Before long, Gouche was juggling gigs with Cleveland, Crouch, the Hawkins Family, and the Winans, as well as stints with Cheryl Lynn and the Jazz Crusaders. Out of the pack shone a new bass beacon.

> "I play the way I feel and let the chips fall where they may."

Early in your gospel career, were you consciously trying to approach the bass role differently?

No, because it wasn't really defined. In a lot of churches the organist played bass on the pedals, and where there was bass guitar there was no real precedent, so I just started my own precedent. When I first met Marcus Miller years ago, he said, "Man, I've heard a lot about you. What can I hear you on?" So I sent him four cassette tapes, and he called me up and said, "How do you get away with playing all that?" Right from the beginning I never had the desire to sound like any other bass player. That said, a key for me was meeting Joel Smith when I was 17. When I first heard him I got depressed because he was so incredible—but then when I got to play with him in the Hawkins Family band [with Smith on drums], it was like going from black and white to color. He opened up my whole approach to bass and enabled me to see all the different musical possibilities, because he had a broader influence base and a bigger vocabulary; he was into jazz and players like Anthony Jackson and Jaco. Bassists know who Joel is now, but back then the only reason I was better known in gospel was because I was traveling more than Joel, who stayed closer to home in Oakland.

What would you say got your name out there more—records or touring?

Gospel fans read album credits and I was showing up on a lot of recordings.

I didn't realize it until I went to London with Andrae Crouch and the crowd responded when he introduced me. Afterwards they were like, "You're the guy who played on 'Spirit (Fall Fresh on Me)'" [on the 1997 Edwin Hawkins Music & Arts Seminar Mass Choir album, *Give Us Peace*]. That song really put my name out there, and the funny part was Edwin didn't like the bass line at first. Another key track was "Use Me" by the L.A. Mass Choir [on 1991's *I Shall Not Be Defeated*]; afterward, you started to hear that groove everywhere in gospel.

What led you to tune your basses down a whole-step?

I knew Joel was tuning down to E♭, which made sense because a lot of gospel tunes are in flat keys. So in 1982 I started tuning my bass down to *D*, just so I would be lower than Joel [*laughs*]. I got my first 5-string, a Yamaha BB5000, right when it came out in 1985, and I tuned it down a step, like my 4-string. Not long after, I was doing a live recording at an Edwin Hawkins seminar and there was a ballad by Thomas Whitfield that had a break on it. I hit the low open *A*, and Thomas tripped out. When he got back to Detroit he had all of his local bass players tune their *B* strings down a step.

How would you describe your style?

I don't really play bass lines as such. My playing is much more melody-driven, and I'm really in tune with the lyrics of the song. On sessions I always ask for the lyrics because they give what I play a meaning, an intent. I can just go in and play to changes, but when I know what the song is about, it dictates the attitude I play with. I've always said, some people like the way I play, some people don't. I play the way I feel and let the chips fall where they may. I tell young bassists to follow their heart regardless of what others say and they'll always be fine. Because no matter who else you try to please, someone is not going to like your playing. Looking back, I have no regrets; I realize there are certain gigs I'll never get because I'm not a model bass player; I don't read music, and some people think I play too many notes. But that's cool; there's enough music and listeners in the world that someone is going to want to hear what I do. And it works the other way, too. I stepped away from gospel briefly in the mid '80s, and in 1997 I left Gladys Knight's gig after six years without anything lined up because of burnout. I didn't want to lose my love of playing. Fortunately, I came back to good playing and working situations both times.

What's your concept when you're improvising a bass line?

When I start playing I never know what's about to come out. I look at my playing like a batting average, and I bat about .800: 80 percent of what I do is cool, 20 percent is not so cool, but I'll take those percentages anytime. For the most part, I start playing and see where it goes, which means much of what I play is a reaction to what I've just played. It's all still relevant to the song and the chord changes, but it gets freer as I go, especially with my gospel band. We'll play the same song in consecutive masses on Sunday, but they'll be totally different from each other. In a pop situation, like with Chaka, there's still freedom, but it's a little more arranged. There are set bass lines that I'll vary slightly, and there are licks that I've figured out work at a certain point in a song, so I'll do them every time.

You're particularly known for your extended licks and fills.

Again, I just go for it and once in a while, in the middle of it, I'll think, I shouldn't have done that! Then I'll laugh because I find my way out of it and land back on my feet. What helps is I have perfect pitch, I can hear every note in the chord—even when I can't tell you exactly what the chord spelling is—and I know my way around the fingerboard really well, top to bottom. I'm not singing in my head what I'm playing, but I hear what I'm going for. Also, I think the joy of what I'm doing has a lot to do with putting it across and making it work.

How about the bass/drums relationship in gospel?

There are certain fundamental rules that apply to whatever style of music you're performing, and the bass and drums playing together is one that applies big time in gospel. The key is, the whole band is playing parts, but it's still open and improvisational within that framework because everybody is listening and aware of trying to play *together*, as a unit. There are those special, magical moments, but it's not smoke and mirrors; there's a lot of looking and communication onstage— plus we know each other's tendencies.

How did you come to be Chaka Khan's musical director?

She had heard about me and came to one of my gigs in 2006. She loves bass players, and she told me I reminded her of Anthony Jackson; she said, "You don't play like Anthony, but you have the same spirit in your playing." She asked me to be her M.D., saying she wanted a different approach to all of her songs. I rearranged everything and her fans revolted a bit, saying the songs didn't sound like the album versions. So we went back to playing more in the style of the records, but with a current vibe and technology—and the Chaka-holics love it. It's been a total blast for me; Chaka can still sing anyone into the ground. The band is myself, George Johnson on drums, Javad Day on keys, and Eric Brice on guitar—all church boys.

21.
HIP-HOP AND NEO-SOUL

★ PRESTON CRUMP: SOUTHERN HIP-HOP'S
SECRET WEAPON BY BILL LEIGH ★

Preston Crump grooves. If you keep your radio tuned to the funkier regions of the
dial, it's a safe bet that Preston has grooved you. Crump is known around Atlanta
as the man to call when the situation requires fusing Old School funk feel with
New School studio creativity. That means he's one of the busiest bassists in hip-
hop and R&B: Preston boasts a résumé that lists nearly every album from
Southern rap groups Goodie Mob and OutKast, not to mention albums and
tracks with En Vogue, Dr. Dre, TLC, Xscape, Mystikal, Destiny's Child, and
many others. When he's not heating up Atlanta's studios with his burning bass
grooves, Preston can be found on the road with Raphael Saadiq, Joi, or Citizen
Cope, all of whose albums he also appeared on. Why does Preston stay so busy?
As Saadiq says: "When it comes to creative hip-hop bassists, Preston is *the* man.
He's got a feel and a melodic thing happening that's all his own."

Preston grew up in Connecticut, where he played funk and R&B and stood
in awe of the funk-bass pantheon. "I listened to James Jamerson, Anthony
Jackson, Michael Henderson, and all the P-Funk guys—Bootsy Collins, Rodney
'Skeet' Curtis, Cordell 'Boogie' Mosson, and Billy 'Bass' Nelson," says Preston,
with an amiable, soft-spoken manner that nearly veils his seriousness and focus.
"Parliament really messed me up—like, *damn!*—but in a good way."

After four years studying at Boston's Berklee College of Music, Crump moved
to Atlanta, where he first hooked up with the hit-making production team
Organized Noize and started his association with OutKast.

Is there a difference between playing hip-hop and funk?

No. I gravitated toward hip-hop because it was the only thing to me that was
original and free like funk. The only thing is that you have to repeat yourself; you
can't get as loose with it. You have to keep it straight for at least three minutes.
Toward the end I'll start slowly bringing in fills and things, but that's the way I
approach it.

How do you make a track work?

I just try to keep my ears open and keep the vibe open. I try to keep hearing
things and try not to get locked into anything. Sometimes I might use my Boss
ME8B multi-effect pedal to explore sounds that may spark something new. If I'm
having a hard time with a bass line, I go to a melody line. Like on OutKast's "Rosa
Parks," they used a sample for the bass line, and I couldn't beat the way it sounded,

so I came up with a sustaining guitar-type line that I played through the whole song.

What are your sessions typically like?

Most of the time it's just the producers and machines, though we did a lot of live stuff with drums and guitar on a few tracks of OutKast's *Aquemini*. I play all the way down the track, unless it's something they want to sound loopy that's hard to keep consistent. They might say, "We'll just pick a section to sample," but I usually try to play all the way down, and they keep most of the tracks.

Did you play OutKast's "So Fresh So Clean" straight through?

All the way down.

How do you get that staccato feel on the song's signature lick?

I rode the kick pattern, muting it with my left hand a little. That was the melody they had, so I just played along and added my little fills here and there. On a lot of tracks I play overdubs and melodic lines; for example, I did that keyboard-sounding line at the beginning of OutKast's "So Fresh So Clean." It's the bass through the pedal. I do that kind of thing a lot.

How would you compare your playing style to Raphael's?

Raphael plays harder and more behind the beat than I do. He plays more like a Larry Graham style to me—not slap, but the way Larry sounded on the Sly & the Family Stone albums. His lines always sounded muted, lazy, and really thick, but still strong. That's the biggest difference I notice. But Raphael has said he based a lot of his lines on the album on stuff I did. My bass playing is Old School—I listened to a lot of Bootsy and Jamerson back in the day—so I want my sound to be thick and solid, and sometimes melodic. I like playing chords; I use 10ths a lot. And right off the bat, I try to get my basses to have a thick sound.

When you're doing a hip-hop session, how much are you creating?

In the early days, I created more than I got credit for. Actually, I didn't get any credit. Many times they'd have a beat going and I'd come up with a bass line totally on my own. Later, people would tap me on the shoulder and say, "Hey, you did that and they didn't give you credit." Then new people started coming into the fold, and they would get credit for chord progressions. They couldn't deny me credit if they were giving it to other people, so from then on, they tried to start having sessions where they wouldn't let people come up with stuff. They would try to have in mind what they wanted before bringing me in—I'd do what they want and then add my flavor. That's the way it should be: Tell me what you want, or cut me in.

What kind of advice would you give people trying to get into the scene?

Know your business, but be flexible with it. You want to be working, but you don't want to get pimped, either. I talk to a lot of guys about the credit thing, and when you think about it, you can't blame anybody, because you allowed it to happen. So roll with it as a learning experience and say, "From now on, this is how I do it." I don't sign work-for-hire forms when I make up the bass line. You need to know what you're getting into and how much you're willing to give up, but don't play yourself out of work.

And learn all different types of music. Even if you don't play it, just listen. Don't be closed-minded. I listen to a lot of old music; I don't think you can learn much from new music besides production.

Why is that?

A lot of those artists are listening to old stuff. The new stuff is all cookie-cutter, really. All I hear is new production secrets. People who stay in the business a long time listen to old stuff, not just their peers.

★ RAPHAEL SAADIQ'S HYBRID VINTAGE VISION BY CHRIS JISI ★

Hip-hop has continued to influence styles ranging from R&B to heavy metal, but few approaches to the musician-meets-machine concept are more cutting-edge than that of Raphael Saadiq, who has merged hip-hop's programmed approach with his Old School R&B roots to create a whole new rhythm section style. "When we're creating tracks," explains Glenn Standridge of Saadiq's production team, "everyone sort of plays to their own beat, with everything revolving around Raphael's bass—so it has that loose, hip-hop quality of samples layered together. The result is a best-of-both-worlds scenario that creates a feel all its own. It's deeper than hip-hop because it's all played or sampled on the spot, mostly on real instruments. It's inspired by great old records, yet it's contemporary. It doesn't sound like just a bunch of people mimicking classic grooves on vintage gear."

Probably the best-known examples of Saadiq's post-modern potion are his groove-breaking collaborations with neo-soul crooner D'Angelo and Lucy Pearl, his short-lived trio with ex-En Vogue vocalist Dawn Robinson and A Tribe Called Quest's Ali Shaheed Muhammad. But Saadiq has been applying his ethic since his frontman days with gold-selling neo-soul trailblazers Tony Toni Toné, and as an in-demand bassist/producer with everyone from Snoop Dogg to John Mellencamp.

Guitar was actually the first instrument Saadiq (born Raphael Wiggins) played in his native Oakland, California. After hearing James Jamerson's upright on Marvin Gaye's "How Sweet It Is (To Be Loved by You)," and being visually attracted to the electric bass in his church's band, he asked for and received an Orlando Jazz Bass copy at age seven. "The first bass line I learned was Rufus's 'You Got the Love' [from the 1974's *Rags to Rufus*, with Dennis Belfield on bass]. My brother taught it to me, and he played the guitar part." With a quick ear in a musically fertile neighborhood, Saadiq soon graduated from jamming with family and friends to having his pals ask their dads if he could sit in with them at clubs. Paying gigs at night followed, with days spent playing trombone in the junior high school jazz band and bass in U.C. Berkeley's Youth Music Program. "I was constantly playing in all kinds of settings, from quartets to solo. I'd go into coffeehouses alone and just improvise grooves behind rappers or poetry readings."

In 1987, while the 18-year-old Saadiq was putting together demos with his brother D'Wayne Wiggins and cousin Timothy Christian Riley (for what would eventually become Tony Toni Toné), a friend called to tell him Sheila E. was coming to the Bay Area to audition singing bassists for her touring band. Raphael beat out 40 other hopefuls, and a month later he was opening for Prince in huge Japanese arenas. What's more, Prince quickly enlisted Sheila's band for his notorious after-concert club gigs. Upon returning in 1988, the "Tonys" were signed, and Saadiq began his musical quest.

One of your trademarks is a super-laid-back feel.

I don't have a name for it; it's sort of like ghosting or shadowing the snare drum. I'm locking with the drums but a step behind, kind of sneaking up on them. You hear the snare hit and then I ghost or echo that. But for it to work, the drummer has to be aware of what I'm doing, and stay right in the middle of the beat, to keep that rubber-band-like tension. It's hard to learn, especially for people who always play on top, so it's best to listen to it being done; eventually you'll feel it. It's not something I've tried, but I suppose you could also practice it by setting up a basic drum loop with a *two* and *four* snare. First play a simple quarter-note or eighth-note pattern that locks with the loop, and then gradually pull back until you're ghosting the snare by playing a split-second after it hits.

It came about when D'Angelo and I first played together on keyboard and bass. We just started doing it, and the more we laid back, the more we'd laugh. We could go so far back that people around us would be like, "No, stop it!" That's the way D sings and plays, but it's something we both felt naturally; I don't think he ever did it with anyone else. When he got his road band together, he found players in Pino Palladino and [Roots drummer] Ahmir Thompson who could do it well—but so far they're some of the very few who can. I would say it has roots in hip-hop's sloppily synced samples, but there's also a link to Old School gospel, blues, and R&B, with bands like Sly & the Family Stone.

Let's talk about how you merge hip-hop and R&B.

My whole thing is, if I want to sample something, I'll play it myself, sample it, and EQ it—rather than sample some old track. People sample stuff because they can't play. I can play. The hip-hop side is the repetition—simple, funky, and tasteful, but banging hard. My measuring stick is that the groove has to make an

MC want to rhyme to it—to make him want to bust freestyle to my bass line. I grew up on R&B, but I was right in the middle of hip-hop, too. I dug artists like Mobb Deep, NWA, Wu-Tang Clan, and A Tribe Called Quest. When I heard the sampling, though, I felt I could do it better through real playing. Some people call my stuff progressive hip-hop or creative hip-hop, but it's not about that. It's just my music.

Who were your early bass influences?

Aside from Jamerson on the radio, it was a pair of great local players, who are still two of my favorites: Joel Smith, who was with the Hawkins Family, and Robert Ball. My godfather, James Levi, played drums in Herbie Hancock's Headhunters; one day, when I was maybe eight, he asked this bassist to drive me home, and he pulled out his bass and gave me some pointers. I later found out it was Jaco. Eventually, I got into Verdine White, Bootsy Collins, Bobby Watson, and Louis Johnson—but my two main guys were Bernard Edwards and Larry Graham. I saw both Chic and Sly & the Family Stone at the Oakland Coliseum.

Can you describe your techniques?

I learned to slap first, because as a kid I didn't have the forearm strength to finger-pluck. I don't slap much anymore because it's not the thing right now. I alternate my two fingers, and I do a lot of what I call thumb-plucking: Holding my thumb parallel to the strings, I use the meat of my thumb on the downstroke and top side of my nail on the upstroke. I can mute to varying degrees with my fingers or palm.

What did you learn while playing live with Prince?

Mainly, how to play all night long, and also the power of simplicity. One night we were playing funk in *E*, and he went over and picked up my bass—but it was tuned to *E♭*, so he just found one note that worked, and he stayed on it the entire song and drove the groove home.

★ MESHELL NDEGEOCELLO: FEELING IT BY BILL LEIGH ★

"It's true," chuckles MeShell Ndegeocello. "I can't reach the tuning pegs on my bass when it's strapped on." Here's evidence that size doesn't matter: Though she stands only five feet tall, the bandleader's giant sense of groove is only a small part of her stature as a creative musical artist. Her albums blend solidly funky bass playing with powerful compositions, provocative lyrics, and considerable flavors of hip-hop, pop, or jazz fusion.

Onstage it's a different stature story: Her seasoned band transforms MeShell's carefully crafted songs into soulful meditations that draw on avant-garde jazz improv as much as deep funk. "I'm just going to tell you some stories," was her understated introduction to one small-town audience. "Is that cool?"

Whether she's singing, rapping, or playing keyboards, MeShell maintains an onstage control of her band as if they were a direct extension of her conscious creative flow. When she straps on the bass, though, the energy intensifies. "She has a conviction on the bass I very seldom see in other players," says David Dyson, who played for years as the second bassist in Meshell's band. "She won't rip off a Victor Wooten solo, but she'll groove you to death. I love those moments on the gig—we never plan it, it just happens—where we're just grooving together, moving in and out of each other. I'll be playing a one-line part like a guitar player while she's in the groove. Then she'll move up the neck, and I know to go down to the bottom and hold it down."

Having come of age in Washington, D.C., MeShell cut her teeth playing go-go music, the city's distinctive funk offshoot with a loping, percussion-driven shuffle beat. After she moved to New York, where she paid additional dues playing with members of Vernon Reid's Black Rock Coalition, MeShell's early demos helped her get signed by Madonna's record label, Maverick. These days, MeShell stays busy not just with her albums and tours but also as a session bassist with artists ranging from Alanis Morissette to Citizen Cope. "I love playing other people's music—sometimes more than my own. I like hearing what they don't hear and adding it. With Citizen Cope, I got to be Lee Sklar—just creatively supporting the songs and adding what was best."

Do you consider yourself a songwriter first or a bass player first?

I love the bass—and the way I play is very much my personality. I'm all right standing way behind whoever's up front, just holding down a groove. I like to make everything lock, gel, and be funky. Compositions move me more than anything, though—the construction of the song, the lyric, and everything. My goal is to be a great writer, not a great bass player.

Most of my favorite bass players are writers. Jaco's my hero because of his virtuosity and craft in composing and arranging. Of course his bass playing is way up there, but the songs are beautiful. Jaco Pastorius is the greatest bass record ever made, but *Word of Mouth* was a big part of me wanting to hear strings and orchestral sounds in my music. Probably my favorite bass player when I was growing up was Prince. His bass lines, like "Let's Work," are like songs within themselves. Then there's Paul McCartney—an incredible songwriter and bass player, and Sting, who writes the lines you remember.

Are there bassists you admire just for their playing?

Rodney "Skeet" Curtis from P-Funk—put him way up on the list; everybody slept on him. Paul Jackson with the Headhunters—he sounds like a bass player. I also had a great mentor: Mike Neil, who played in a go-go band when I was growing up in D.C. Our playing is very similar. He played on the first Maxwell record. He's been my teacher as far as developing my bass personality and just holding it down. He always said, "You've got to know what *not* to play. Just hold it down—it's a waste of time if nobody can dance to it." I definitely got that slide stuff I do from him. It's the period, the end of the sentence.

What does writing bring to your bass playing?

Simplicity and flow. Bass is the harmonic and rhythmic foundation, and I like that. I like to make it feel good and give it a personality. I'm okay not being a solo bass artist; I don't want to be so alone. I'm never going to be Victor Wooten. That's not my gift; I didn't get virtuosity in bass playing.

What is your gift?

I have virtuosity in creativity. You can sit me onstage now with a drummer and I'll come up with a bass line. You can put me in any setting and I'll make it work. I can play with anybody: I could play with Incubus, with Lynyrd Skynyrd, or with Joshua Redman if he didn't mind me playing electric.

How do you keep the ideas flowing?

I know when to stop. When it's not coming, I stop, go watch some movies, eat some food, and hang out. When it comes back, I try to address it. Don't push it; when it happens, it happens. I realize it's not under my control. Sometimes the spirit hits you, and sometimes it doesn't.

It's like having shows night after night. Sometimes you're *killin'*. Other times you feel like, Whew, glad I got through that! Hope we didn't hurt anyone! Hey, I've seen a few famous people that I love have rough nights. That's just how it is.

The moods on your albums are totally different. Are there some moods that make you want to pick up the bass more?

Oh, no. There's years between each of my records, and in between I change and grow and hear new things I like. I just get in these moods. That's how I am about basses, too. People call me for gigs, but sometimes my Fender doesn't sound good on those gigs, so I have an array of basses. I'm a painter, and I'm going to have a lot of brushes. I don't believe you have to stick with one sound. I have a bunch of different sounds. In fact, I'd be afraid if somebody said I had a sound. I'd rather they say, "She has a certain feel."

★ LAMARQUIS JEFFERSON: THE FUNK IN THE CRUNK BY KEVIN OWENS ★

In addition to being the exclusive bassist for multi-platinum producer Jermaine Dupri, the "king of crunk" Lil Jon, and contemporary R&B singer/songwriter Tony Rich, LaMarquis Jefferson and his grooves have graced recordings from OutKast, TLC (that's him on "Waterfalls"), Da Brat, Lil' Kim, MC Lyte, Petey Pablo, and the decidedly un-crunk Michael Bolton, among others. He received a

Grammy for his contributions to Usher's 2004 mega-hit "Yeah!" Thanks to his mastery of his instrument, his studio savvy, and his business smarts, LaMarquis has carved out a niche for himself as a first-call studio bassist in a scene long dominated by synthetic low end.

"I don't remember not being able to play the bass," says LaMarquis, who says his defining bass moment came at age 11, when he learned Verdine White's solo from "New World Symphony." LaMarquis continued to hone his musical skills, mostly in church bands, after his family moved to Atlanta. His first big musical break came in 1991 when a gospel song he penned, "Ain't No Rock," earned him the grand prize in *Billboard*'s Amateur Songwriting contest. "I was working as a maintenance man at an apartment complex when I got a call saying that Quincy Jones had chosen my song out of 60,000 entries." Jefferson invested the $25,000 prize money in equipment and began to develop his skills as a producer. In 1993, when a demo pitch to Organized Noize's Rico Wade wasn't going well, LaMarquis impressed him with his bass skills.

> ### "I don't remember not being able to play the bass."

"At that point, Rico wanted to put me in the studio, so I went down with my fretless Fender Jazz Bass. When I got there, there was no music on the track, and Rico said, 'Play what you hear.' All that's on that track are the voices of the four girls and my fretless line. The name of the song is 'Tonight,' and it's on Xscape's first release, *Hummin' Comin' at 'Cha*. That was the song that got me into the Atlanta music scene just in time for that scene to explode."

How do you avoid becoming cliché with your lines?

I try to get a vision of what the producer wants to accomplish with the record. And sometimes from listening to him I'll figure out that the sound he's looking for is a '71 Fender Jazz with flatwound strings. So that's what I'll give him. Also, when I'm working with a producer and he has a drum pattern going, I try not to add too much. If there are vocals, it helps even more because then I know exactly where I need to go, and more important, where I don't need to go. But for the most part, I just try to give drum patterns life. I feel like that's what bass lines do: They help provide a pattern to the bottom end that gives the song the sonic flexibility it needs to really stand out.

How'd you cross over from R&B into hip-hop?

Hummin' Comin' at 'Cha was released on Jermaine Dupri's label. He had a lot going on at that time, and I told myself that if I ever got the chance to meet him,

I wasn't going to ask him for anything. So when I saw him one day, I introduced myself and thanked him for the opportunity to play on the Xscape record. The next thing I knew, he invited me to play on some more records. So I went to his home studio and laid down some bass lines for Da Brat's remake of Rick James's "Mary Jane" and a song called "Give It to You." I used a fretless MusicMan Sterling that I ran through a Mu-Tron pedal, and it came out sounding real crazy.

How did you and Jermaine develop those lines?

It was a mixture of him telling me what to play and me coming up with things on my own. Sometimes he would ask for bass lines that were repetitive and right on the *one*, almost like a drum machine. And I would say, "I can do that, but let's keep *a little* live element in there; let it vary every once and a while, and maybe let me lay back behind the *one* every now and then. Let me play the line all the way through instead of just putting a three-second sample into your drum machine and looping it down." There were times when a repetitive bass line was exactly what the song needed, and then there were times when the bass line needed movement. It was in those times that I was able to do what I wanted to do.

What's the songwriting process like with Lil Jon?

Sometimes he'll come up with a drum pattern and a few synth parts and then relay what he wants. And sometimes when we're vibing he'll be like, "Yeah, I like that—put it down." The songs get built around whoever has the idea. It's a beautiful situation, because Jon is not selfish about writer's credits. He's more into getting a good vibe. It makes the creative process easier because you know he's not going to take what you do and keep it.

Does any of the "crunk" subject matter ever get to you?

To be honest, I can't listen to *Crunk Juice*. A lot of that music was done during a six-month stint in Miami last year. We did about 300 tracks—we made a *lot* of beats. The beats were sent out to various artists, and they wrote whatever they wanted to write to them. I never knew what was going to be on those beats until the songs began to come back. And for some of them it was like, "Wow, cool!" and on some others it was like, "Whoa, that's kind of hardcore." But I can't control what someone does over my music. I've had to look at it like any business.

★ PINO PALLADINO: WORLD'S MOST FLEXIBLE BASSIST? BY CHRIS JISI ★

To forge a much-imitated style on bass guitar is rare, and to do it as a session bassist is even rarer. Then there's Pino Palladino. Over the course of a three-decade career, he has reinvented himself twice, pulling a legion of bass followers with him each time. During the '80s, the Welsh-born bassist put fretless on the pop music map via his soaring sub-hooks on hits with Paul Young, Don Henley, Tears for Fears, and numerous others—in the process placing second only to Jaco Pastorius when it comes to smooth-fingerboard impact. In the '90s, when Top 40 turned fickle to the fretless, Palladino favored his fretted axes and continued to bolster his résumé with a wide variety of artists, such as Eric Clapton, Seal, Melissa Etheridge, Elton John, and jazzers ranging from Chris Botti to Al Di Meola. Next came a chance meeting between Pino, his flatwound-strung '63 Fender Precision, and D'Angelo, culminating in the singer's heralded 2000 CD, *Voodoo*. The album's greasy, laid-back feels caused quite a buzz among rhythm sections everywhere and led to a Who's Who of hip-hop artists summoning Pino and his P-Basses to their recording studios.

While Pino-inspired pluckers worldwide were hanging back in the groove with vintage 4-strings and flatwounds, Palladino got two starkly contrasting calls: replacing the late, loud-rocking John Entwistle, who died just as the Who was launching its 2002 tour, and supporting mellow folk-rockers Simon & Garfunkel on their late-2003 reunion tour. So what is it about the modest Londoner that appeals to such diverse employers? Feel. When Pino lays it down in any style, his grooves pulsate with a rhythm and energy that oozes between the deepest cracks and frequently boils to the surface.

Are you seeing a trend toward having more real bass and drums on dates, and having the rhythm section record together, as opposed to overdubbing a part by yourself?

I think in the States there are more records with real bass and real drums. Thankfully, people like D'Angelo and Raphael Saadiq are introducing generations raised on machines to real instruments. Other artists ask, "Wow, how do they get that feel?" You can't get it with machines. Personally, I try to make a point of taking sessions that have a live section playing together. That's always my first question: How are you going to cut the track? I'd say I do 75 percent live-section dates versus 25 percent overdubbing by myself. A lot of young producers bring me in with the idea of adding drums later, and I'll say, "Why don't you do the bass and drums together; that way we can work off each other," and they'll say, "Hey, that's a great idea." There is something to be said for coming in at the end and finding the space to put something special on the track, but I don't get much of that anymore. I'm open to both situations, but for me it's most satisfying to interact with a section.

How do you come up with parts? Do you think in terms of chord changes, melodies, or rhythmic ideas?

I just wait for something to come into my head. Sometimes I let the track play without any bass a few times to see if I can imagine the bass line, or I'll ask the rest of the rhythm section to play while I try to find a part. It varies; in the writing team I have with [keyboardist] James Poyser and [Roots drummer] Ahmir

Thompson, we just play together until we mold something into shape, which is the most enjoyable way for me—reacting to whatever I hear. Technically, there's a degree of musical knowledge in the equation—knowing the changes and being aware that you can play something nice over this *Em9* chord coming up. There are certain places in a song where each musician gets a little spark and thinks, Well, I can put something special in here—this spot is where I can do my thing. The rest of the time it's a probably a good idea to just keep it simple.

Part of what makes your fills jump out is the way they're phrased. Do you get into a separate mindset to play fills as opposed to a groove part?

Yes. It's almost like I'm playing the support line and occasionally I feel like singing something. I find when I go to the upper register and play something that's going to stand out a little, it's a natural for me to phrase it in a more vocal, soloistic fashion. It's a matter of being aware that you have to let go of holding down the root and locking with the drums, and step into a different frame of mind to get it to come out more loose and relaxed.

Who are the key influences on your bass approach?

The key players for me would be James Jamerson, Jaco, Anthony Jackson, Michael Henderson, Stevie Wonder's keyboard bass, Larry Graham, Marcus Miller, and Bootsy—his part on James Brown's "Talkin' Loud and Sayin' Nothing" is one of my all-time favorites. Michael's solo album *Going Places* was a huge inspiration; he's similar to Jamerson, but with his own take on it. I also loved the early fusion stuff with Stanley and Jaco; a lot of it was funky, like George Duke's *The Aura Will Prevail* with Alphonso Johnson, and Lenny White's *Venusian Summer*, with the late Doug Rauch—he played some stinky funk that blew me away.

What do you retain from your fretless approach in your current fretted style?

A great deal. Playing so many fretless bass lines that were featured as important parts of songs gave me the confidence I have today to try ideas and step out a little. Technique-wise, I keep the phrasing and vibrato aspects in mind, although I was using vibrato and moving my hand on fretted bass before I ever got a fretless—in the vein of Paul Jackson and Abe Laboriel. The last time I recorded on fretless was while doing some tracks for D'Angelo. He wanted a certain sound, so I used this hollowbody Status I have, with black nylon strings and a piezo pickup. It was pretty scary because I hadn't played fretless for a while.

Your work with D'Angelo symbolizes your move back to your R&B-rooted influences and fretted bass.

My roots and the music in my heart have always been R&B. The move back really started around 1994, after I got my '63 P-Bass and put flatwounds on it. I'd been writing with [drummer] Steve Jordan, and I used the bass on a great album we did for Tom Jones that unfortunately never came out. [Bonnie Raitt bassist] Hutch Hutchinson heard the tracks, and he recommended me to producer John Porter, who called and asked me to bring the P-Bass for B. B. King's *Deuces Wild* CD. That's where I met D'Angelo, and we hit it off in a big way. Whenever he sang, I played better! He said, "You've got the sound I'm looking for—come and play on my album." That was incredibly fortunate, because it also led to sessions with a variety of other hip-hop artists, and the formation of the writing team with James and Ahmir, who are D's sidemen.

D'Angelo's behind-the-beat grooves have intrigued many musicians. What light can you shed on the subject?

It's something D and Raphael Saadiq got from hip-hop—where the samples are not always in perfect time, creating a certain sloppy feel—which they incorporated into the way they feel music. Actually, that loose feel has always been around; I don't think it's anything new, really, but D's take on it and the way he arranged it on his tracks is the key—he brought it to the next level. For whatever reason, I took to the feel completely, and I felt fortunate to get it first-hand from one of the originators.

How do you approach the feel from a bass point of view?

The only way I can play that style of bass—really hanging back—is for the drummer to sort of ignore what I'm doing. The tension is created by the drummer keeping the beat strongly in the middle and maybe even pushing slightly. If the drummer tries to hold back with me, the tension is gone. I like to feel the snare just on the edge of pushing, and then I can sit back in a certain space that makes the groove wider. It's not about listening to the drummer and playing an instant later; I'm still locking with the drums, but I'm feeling the groove in a different rhythmic dimension.

CONTRIBUTORS

Chris Jisi is *Bass Player's* senior contributing editor and editor of Backbeat Books' *Brave New Bass* and *Bass Player Presents the Fretless Bass*.

Jim Roberts is the founding editor and former publisher of *Bass Player*, and the author of Backbeat Books' *How the Fender Bass Changed the World* and *American Basses: An Illustrated History & Player's Guide*.

Richard Johnston is a former editor of *Bass Player* and former executive editor of Backbeat Books. He's the editor of Backbeat's *How to Play Blues Guitar* and *How to Play Metal Guitar*.

Karl Coryat is a consulting editor and former editor and senior editor at *Bass Player*. He is the editor of *The Bass Player Book* (Backbeat) and the author of the Backbeat titles *The Frustrated Songwriter's Handbook* and *Guerrilla Home Recording: How to Get Great Sound from Any Studio (No Matter How Weird or Cheap Your Gear Is)*.

Scott Malandrone is a former *Bass Player* senior editor.

Gregory Isola is a former *Bass Player* managing editor.

Jonathan Herrera is *Bass Player's* senior editor.

Brian Fox is *Bass Player's* associate editor.

E. E. Bradman is a former *Bass Player* associate editor and the former editor of *Guitar World's Bass Guitar*.

Kevin Owens is *Guitar Player's* managing editor.

Jimmy Leslie is a contributing editor to *Bass Player* and *Guitar Player*.

Bill Milkowski is a freelance contributor to *Bass Player* and the author of *Jaco: The Extraordinary and Tragic Life of Jaco Pastorius* (Backbeat).

Allan "Dr. Licks" Slutsky is a freelance contributor to *Bass Player*, and the author of the seminal James Jamerson book *Standing in the Shadows of Motown*. He also served as producer and music supervisor for the 2002 documentary film of the same name.

Chuck Crisafulli is a freelance contributor to *Bass Player* and the author of several books, including *Teen Spirit: The Stories Behind Every Nirvana Song* (Fireside).

Mikael Jansson is a freelance contributor to *Bass Player*.

Alan Goldsher is a freelance contributor to *Bass Player* and author of several books, including *Hard Bop Academy: The Sidemen of Art Blakey and the Jazz Messengers*.

ACKNOWLEDGMENTS

This book is the result of more than 20 years of work by a group of musicians-turned-writers who have devoted much of their careers to telling the stories of musicians who, despite their outsized cultural contributions, have largely remained anonymous. This is more true of bassists than other musicians, and it's especially true in R&B, soul, and funk music, where players who helped an angst-filled generation cope have too often disappeared into obscurity, poverty, or worse.

I feel fortunate to have been able to work toward helping make sure these players escape obscurity, through telling their stories and sharing their wisdom. I couldn't have done it without the opportunity, guidance, and inspiration from many talented colleagues. *Bass Player* founding editor Jim Roberts gave me my first opportunity. Bassists everywhere owe Jim a debt of gratitude for his steady helmsmanship in the magazine's first tentative years, which ensured the longevity of an ongoing means for bassists to learn from each other and honor our history. Karl Coryat, Greg Isola, Scott Malandrone, Greg Olwell, E. E. Bradman, and Scott Shiraki each taught me a lot about writing for musicians, and about bass in general. Richard Johnston and former *Guitar Player* senior editor Jas Obrecht gave me early encouragement, and Richard in particular has been a patient and supportive mentor, as has Paul Haggard, from whom I learned a lot about the visual aspects of storytelling.

Major props must go to Chris Jisi, who is likely the single most prolific interviewer of bassists, and is therefore probably the best friend that bassdom could have. Also inspiring is Allan Slutsky, whose dedicated and often thankless work at acknowledging the contributions of anonymous studio musicians has in itself had a far-reaching cultural impact.

Most of all, heartfelt thanks to my supportive family, my parents, Fred and Barbara, my sister Tracey, my lovely daughter Olivia, and especially my wonderful wife, Chandrika.